REGIONAL FLASHBACKS

THE REGIONAL FLASHBACKS SERIES IS PUBLISHED BY THE
EUROPEAN ETHNOLOGICAL RESEARCH CENTRE
CELTIC & SCOTTISH STUDIES
UNIVERSITY OF EDINBURGH
50 GEORGE SQUARE
EDINBURGH EH8 9LH

REGIONAL FLASHBACKS

REGIONAL FLASHBACKS

Stranraer and District Lives: Voices in Trust

Edited by
Caroline Milligan

THE EUROPEAN ETHNOLOGICAL RESEARCH CENTRE
AND NMS ENTERPRISES LIMITED – PUBLISHING
NATIONAL MUSEUMS SCOTLAND

GENERAL EDITOR
Mark A. Mulhern

Published in Great Britain in 2017 by
European Ethnological Research Centre
Celtic & Scottish Studies
University Of Edinburgh
50 George Square
Edinburgh EH8 9LH

and

NMS Enterprises Limited – Publishing
NMS Enterprises Limited
National Museums Scotland
Chambers Street
Edinburgh EHI IJF

ISBN 978-1-910682-11-1

The rights of Caroline Milligan as editor
and all named contributors to be identi-
fied as the authors of this book have
been asserted by them in accordance
with the Copyright, Designs and Patents
Act 1988.

**British Library Cataloguing in
Publication Data**

A catalogue record of this book is available from the British Library.

Cover design by Mark Blackadder.
Cover photograph: (front) Bathing at
   the Creamery diving board, Stranraer
   1937. HMS *Spey* can be seen on the
   right and flying boats on the left
   (Reproduced with kind permission of
   the Nelson Collection); (back)
   Telegram boys Danny Hunter (left)
   and Davie McColl (right) on their
   BSA 250cc delivery motorcycles at
   the far end of the East Pier, Stranraer.
   The Creamery, built in the 1930s to
   replace the earlier building is visible
   in the background, 1953 (Reproduced
   with the kind permission of the pho-
   tographer, David Brown).

Internal text design by
   NMS Enterprises Ltd – Publishing.
Printed and bound in Great Britain by
   Bell & Bain Ltd, Glasgow.

For a full listing of related NMS titles
please visit:
www.nms.ac.uk/books

CONTENTS

ACKNOWLEDGEMENTS

The EERC are indebted to the Stranraer and District Local History Trust for donating copies of their fieldwork interviews made between 1999 and 2016. These were the first recordings to be deposited with the 'Dumfries and Galloway: A Regional Ethnology Study' and are the focus of this *Regional Flashback.*

Thanks are also warmly offered in recognition of the tremendous support, in time, energy and enthusiasm, given to the preparation of this *Regional Flashback* by Christine Wilson, Eric Wilson, Donnie Nelson and Nancy McLucas.

Caroline Milligan
Edinburgh 2017

LIST OF ILLUSTRATIONS

GLOSSARY

battle (of straw)	a bundle
broo	unemployment benefit office
chaff	chopped hay and straw
chimley	chimney
coup	mound
cuddy	donkey
eens	eyes
fecket	a woollen garment with sleeves and buttoned front
forrit	forward
gibs	(metal props for rabbit nets)
graip	iron-pronged fork
mim	prim, restrained in manner of behaviour
riddling	a sieving of potatoes to remove the loose earth, stones, etc. as they were gathered.
schuil	school
snedded	cut the tops off (turnips)
timmer	to beat, thrash, hammer with a stick
trogs	(wooden basket)

PREFACE

This work is an addition to the long-standing series of oral histories, memoir and diary accounts of lived lives published by the EERC in association with NMS Enterprises Ltd – Publishing – *Flashbacks*. It is also the first such work to be published based upon the work undertaken by the EERC in its current research programme, Dumfries and Galloway: A Regional Ethnology. This study is part of a wider research programme being conducted by the EERC – The Regional Ethnology of Scotland Project (RESP).

One of the main strands of this research programme is the conduct of new fieldwork using recorded oral interview as a means of inquiry. The particular approach adopted by the EERC has been to train the people of Dumfries and Galloway to conduct this work themselves with the guidance and support of the EERC and Alison Burgess, Local Studies Officer with Dumfries and Galloway Council Libraries and Archives. The interviews which form this work come from the Stranraer and District Local History Trust which had undertaken interviews prior to the EERC starting their activity in Dumfries and Galloway. This collaboration is another way in which the EERC has sought to work positively with groups and individuals across Dumfries and Galloway so as to get the greatest coverage.

The RESP is seeking to build-up an understanding of life and society across Scotland at a local and regional level. To do so it was held to be important that space was left for the people of the regions – in this case Dumfries and Galloway – to give *their* view as to what was and is of importance to them. By allowing the people of Dumfries and Galloway to establish for themselves what was and is important – we contend – allows for the synthesis of a more nuanced and complete understanding of lives in a time and place. The manner in which we worked towards meeting this objective was by enabling to people of Dumfries and Galloway to interview each other without being directed as to what they should discuss.

Thus far this approach has encouraged participation of 49 volunteer fieldworkers who have interviewed over 300 individuals. The range of topics discussed is extensive and provides, to some extent, a statement about what life and society in Dumfries and Galloway during the latter twentieth century was like and how those who lived those lives felt about that time and about the places in which they lived, worked and spent time. In what follows, just such an account of life in and around Stranraer is provided. That account is set out thematically. The balance of material presented is a reflection of the level of detail on a given theme contained within the interviews. It does not represent an editorial assessment or view on the relative importance of various themes. That is, what follows is a broad account of the content of the interviews. Such is the richness of recorded oral interviews that there remains scope for others to look at the interviews to seek information on other aspects of being which are, to them, of interest. The EERC will further enable such inquiry by, in due course, establishing a freely available repository of the interview recordings – both in audio and in transcription.

This work is the culmination of much endeavour on the part of the EERC, Dumfries and Galloway Libraries and Archives and the Stranraer and District and Local History Trust. Most importantly, however, it is a representation of the contribution made by those interviewed to our understanding of a place within a place. This is ultimately a work of the people of Stranraer and district. A work in their own voice in which they tell us what it is they know and understand about their place and about themselves.

Mark Mulhern
Research Fellow, EERC

INTRODUCTION

Shortly after Dumfries and Galloway: A Regional Ethnology Study was launched, members of the Study team travelled to Stranraer to meet with Christine and Eric Wilson and Donnie Nelson of the Stranraer and District Local History Trust. The purpose of this visit was to receive copies of the fieldwork interviews (with transcripts) which had been conducted by the Trust since 1999. This was to be the first material deposited with the Study's repository of fieldwork recordings and it is this donation, 42 recordings with 46 contributors, which forms the content of this *Regional Flashback*. The EERC collection now extends to 316 recordings, made with 276 individuals and continues to be added to. Some of these recordings have come, like those made by the Trust, as donations but the majority have come about as the result of extensive, volunteer-led fieldwork which has been a central activity of the EERC team over the period of the Study.

The initial donation by the Trust was an important early acquisition for the Study and this *Regional Flashback* is an opportunity to showcase the wealth of information contained within the interviews. Rather than present all the interview transcriptions in full, a selection of full transcripts are presented here alongside chapters which bring together extracts from individual recordings that share a common theme. The selection presented here reflects the content of the collection and will hopefully encourage readers to listen to the original recordings. Copies of the Trust recordings are available to consult in Stranraer Library and it is intended that the recordings, as part of the Dumfries and Galloway: A Regional Ethnology Study will, in due course, also be available to listen to online.

The Trust interviews illustrate many different aspects of life in the Stranraer area: from a childhood in rural Rhins in the early twentieth century to the challenges of being a lawyer in the early twenty-first. Given the range and quality of material available for inclusion in this publication the process of selection presented quite a challenge. After completing a detailed survey of the material, a broad thematic approach was chosen to reflect the diversity of content and to allow for the inclusion of interview extracts from all of the interviewees. A key theme in the interviews, and therefore of this collection, is, change over time. The early decades of the twentieth century were a time of rapid change with a move away from a labour-intensive means of production to one of increased mechanisation. This change was associated with a significant decline in rural populations and relocation of many people into an urban environment. In an interview with Bill McCaig of Challoch farm, which at one time supported a community of 36 people, he observed, 'There are very few people on the farm now. You can go to a farm and hardly know it was inhabited, because if the cows are out in the fields there is no one about the steading in the way there was in the old days'. (p. 53) It is details such as this that make the oral history interview such a valuable resource. We can know that the process of mechanisation in farming led to a decline in people working rurally, but listening to a testimony like this helps us to more fully understand and appreciate what that must have felt like. Going on to read several accounts on a similar theme can provide us with a more comprehensive understanding of the given theme and this principle has dictated the structure of this book whereby thematic sections on rural and urban life, covering key themes such as rural work, farming, community life, shops, health and war are presented alongside interviews which are given in full. The complete interview transcriptions in this collection includes the first interview conducted by the Trust, which opens this collection. Helen Davies, then 87 years old, was interviewed by Harriet Collins on 29 January 1999. During the interview, Helen spoke fondly about her childhood and early life in rural Galloway. Although primarily about life on the farm, Helen's recollections also encompass school life and education, Armistice Day 1918, and her first impressions of Stranraer town life. In the complete interview transcriptions, it is the small details which are often the most enlightening. This is the case here where, for example, Helen recalls that only the farmer's wife had a washing line and for everyone else the hedge was kept well trimmed and the clothes simply thrown on top of that to dry (p. 15).

The overall structure of this book moves, for the most part, from rural to urban, reflecting the movement of many people at this time. Following the opening interview transcription from Helen Davies there are thematic chapters on 'Tattie Howkers' and 'Tramps & Travellers' with both illustrating the changing rural landscape. Tattie howkers were an important part of the rural economy in the region at one time and interviewees recalled how the same workers often returned to the same farm community year after year. This practice changed with mechanisation. Initially, farmers chose to give what work was available to their own farm workers, but before long mechanisation developed to such a stage that manual harvesting was no longer needed. The Irish tattie pickers worked hard but, as Bob Grierson recalled, there was time for fun too: 'In nice weather they used to go down to the sea, nearly every night after they finished work. And a big lot of them had a swim in the sea just below us here.' (p. 28) The chapter on tramps and travellers adds to what we already know about this diverse group of people. Again, change is central. One group of travellers brought useful resources to the remote communities while others were simply displaced people who were wandering around, tramping the country. As Bill McCaig remembered, 'tramps were universal in the twenties and thirties' (p. 37) while Andrew Love recalled that these folk were known locally as wheelers, because 'they went round the country lik a wheel'. (p. 34)

Following this is a complete transcription of an interview made in 2013 with Vivien Delf. Although quite a short interview, only a few pages of transcript, but full of rich detail, providing more information on tattie harvesting and tramps as well as introducing a new subject, catching rabbits. Rabbits are central to the next item, a transcription of the interview with Hugh Reid about his poaching experiences. Hugh was 91 when he was interviewed by Nancy McLucas in 2006 and part of his interview is represented here, while the rest forms the final transcribed interview presented in this collection. The complete interview is full of laughter and emotion, and it is clear that Hugh enjoyed sharing his life experiences with Nancy.

Change is again the central theme in the next chapter, 'Agriculture and Farming'. This selection includes a substantial extract from the interview recorded with Andrew Hannay in 1999. Andrew's family firm was once a central part of community life and his interview records the history of the firm. As John Carruth recalled, 'At the west end of the town [Stranraer] was Hannay's Oatmeal Mills which employed a considerable number of men and, as was usual then, nearly everybody lived as near their work as they possibly could. So Hannay's men all lived really in Sheuchan Street and Agnew Crescent'.

The next chapter, again thematic, examines changing 'Rural and Urban Living Conditions' and includes short interview extracts relating to, for example, the arrival of electricity or indoor loos. What might surprise the reader is the progression of this change and how this was distributed across both rural and town areas. In 2007 Nancy McLucas recorded her own memories of living in Bishopburn and an extract of that interview is included here. During an interview in 2016 she spoke about how this community had been built after World War II to encourage young professionals to come into the area. Tenants usually stayed for two years or so, before moving on to purchase property in the town. She remembered it as a great melting pot where New Year went on till Burns' night, the recollection of which all these years later, she said, was strong enough to bring on a hangover!

The following two sections are complete transcriptions of a two-part interview with Bobby Gemmell. In terms of the overall structure of the book, this interview takes us from the rural context of the earlier chapters into the urban setting which will be the context for the remaining chapters. The first part of the interview concentrates on Bobby's early life in the family home on Lochnaw Estate where his father was head gardener to the Pollock family. This is a period, prior to World War II, when the large estates still played a central role in rural areas. Bobby's description of estate life is fascinating, such as when he recalls the square house which operated as the fruit store: 'Beautiful big cases, all drawers, and the peaches and the pears and the plums, everything was kept [in there]. Every Saturday mornin [the fruit] was lifted out, inspected and put back in …'. (p. 67) The second part of the interview is on a very different theme. The arrival of World War II provided an opportunity for Bobby to begin an apprenticeship and this change in his own circumstances is reflected in the changing life at Lochnaw. Lochnaw was requisitioned by the army and the Pollock family left the Lochnaw Castle for good while Bobby's parents subsequently moved into town where his father was Parks' Superintendent until he retired.

Change is again central to the next interview transcription with butcher Ian Jack whose family firm had been in Stranraer for almost 100 years when Nancy McLucas interviewed him in 2007. Now firmly in the town environment, the subject of shops and businesses feature in many of the Trust interviews and this is the first of several complete interview transcriptions with a focus on this theme. In his interview Ian talks about the changes that he has seen over his time in the family business and reflects on how he has responded to the impact of, for example, the closure of the local slaughterhouse, the challenges of supermarket competition and the rise in demand for organic produce. This is a fascinating long-view of change. Again, it is in the detail that we find the most striking images, such as that conjured up by Jack's description of the cellar full of poultry at Christmas, 'You would go home at night with the lice crawling off you. You had to take your clothes off at the foot of the stair … and upstair and jump into the bath …'. (p. 90)

Next is a full transcription of the interview Nancy McLucas made with Mrs Agnes McClymont in 2008 which paints a similarly vivid picture, this time about working with the Scottish Gas Board in the 1960s and early seventies. This interview is interesting for a number of reasons, not least in exploring the role of women in the workplace, and the coal-gas industry before the introduction of natural gas and a national networked gas supply. This interview also demonstrates the skills of the interviewer.

Nancy has carried out all but five of the interviews made on behalf of the Stranraer and District Local History Trust. It is a job that she was 'volunteered for' at a meeting she did not attend. The interviews cover a wide range of themes, yet Nancy is consistently curious and interested in her interviewee and for this reason the interviews are always illuminating and full of content. Within the discipline of ethnology, there is always a lively debate about the dynamic between the interviewer and the interviewee and about whether the interviewer needs to be a specialist on a particular subject or theme in order to conduct a meaningful interview. This is certainly something volunteer fieldworkers participating in the Dumfries and Galloway Regional Ethnology Study have had to be aware of. Getting the balance between knowing enough and saying too much can be, for a novice interviewer, difficult to achieve. The interview with Agnes McClymont is a model in fieldworker techniques – from not being afraid to ask for details or clarification, to admitting you just do not know what the interviewee is meaning. If the fieldworker is confused, then it is equally likely that someone listening to the interview decades later will be too.

The next chapter, a collection of interview extracts dealing with 'Shops and Businesses', is the largest thematic collection presented in this volume. Many of the people interviewed by the Trust were themselves shopkeepers or businessmen, and many of the others recalled the shops of their youth and early adulthood. At a time when each community could support any number of businesses the interview extracts presented here provide us with rich details of street scenes, including where individual shops were located and also what each shop sold. The chapter begins with a description of McHaffie & Sons, purveyors of everything from sou'westers and linoleum to try-and-buy spectacles and finishes with an interview extract from Olive Murray and her daughter, Debbie, in which they reflect on the history of the family business, Moodies. Throughout this chapter we see how outside factors, such as increasing domestic transport and the arrival of the supermarket, have influenced mercantile history in Stranraer and the surrounding communities. In March 2016 Nancy McLucas reflected on this, 'In these days you went to Ayr for a treat, not to pop into M&S!'

This selection is followed by the transcription of part of the interview held with lawyer Alan Smith in 2007. This is an account which takes the reader from a very personal law service which focussed on the individual clients, to the pressures facing the law in Stranraer in 2007 where drug trafficking, abuse and illegal immigration were becoming an increasingly prevalent part of the working life of a local lawyer. This discussion of the law resonates with Hugh Reid's comments (in the earlier transcription) on the lawlessness of his parents' time.

Alan's transcript is followed by the interview held with Betty Findlay in 2008 in which she talked about the family drapery business. Mrs Findlay's account is again rich in detail and includes information on how staffing levels and stock changed over the decades as the business moved from being one which stocked just about everything, to a more specialised retailer operating in the context of wider consumer choice and people shopping further afield. Here too we see the shopkeeper as a central character in the community and an important part of the social structure of the town.

In a 2016 interview with members of the Trust, Nancy McLucas remarked that she purposefully did not ask her interviewees about personal matters, such as religion, as she felt these to be outwith the scope of the project. However, some comments and observations did come up during the interviews and a number have been included in the next thematic chapter, 'Community Life'. Also included here are accounts of how individuals participated in their local community and social life, and includes a very short account of curling at Leswalt where, in the freezing conditions in the winter of 1947–48, Bill McCaig and his fellow enthusiasts simply stopped the cars to curl on the roadways.

The next two chapters look at important areas of public health and welfare and demonstrate how much has changed in these areas over the past 80 or 90 years. In the chapter on 'Education' we gain an insight into what school was like in a time when one-teacher primary schools were commonplace as was a two or three mile walk to school – whatever the weather. Many readers may feel a pang of recollection from their own family memories when they read John Carruth's account of being punished for using his left hand to write. What might be less familiar, in the accounts given by Agnes Lamb and John McColm (and also reflected in the earlier interview transcriptions from Ian Jack and Mrs Findlay) is the expectation that young people did what the family expected of them, unquestioningly. As Agnes Lamb told Nancy McLucas in 2005, 'You werenae allowed to choose what you wanted to do, or what your education was. Because if you were needed, you had to go home and help. That was the way it was long ago'. (p. 142)

The subsequent transcribed interview, with Margaret and Jean Templeton, tells of their own school life and youth and also recalls their father's opticians business, including information about the transition to the National Health Service which brought a significant increase in business. Similarly, the following chapter, on health, includes the period before the introduction of the NHS and these few short extracts provide fascinating details of health and illness around this time.

The next chapter, 'Travel and Transport' highlights some of the issues with travelling in an area where, at one time, the train was the central means of transport and transportation. At a time when most goods were transported by train John Barr recalled, 'The station was the hub of the community'. (p. 157) Other interviews collected as part of the Study have illustrated how significant the loss of some of the rural train lines was to the region when commodities such as soft fruits and snowdrops were only viable when transported quickly and smoothly by train.

World War II had a tremendous impact on the Stranraer area, which was a significant military base for both the Royal Navy and the Royal Air Force, and it is perhaps no surprise to find that the majority of people interviewed by the Trust shared War-related memories during their interview sessions. The selection collated in the next chapter, 'War', takes us from Agnes Lamb's recollection of the declaration of World War II and her annoyance at not being able to go off to join the War effort, to an extract from Geoffrey Wardley's interview in which he recalls his National Service deployment to Wig Bay in 1950.

One of the interview transcriptions included in this selection is from James Blair, who served with the Royal Navy during World War II. This poignant recollection from him is one of the visual images which stays in the mind long after the transcript has been put aside:

> On November 14th 1940 I travelled from Stranraer to Skegness. I had never seen such flat country as Lincolnshire. Scarcely a tree to be seen as far as the distant horizon, and I realised this was it. The landscape was so depressing it brought to me the thought of how I might never see home again. I felt like weeping. At Skegness … we were rigged out in sailor's kit consisting of two suits … [we were also] issued with a sheet of brown paper, this was to parcel up our civvy clothes to be sent home.

The chapter on 'War' is followed by a short thematic selection which recalls another sad episode in the history of Stranraer, the *Princess Victoria* disaster of 31 January 1953. The two short accounts given here provide an insight into the horror of the accident and the impact it had on the local community. The Trust has published a full account of this tragedy in 'The Loss of the *Princess Victoria*' by Jack Hunter (1998 and 2010).

The material presented thus far has taken us from early childhood memories through to schooldays, home and working life against a backdrop of both peacetime and war. Many of the themes explored have been present in each of the interviews, and together then enable us to understand more fully what it must have been like to live in this part of Scotland in the earlier decades of the twentieth century. In the next two chapters of this collection we move into the realm of anecdotes and storytelling.

First is a chapter on the storm which occurred during the winter of 1947–48, with two accounts of a train stuck in the sidings outside Glenwhilly station during the great storm in the winter of 1947–48. The recollections given here both relate to the same incident, but from very different perspectives.

For the final chapter 'Ghostly happenings', we return to poacher and story-teller, Hugh Reid, who relates some of the many tales and anecdotes about murders and supernatural incidents which were obviously an important part of his childhood. One of the stories relates to Dr Orgle, a Burke and Hare type character who rode in a carriage drawn by horses whose hooves were shod with rubber so you wouldn't hear their approach. Another tells of how his father was seen to be kicked and abused by an invisible presence, and this calls to mind the phenomenon of the sac ban found in many Gaelic tales: a disruptive apparition which is often used to explain the dishevelled appearance of the, often drunk, victim but which could also, quite literally, scare the life out of its victims.

Images can provide important supporting evidence for ethnologists and historians, and this is especially the case if these images are then interpreted by someone with a great depth of knowledge of the context of the chosen image. Moving away from oral testimonies, and into the realm of material culture, the final selection in this *Regional Flashback* is a chapter describing some of the highlights from Donnie Nelson's vast photographic archive. Donnie, who has been an active member of the Stranraer and District Local History Trust since it was established in 1998, worked with the *Stranraer and Wigtownshire Free Press* for 40 years. For almost 20 years of that period he ran a column, 'Peep At The Past', which showcased photographs of the local area and explored the history behind the image depicted. With a foresight that would be the envy of any archivist, Donnie always accepted images on the grounds that he (and the Trust) could use the image in the future in any way they saw fit, and the resulting archive is a great asset to the local area.[1] Known to his friends as 'Mr Stranraer', Donnie has an impressive knowledge of local history which was encouraged by his granny when he was a small child and which he continues to add to. Many of the images he has chosen for this chapter are on themes which are important in his own life. This is especially the case with images relating to World War II, which Donnie experienced as a child.

For ethnologists the purpose of collecting oral testimonies, and then exploring those within the context of the available material culture, is to enable us to build up a more complex history of our society and thereby more fully appreciate and understand the role of the individual in creating and shaping that society. The 42 interviews collected so far by the Trust help us do just that. Through the interviews and images presented here we can better understand how the process of change has unfolded over time, and how this has impacted on the local community. Many of the themes explored in this *Regional Flashback* are ones which would be highlighted in other areas and regions, but experience and the impacts will be unique, and the material collected by the Trust and presented here enables us to build a more complex and diverse record of that change.

In an interview with members of the Trust in March 2016, Nancy McLucas said that she might just do some more interviewing as she had her eye on a few other possible interviewees. Let us hope she does.

A NOTE ON THE TRANSCRIPTIONS

Interview transcriptions were made shortly after the interviews were conducted and these formed the basis of the transcripts represented here. The act of transcribing fieldwork interviews is not for the faint-hearted and the editor recognises and applauds the great contribution made by the transcribers who worked with the Trust over the years: Davida Allison completed transcripts for the first interviews while Irene Heron completed the subsequent transcripts over a period of many years.

The agreed style for representing the spoken word in print is something which changes over time and presently we tend towards finding a 'narrative voice' in transcribing speech: somewhere between written and spoken language. This is done to bring the reader as close as possible to hearing the narrator's spoken voice in the text, whilst also respecting that the interviewee would represent themselves rather differently if they were writing their account themselves, rather than reporting their thoughts via an audio interview. To this end, a number of the texts represented here have sometimes been modified from the original transcriptions.

The First Interview

Helen Davies was 87 years old when she was interviewed by Harriet Collins in January 1999. This was the first recording made by the Trust. Helen spoke about her early memories of life on a farm in rural Galloway, schooldays and her first impressions of Stranraer town life.

Helen Davies

The beginning is a very good place to start, isn't it? So tell us where were you born and when?

A wis born at Barnchalloch Croft on the 27th September 1911. My father at that time had two cows and he went out working to other farms. And A wis the youngest of a family of six.

How many boys and how many girls?

Three girls and two boys and finally, after four years, A came along.

So you were the baby of the family?

A wis the baby of the family, but not spoiled. No by any means.

How did your parents earn their living?

... my father was a dairyman which meant that he looked after the cows, the milking and all that sort o thing, and the family helped. My mother's day started in the morning – she was always first on the floor, at half past four .... Our oven ... it wasnae a real range. Jist a small [thing] wi two hobs, a little oven that you kindled a fire underneath – which we never baked cakes in, but we dried sticks in it. And she boiled up the kettle – and the house was awake by that time – and [they] had a cup o tea before they went to the milking.

But, in the wintertime, it was nice to go into the byres. Warm, and it wasnae unusual to find maybe a wee baby calf staggerin around. Then sometimes there was difficulty [and] my father – he really had to be a part vet as he had to help when the cows were calving. Sometimes things went wrong and they had to get the vet proper, but he [mostly] had to attend to all the little illnesses. When they went out to the spring new grass, in the summer an the spring, they used to swell away up and there was a certain place you had to pierce them to let the wind out, otherwise they would aa died. And also he had to pare their feet (I suppose jist like us cuttin our nails) and if they had bad feet they were treated with stuff called Archangel Tar.[2] I can smell it yet, I can still smell it, yes.

In the meantime my mother, she came along after she had got things sorted out. The porridge was always put to the side on the hob. We'd had porridge the day [before] for tea, before tea. And then we had porridge in the morning before breakfast. Well, it was back-het with milk in the morning. And then she came up to the dairy and [the] milk had been put down in two big – I think they wid be sort of stone – flat coolers. And the cream had to be skimmed off and put in a crock for churning farm butter, which I didn't like. [*laughter*]

Well. I must tell you a wee story in connection with this. … [They] reared a lot o chickens on the farm, which belonged to a Mr McDowall at High Three Mark. They were very good people. They were the nice farmers. And this [one chicken] wis a wee oddity. It never really grew and it … followed everybody about. And this morning it had followed ma mother into the dairy and A wis there. And she turned her back to do somethin and it jumped up on the side of the cooler and it was at the cream. And she hit it such a slap. [*laughter*] This is true, they talk about runnin about like a headless chicken, but it really happened. The head come off and the little thing ran about – the little body. Well, it disappeared intae the big steam boiler fire – the one that supplied all the steam for everything else. [*laughter*]

In the wintertime there wasn't a lot of milking really … but it was heavy work for my father, because the cows stood-in then. And my mother had to hurry back home when she was milking like, and after that, and have his breakfast ready. And then he took the milk to the creamery. And when I was a wee girl that was what I loved, going to the creamery wi my dad in the horse lorry. [That] was really wonderful. So, he came back home and no even time for a cup o tea. My mother meantime had been washing our milking pails. They weren't metal, they were wooden. Luggies we called them, and they had to be scrubbed, really scrubbed. And then they were put in a boiler of boiling water. And after they'd been in so long they were put out on a shelf to dry. I can't remember where the milking stools were kept, but every milker had their own …

But, I'm getting away … . My brother, Bob, the second youngest, well he was four years older than me, he got a bursary and went to Stranraer High School. And yours truly followed him four years [later]. [*laughter*] Now, I don't know what it would be worth, it seems a very paltry sum now. But, eh, there wis £2 in the spring, £2 in the autumn –

this was for three years. No, I'm wrong. There was £4, and then £4 and £8. It came to £16 anyhow – in the year. And A went to the High School for three years. A lot of good it did me. [*laughter*]

Can we go back to the farm, to your earlier days? Tell us about the accommodation that was available on the farm? What was the cottage like?

Well, now, actually it was jist very, very basic … . Ah, there were two bedrooms, neither o them very large, and a great big kitchen. And a concrete floor … . And, as A said, ma mother, she had to wash all up at the dairy, like [at] first until my brother, Jim, was old enough to help. We did it unquestioningly, it was all part of the job. Aa the family worked to keep them togither. And, Jim, he must have been a really square peg in a round hole because he was a very artistic person. He loved good music, he loved flowers and he could play the fiddle by ear, and get a tune out of a piano if there was one available …

He would feel hemmed in?

But he never showed it, if he did. We just did it, it was a way of life. We just did it, we never questioned it.

Your mother must have found it very hard, not least the child bearing, and she would have to be up and about just as soon as she could after having a baby and back to her dairy work?

Back to work. And this happened to all the wives in the country. In fact, I know of one wife that actually had er baby one day, and she was out in the fields the next day.

Goodness me. And there were, of course, no labour-saving devices in the home?

No labour-saving devices at all. The water had to be carried from a well – that would be about 300 yards away. It was a proper well, concrete [surround], and wired off, and the cattle trough outside that they could drink [from]. And it was lovely water. I wid give anything for a drink of that water … instead of what we get to drink [now] – different altogether. And for washing we had a water barrel, or butt as we called it, where it came off the slates in a downpipe – a drainpipe. And we always had the rain water too … there didnae seem to be so much rain then as we have now. Maybe because I was young, I always thought the summers were nice, warm and nice … . A lovely thing about it – I used to have to go up when the cows were out in the summertime. I used to have to go away, and I'm sure it would be a half-mile or so, tae let the cows … out of the field and let them in. The mornings they were beautiful, they were really lovely, I cannae explain to you what they were like.

And what about your diet at this time? Tell us what kind of meals [you had]?

Now, we had porridge in the morning. The porridge was made in the afternoon. The previous afternoon – and we had a bowl of porridge before our tea … . My mother baked every day, it wasn't one day. They had, after their meal at twelve o'clock – they were lucky [if] they maybe snatched 15 minutes in the chair, and then A washed up the dishes. By that time, as I told ye, the others were away and she got the baking-board down. It was just a flat piece of board wi·four sides on it, mibee about four inches high and a wee opening where you brushed the flour out, and the girdle hung over the fire. It had to be just right. Not too much smoke. No smoke at all, and not too much flame. And there was just a certain thing, and that was potato scones, oatmeal scones, soda scones. And some days, instead of doing oatmeal scones she did oatcakes. And they had a sort of wire contraption which pushed in in front of the fire and the oatcakes were put on it, the farls, and they curled up on each side. Well, porridge was really our staple diet. We had very little, in that we were lucky if we saw a butcher once a week until my brother Bob started work in the town, and at weekends … she always sent for a bit of meat or something.

Did you get vegetables off the farm?

My father had a garden, we all had a garden, and never was there such nice potatoes or such nice vegetables. They were really lovely. And my brother Jim had a part fenced off for flowers. It wasnae fenced off, it was just a part o the garden kept – and that was his. His great love.

But your mother would be able to make good pots of soup?

Oh, yes. We had plenty soup, plenty o good food. We never wanted for milk or butter although, I didnae like farm butter. … although my mother was a butter maker, and in her early married life she made the butter for Glenapp Castle. My father and her were up there. That was before the family came along. But getting away back again, it was the missus that did the churning and them that wanted butter, got it. As for getting our supplies in, there was MacKenzie's van from Sandhead. He had a great big van on the road and it came every Friday night about, maybe, four o'clock and brought what had been ordered the Friday before. And these were paid for and then took the [order] for the following week. That's how we got our main supplies. And a very occasional treat, and she was a dab hand at thim, she made a cloutie dumpling. If it was a birthday, there was wee charms put in it. A wee thimble and a thrupenny bit. Wee odds and ends, and she was a dab hand at them, I will say. And if there was a bit [leftover] we very often had that on a Sunday. But as I say, if it was a birthday, it was a special one.

What about when it came to washing day?

Now, washing day. Ma dad [had] built a wee boiler at the end o the house. He rigged up a shed with bits o this and bits of that because, well, I suppose they couldnae just afford to get wood. And, as I say, there was only the four walls o the house. So he built this little boiler, which was a godsend, and she had it kindled up and the water boilin ready to get the tubs out an the scrubbing board.

And was this a zinc scrubbing board?

Yes, it was. As far as A remember, yes it was. That was before the glass ones. The glass ones came in later on, but this was the zinc one. And we didn't have a drying line. There was a big hedge outside, it was kept trimmed, and the clothes were thrown on top of it to dry.

You didn't have a washing line?

We didn't have such a thing. No, the only people that had a washing line was the farmer's wife.

Oh, was this a status symbol?

Now, I couldnae say, because A never knew them done any other way than just being dried on the hedge.

They say the sun bleaches?

Yes. Well, that was another thing. Now, if there was white things, if the cattle wasnae in the field, they used to put them out on the grass for so many days … to bleach. Well, the morning dew just did one thing and another. Then they were rinsed and used again and they were always lovely. And, our beds, now believe this or not, the mill came in, the travelling mills. McDowall's had their own mill and engine and did their own thrashing, or threshing I should say. But now and then, if they needed to get a bit extra done, they had the travelling mill in. And we filled sacks with the caff, we called it. I suppose the word is chaff, and that is what our beds were. They were filled with this chaff and they were really lovely. Comfortable. And I slept in a big settle bed. Have you seen one? … Now, it folds up and it's just like a seat. And then at night – it hooks at either side – and at night it's put down and that's the bed. And all the things is inside it providing a seat and a hidey hole. … It was lovely.

I suppose the equivalent of today's bean bags, maybe?

I would think so, but maybe I think the chaff would be even softer than the bean bags. Although … I don't know what the proper name of them was, we called them Barley Anns. They sort of pricked you. There was something come through the ticking. But it was great for a long time … you were away high up. Of course, with wear … it flattened down through time, but then there was always a refill to come.

And tell me about clothing? How did you come by the clothing?

Now, my parents only drew so much o their wage every week. And at the term time, which was hiring time for the dairymen – it was the 28th November and for the ploughmen it was the 28th May – and they borraed a spring cart and the pony from the farm …

A spring cart?

You know what the heavy farm carts are like? You've seen them? Well this is a light version, with springs and the pony. And they went into town an did their shopping – and that was for six months. My mother had a sewing machine which was her pride an joy. And she made the menfolk's feckets, which you have probably never heard tell of … . This was [made from] a blue material with a white stripe, and a sort of band round the bottom, and long sleeves. And my father and my brother wore them. That was their working clothes, as well as overalls. So, A think … now, A can remember her makin a coat for me. And A thought there was nothing like it, because she had put a wee bit fur round the neck … . That was luxury.

Did you ever find that because you were the baby in the family that you were on the receiving end of hand-me-downs?

No, because I think my three elder sisters … the younger ones of them would get the hand-me-downs from my elder sister and then … the two boys, well there was nothing would do for me … . There was too big a gap. … There was nothing left by then. They were all worn and done.

When you turned five years old and went to school, where did you go to school?

I started school at Stoneykirk. It was a Mr Robinson was the teacher – there wid only be two teachers at that time. And I can remember the first day. He let me sit with my big brother Jim and I was quite happy about it, and A never looked back. I don't remember an awful lot about it, my school days there, except the day the 1918 war finished, when peace was declared and the Armistice. The school children were all out marching along the main road, waving little flags and singing. We thought we were doing lovely, and I don't suppose we understood much about it really. I still can remember having the dark blinds, even then, that we had to have in the windows. I can remember my mother … she had navy blue blinds on the window.

And how far did you have to go from home to school?

Well, believe it or not, I walked three miles … . There was no bussing then back and fore. … [And] with my father being a dairyman, if they saw something better they moved on … at term time. That was the time for shifting. And would you believe it, I've known ma mother … . They put these rails on the carts that they use in harvest time for building the high [loads], and that's what the furniture was moved in. By horse and cart with these [sides] that was built up. When we went to our new house, I can remember quite well, the kitchen furniture was gathered in the middle of the room and she was puttin the distemper on the walls. Yes, she didnae have to go to milking then. Being November, there was no need for a lot of milkers at that time of year.

All the milking then, of course, was done by hand?

And, mind you, most of the cows were gentle and liked to be milked. But there was the odd one or two that would like to put their foot in the pail, and kicked. Well, I've even seen it that they tied their back legs with a rope, you know. The cows – they were tied tightly with ropes. And the very bad ones, they put humbugs in their nose. These was a thing that clipped in their nose, and held them by a rope … humbugs they called them. I have often thought this out as I got older. What was the sense of keeping an animal like that, really? I suppose they must have been paying their way, or they wouldnae have bothered.

So you didn't have all of your primary education at Stoneykirk?

Oh, no, I moved to Meoul, Meoul school.

How many teachers were there?

Two, just two. A Mr Fyfe taught me there. They were Glasgow people [and] they had no children. A very nice man, and he must have done quite well. A lot of the folk thought he was lazy, but I thought he was a nice man. And I know my brother and two girls, he got them through to the High School, and a year or so after he got yours truly to the High School. Altogether, I think he achieved quite a lot. He had the children doing a concert now and then. … and this was to help with the wee treats.

It would be away long, long before there was any free milk, school dinners, etc. at school? How did you manage for sustenance all day?

There was none such thing. We just took a piece, to be quite truthful. At Meoul, there was this about it. There was a wee cottage, and one end of it was the soup kitchen and there was a woman lived in the other end and she made the soup – a great big tureen thing of soup, a big huge thing. The farmers gave in vegetables, rabbits, and we didn't lack for a bowl of soup at a penny, that was the charge. I never found anything wrong with it. I thought it was lovely.

Any other schools you went to?

That was Stoneykirk, Meoul. I went to Portpatrick for a wee while. Not because my father had moved. But my eldest sister was there and she had to milk and she had a baby, and I had to go and stay with them and look after the baby while she was milking. And [so] I went to Portpatrick School, which I hated. I didn't like it at all. I felt just like a fish out of water. I was very unhappy there and I was glad to get away back again.

Looking back over all your primary education, it was a happy enough time?

Oh, it was, yes. [If] it was the wintertime we had the soup, but in the summertime Mrs Fyfe, anyone that liked to take in a tin of cocoa and some sugar or milk, … and she made it for the children. And I was one of the ones that had cocoa and my piece. We always had it in the wash house.

What about toilet accommodation at the school?

Very basic – just a piece of wood with a hole in it and exactly the same in the cottages. Don't think there was any toilet at the cottages because there was not. Everyone had to find their own. As I say, my father put this shed up and I think that was the main place.

Then you moved on, as you said, to the High School, because you were a clever girl and you won a bursary?

Not very distinguished.

Did you enjoy your time at Stranraer High School?

Mostly, with reservations. One or two of the teachers that I didn't really …

How old were you when you left school?

Fourteen. I had just turned 11 when I went.

Was there then, whatever it was called then, a qualifying exam?

There was a certificate, I suppose. But both Bob and I left after we did our three years.

I was meaning to gain entry to the High School?

Yes, I remember coming to sit an exam in Stranraer Academy. I can remember my mother taking me, and another girl and her mother. It was so strange.

Can you remember who the head teacher was in the Academy?

I think it would be Mr Hood, Joe Hood.

After you left school, of course, you would have to seek work?

Yes, well, by that time my mother was getting a bit tired and my father was getting a bit tired. Jim was kept to help my father and I helped my mother and graduated into doing the dairy too. There was pigs to look after and … I couldn't tell you – every sort of thing.

So you were able to turn your hand to anything really on the domestic front and what your mother would have done on the farm had she been fit enough?

Yes, I don't know, I was happier, I must say, in the country than I was in Stranraer. The first time that I came to Stranraer was with one of my sisters, my second eldest sister, she had two ladies that she visited in Fisher Street. I didn't know one place from another then, it was all new to me. I used to think it must be lovely to live in the town. No muck, everything was so clean and polished and all the rest.

[It] seemed so up to date and modern?

Compared to a farm, [yes]. She took me to visit these two ladies that she was friendly with, and we had to go through a sort of tenement in Fisher Street. We went through this place and up into their house, which was like a little palace to be fair. But the smell as you went through, the smell of urine and all sorts of things. It must have been all through the place. Although their place, as I say, was like a little palace. They were two very nice young women. I sort of changed my mind after that and I thought to myself, well, there's something to be said for living in the country.

So, really at heart, you've been a country person?

I've been a country lass, beyond a doubt. When I was wee, if I got lost they always knew where to find me. I was in the stable among the horses. I loved horses. I loved the old cows too, everything. But then there was a lot of things on the farm. Now it didn't occur to me then because it was just a way of life, but with hindsight there was a lot of cruelty went on, which was not nice.

Animals not treated [well]. It has obviously made an impression on you?

A very, very big impression.

But then the veterinary care wasn't freely available?

No, there were no such things as to think to get a cat or anything like that sorted out. They were just the lowest form, for keeping down vermin and things, and if they got hurt … . Well, I can remember one old thing, poor old thing. Her leg would have been better off – and it would have been so easy to take it off – and it just always stuck out. It was very distressing, and it bothered me even then.

And then the years went on and you did go to work and eventually married and had a family?

Yes, and that's another story.

2

Tattie Howkers

Potatoes were an important crop in the south-west, and farmers were keen to grow early potatoes and get these to market before the Ayrshire crops came in. Initial planting was often done by local people and then, later in the season, as noted by Agnes Lamb in the first extract below, the locals would often come out in the evening, after the tattie howkers had harvested an area, and look over the ground for missed potatoes which they would then take home for their own pot.

In the extracts which follow we learn more about the tattie harvest and the important role that Irish potato workers played in bringing this in. The workers would arrive, from County Donegal as well as County Mayo and Achill Island, in late May and stay until the end of October. These tattie howkers were hired by the potato merchants who bought the potatoes 'in the ground' from individual farms. The work was hard, and the picker's day started around six in the morning and finished up around four in the afternoon when the potatoes were taken by lorry to Glasgow for sale at the markets the following morning. If the market was overloaded, the potatoes were left in the ground and the pickers would not get full pay.

Individual farms provided accommodation for the visiting squads. Accounts given here describe the different types of accommodation available on individual farms. A farm might support a team of 20 or so pickers, with neighbouring farms having a similar number of temporary workers living-in during the tattie season. Even so, very little disruptive behaviour was noted. By the accounts given here, the potato howker's diet was likely to be potatoes, often eaten with locally gathered shellfish, although it is also noted that the influx of workers provided a welcome boost for local merchants. The local priest would often visit those who could not easily get to church, and a nurse was able to come in to treat anyone ill or injured.

As well as learning about the workers themselves, we also hear about the equipment used to harvest potatoes and how this changed over time. Initially done by individual workers using a graip, this work has now been replaced by machines which can achieve in an hour what would have previously taken a tattie squad a whole day to harvest.

The interviews also provide details about the potato merchants, the move away from barrels to jute bags for transportation, and the links with Achill Island, in Ireland, via the Railway Hotel.

The tattie work is an important part of the history of this area and these accounts provide some fascinating details about the way of life of the people involved in the production process.

Agnes Lamb

Well, I was born in St John Street, [Stranraer]. Ma mother – it wasn't like it is now – there … was dwelling houses, and we had a byre. And the cattle were grazed up near where Dalrymple Hospital is now, and were brought back and forward by ma sisters and brothers … . Ma mother, she milked the cows and sold the milk, which was part of her livelihood I suppose. Ma father had the stabling at what was the Buck's Head Hotel in those days. And horses were used like taxis. Then, he went to the War … this would be the First World War. And I am trying to think this now. I was a year old, oh aye, it must have been after the War because I was a year old, and he got the tenancy of the Drums Farm which belonged to Stranraer. It had been left by some old lady to Stranraer Council, but it was eventually to be a golf course. But Stranraer wasnae interested then because they had the golf course out Cairnryan Road then. However, I'm no doin it as I am doing it here, Mrs McLucas. I'll skip about the bits about the Drums, because during the War the Americans decided that they would have tae extend the Wig Bay. And of course the usual option was come on down the shore, so [they] commandeered the Drums – which we had to leave. My father had just died, and it was a bit of rumpus really. But my father had the tenancy of the Larg, where the houses are now, but it was a wee farm [then]. Ma brother, sister, mother an I moved there and had the tenancy of fields round Stranraer, which are now housin estates. And that augmented our income. But A suppose the interesting thing when I was young, we had to grow new potatoes – because it was good soil for new potatoes. And … we got locals from Stranraer to come out and lift them, an sort them out. And these potatoes in those days all went away in barrels. They were not like the way things are transported now, they were just put into barrels an taken away …

Who took them away?

Well it was a merchant, a merchant came and bought them in the ground … And this is the interesting bit, he had workers came over from Ireland and they were very, very decent people. They were wee crofters from the west coast o Ireland, and to augment their income, they lifted potatoes over here in the summer.

And where did they stay?

You had to provide, you had barns and you had to put [in], well A suppose
it was potato boxes an hay an stuff, for them to sleep on.

And what did they do about food?

Well, you had to have a, well, A suppose it was a fire. It wasnae a range or
anything, just a fire. They boiled potatoes, and they gathered shellfish off
the shore, and that is mostly what they ate.

Your mother did not have to provide for them?

Oh, no, no, no. And they had, what they called a gaffer. But he was a man
that the potato merchant sent down. And he stayed in town, but he come
out and oversees them. And they were very strong Catholics all these
people, and it was absolutely amazing on a Sunday to see them going to
Chapel so beautifully dressed. And yet there they were, that was their
livelihood, lifting the potatoes.

And did they have children with them?

Well, not really, no. I've never really noted. I can't remember much. But
obviously that's where I got my love of shellfish. I do love shellfish, you
know, and they boiled the ... cockles and mussels, and everything were
boiled up. It goes without saying, they were very clean people. And then
they moved fae one farm to another ... they would do two or three places
roundabout. And then at the end o the season they went back to Ireland.
But you sometimes got the same people comin back year after year ...

And none of them actually ever settled in Stranraer?

Not really because their homes were there, I think it was the Achill Islands
off the west coast they lived. But some of them spoke Gaelic. But they
could manage, with help ... [they] were very, very decent people.

And did they come straight ... to Stranraer or did they come via Glasgow?

Well, it would depend. A can't remember ... they might have been workin
in Ayrshire. But these merchants would bring them over, and they would
work round whatever farms they were involved in. And A suppose this
gaffer A'm talkin about, he would pay them. You didnae pay them,
because you were workin with this merchant. And these great big barrels,
they were huge. The lorries used to dump them off and they were filled
and then they came and picked them up. And took them away to Glasgow
or wherever, wherever the potatoes were being sold.

And how often did they collect them?

Well, whenever they were full. Depending on how much [you grew] ... .
We didnae have a lot of ground. And the locals in Stranraer, at the west
end of the town, they used to come at night and go round the ground to
pick up what was left. Because there wasn't machines, [the howkers] lifted
them with graip and baskets, there were nae [the] machines there are
nowadays. And people used to come and gather [potatoes] to take home.

And that was allowed?

Oh, yes, because there was very few. But then, money was very scarce in them days, an folk … whatever would augment what little they had, they would gather them.

And this would be before the War?

Before the Second War …

John McColm

I was speaking about our farm at Cairngarroch. We let about ten or 12 acres of land each year to Thomas Harper and Sons. This land was on the shore, and we grew early potatoes. They were Epicures, and we still grow Epicures. They were planted by people from Stranraer who lived in the Dicks Hill area. But for the harvesting of the potatoes each year we had many people from Donegal and County Mayo to dig those potatoes, and they stayed on the farm – and pretty primitive it was. These potatoes were sent to Glasgow for the Glasgow market. Usually we started digging in early June and that went on for many years, right up until the Second World War.

John Barr

When ma father came to Auchneel in 1920 he started to grow potatoes, and to grow potatoes he needed humus. And he was a great believer in hauling seaweed off the shore. And he hauled the seaweed, it would be hauled by horse and cart to begin with, and it would be put out in coups in the field and then spread. Later on the tractor come in and we hauled it by tractor and trailer. But in these days the potatoes were dug by Irish people. Irish squads come over and they stayed on the farms … . And, of course, the staple diet was potatoes. And they would start very early in the morning, they would start about five o'clock in the morning, and they would be diggin for a couple of hours. And they were digging by graip, of course. The man would dig with a graip, and he would be digging two rows at a time. And then there would be a man [or woman] behind would be lifting them and putting them into a basket, and then into a barrel. And then from the barrel they went to the station. Later on that was changed to jute bags … the jute bag was a very important thing – it cut down on … barrels. But I do remember a store at Auchneel where … 40 or 50 of these barrels were stored. Where they were stored for the next year, you know. They were still used for years and years after that because that was the main measure for your hundredweight … . And even when we were diggin by machines [with] the tattie digger, they filled the barrels. And you had timmers who went up and timmed the barrel into the bag. And then you had a man stitching them up, and then they were lifted and taken to the steading for transport, mainly by road, later on.

Were these people actually called timmers? A good old Scottish word.

Yes. A good old Scottish name. Going back to the potato squad. When the Irish workers, I'm talking practically pre-war, when they lived on the farm and they came from Ireland – and some of them were very, very poor. In fact, a lot of them stayed in the area. There was one or two of the workers, who were at Auchneel, came from Ireland and stayed on. And were there for 20 to 25 years, stayed on at Auchneel. There were the McClorey's who a lot of people know locally. And there was the McGrath's and they stayed on. But a lot of them never went back to Ireland. As I say, it was a great boost to the local trades when the Irish workers were on the farm. I mean, you're talking about 20 or 30 workers living on the farm, and it was a great boon for the small grocers because they made a run to come up to Auchneel, and then they would go on to the Chlendry. [The Irish workers] were very keen to buy their groceries from them.

Did the grocers come up in a van?

They had a van. Well, I'm talking, really, after the War. But it was just shortly after that they really stopped employing the Irish workers. We started to employ local people, local squads. We got a squad from Leswalt. We got a local gaffer. And it saved the people living on the farm, and I think that was a good thing. In these days, when you think of it … . The sheds were adjusted for the men on one side and the women on the other side. And the beds were made up of potato boxes, and then they were covered with mattresses which were just filled up with straw. And that was their main bedding for the workers staying there. And, of course, there was no light in those days, there was no electricity. The electricity didn't come in until 1939. I just can remember, just before the outbreak of War, the line went over the back of Auchneel.

John McColm (JMcC) and Bob Grierson (BG)

Mr Grierson, you have been involved in farming and particularly in the growing of potatoes all your life would you like to start off and tell us about it.

BG: Well, I started as soon as I left school, in farming, and my father was always growing early potatoes … about 24 acres o early potatoes to begin with and then it gradually got more. And it was difficult gettin labour, and we got quite a lot of Irish people. And they were brought over from Ireland. And we had two different gangs came over here and they were paid maybe £5 a week … each. We had a gaffer, Kilcoyne was his name, and he was in charge of them, and he brought them over. I think there was 21 men and women and youngsters, and they stayed on the farm. The women stayed up in the granary, where it was nice, and the men they stayed above a hen house, in the shed. And they had straw bales … for beds. And, it was quite a thing. They got what they wanted, potatoes and stuff like that, and milk on the farm … . It was quite a job.

Did they get the milk and potatoes for free?

BG: They got the potatoes because they worked with them, and they brought them in and cooked them themselves.

You said children came?

BG: I don't mean children, but one or two had family and if the woman was working inside, there was always one woman did the cooking, and if they had family they were looked after.

If they had little children did they go to school while they were here?

BG: No.

How did you get hold of the man who organised it?

BG: The potato merchants had these squads, and they got hold of them … . The one that I was working with in business, Kilcoyne, and his family was over there and then he got the workers from there. But it was quite an experience to begin with, all these people. And they were all, usually, very good people, genuine people.

When did they come and when did they stop?

BG: Well, at the potato time, this firm that Kilcoyne had … after the new potatoes were finished, they kept a few of them to work on but most of them went back home – the women and the younger people.

Did the same people come every year?

BG: Quite often the same. A lot of them came for years.

So, when you were a boy you would be quite used to some of them?

BG: Oh, yes, you got to know them.

Did you ever work out with them or did they just get on with it themselves?

BG: I was there, but not with them, being the foreman, the boss kinda business. Then I had a potato business in Glasgow and this man that worked for me from there for about seven years, and he kept the business goin.

When you say you had this potato business, did you then send gangs anywhere?

BG: … After he left me, he would go to different farms.

You must have quite a few memories of them then. Were they law-abiding?

BG: Most of them were quite genuine nice people. There was always one … maybe took too much drink, or something like that, which is not a bad thing. [*laughter*]

Were there many fights?

BG: Not really amongst them … . This place here next to me, they had a big lot of workers, and that was a different crowd – maybe they would fall out there. Then another farm next door [too], so we were surrounded by them for a month or so.

And sometimes they fell out?

BG: Well … not really too bad.

Can I turn to Mr McColm now? What was your experience of the tattie howkers?

JMcC: Very much like Bob's. We had different potato merchants in Glasgow than Bob had. We had two firms, W & A Graham and Paul & Weir, and they each got the squads over here. And [the workers] stayed on the farm, just like at Bob's. And each year the same people came back and Achill Island especially, needed the money. £5 a week they got and sent £4 back home, for the people in the west to live. These people from Achill Island were very fine folks. They were all Catholics, and the priest from Stranraer came out every weekend and spoke to them. And we had one particular tattie gaffer, Kilcoyne, and … yes, I think it would be the same Kilcoyne as Bob had, and his brother was a priest. And … I remember him coming to Cairngarroch to see his brother. And we were led to believe that the eldest of the family always went into the ministry. And Achill Island was a lovely island, and we visited them on numerous occasions. Just before you go over to Achill Island there's a huge hotel there, the Railway Hotel, and it is now closed down, but at one time this hotel was used by wealthy English people. They would go out there to this hotel, take all their staff with them, and stay for a month. And that helped the economy, and I think it would be through these connections that we got the Irish potato workers. It has been suggested by some they were treated badly when they come over here, that's nonsense. We looked after them well, and we enjoyed their company. Every year we looked forward to them coming over. They came from West Mayo and Donegal. They travelled by train to Dublin, got the ferry at Dublin and came to Glasgow. At Glasgow the potato merchant had a lorry and all the equipment for digging tatties by hand, graips and the lot. They got onto the lorry in Glasgow, came to the farm and had to fill their hassocks … with straw.

Back to Mr Grierson, was £5 a week not quite a lot of money?

BG: Well, I was only 14 or so at the time, and I had nothing to do with wages. But that was what I reckon that they were gettin.

And who did the wages …?

BG: The gaffer, whichever [one was working] for the firm paid the wages.

Presumably the farmer gave him the money?

BG: No, afterwards. We sold the potatoes as they were in the ground. [The farmer sold the potatoes, as they grew, to the merchant.] The merchant got his own squad, he kept his own squad all summer. As far as we were concerned, it was just so much per acre.

So, would the merchant be making off it?

BG: [*laughs*] They would make of it, oh yes!

So, he could afford to pay them £5 a week?

BG: Oh, yes, for sure. It was quite a bit of money then, but it wasn't a great life. The £5 would be nothin.

Do you remember the priest coming out here?

BG: Oh, yes, the Stranraer priest come out here.

They didn't go into the church?

BG: An odd one. But he came out here mainly, nearly every week.

Did he conduct a service?

BG: Well, he went in amongst them anyhow. That's all that I can say. There was a squad here, a squad at Glenside and squads here at Kirranrae, so he would go round them all.

He didn't gather them all together?

BG: No, no.

Did you ever have any weddings then?

JMcC: I can't recall any of the workers bein married over here. No, we had ladies with family. The young ones were about 11 or 12 when they started, and they worked with their mother. And they came in late May, after the peat had been cut in Ireland. They came over and they went further north as the Girvan potatoes became available. And then they went right up to Glasgow, digging until October. About the end of October, they left to go home, to Ireland. Some of them stayed on, and they would marry later. But they were always very nice people, and I could never cast anything against them. They did it tae live. It wasn't slave labour. No, I don't believe in that. They worked here to send the money home to their folks in Ireland.

Did they have a party when it was all over?

BG: No, not really. Some nights they had some music and stuff like that. But they were quite happy.

Did you ever go to these?

BG: Oh, well, I looked in amongst them and stuff like that, sometimes. Sometimes they didn't want you.

You must have some anecdotes about them. Is there anything that sticks out as being particularly funny or anything like that?

BG: Talking about marriage, we had a marriage once. A son of the foreman got married to one and they had [the wedding party] in the byre, just off the byre. It was a turnip shed that was cleaned out, and they had quite a party. I can always remember it.

Did the priest come out to marry them or did they go into Stranraer?

BG: They went into Stranraer. In fact I took them in. I ran them in … .
He was the son of Kilcoyne.

In nice weather they used to go down to the sea, nearly every night
after they finished work. And a big lot of them had a swim in the sea just
below us here.

Did they manage to come over during the War?

BG: They did. Oh, yes, they came over just the same.

There was no difficulty?

BG: No.

These were southern Irish people?

BG: That's right … . There was always new ones every year came but the
older ones and that, [they] came every year.

There was no difficulty? [Did the police come out to see them?]

BG: The police usually had a run round, but we never had any bother at
all.

*When did they stop coming? What happened in farming that the tattie howkers
stopped coming?*

BG: Well, I don't know … . There are different ways of lifting potatoes
now.

JMcC: We don't need the Irish workers because the potatoes are now dug
wi a big machine and three people operate this machine. And so, there is no
work now for these Irish people as it used to be. Everything's mechanised
now, and my nephew, at Cairngarroch, Drummore, he can dig enough
potatoes with this machine in an hour that it took a squad a full day.

When did this mechanisation really take over?

BG: Four or five years ago?

JMcC: No, earlier.

BG: Well, it was different then, they had smaller ones. But the machines
now are tremendous. They will lift, in three or four hours, an acre? Which
used to take two days to lift.

What happened if any of them took ill?

BG: Oh, they were always attended. Here, we had a nurse in the village
here, she would go in amongst them any time. And if it was necessary she
would get the doctor. They were well looked after that way here. I have
never seen other places.

*Nowadays there is so much of this Health and Safety at Work. I wondered did you
have any kind of particular regulations?*

BG: No, there was no regulations at all. [*laughs*] Here, I must say, my
father was pretty good at giving them a little bit.

Did they ever get any time off?

BG: Not when they were working. They had, I think it was about a nine-
hour day in those days. And then, if it was too wet they didn't work.

If it was too wet did they get paid?

BG: I think so … . It was more a weekly wage.

JMcC: I would say that if they weren't working, they weren't being paid. But normally it was a £5. But occasionally, if the market in Glasgow got overloaded with potatoes, the workers wouldn't get full pay and they objected tae this very strongly. If they couldn't get work because of the market being overloaded, it was pretty hard on them.

It would be pretty hard on you too?

BG: Oh, yep. Sometimes it was very bad … . When Ayrshire got started above there was more potatoes going in … the earlier you were, the better it was.

Did you ever have that situation where you couldn't get rid of your potatoes?

BG: Oh, well, you just didn't work … . Some years were worse than others. The like of John, he was always early first, and we were kind of second. We werenae too bad, a day or two before Ayrshire.

Once the Ayrshire potatoes came in to the market then that was … and they were nearer Glasgow.

BG: I was friendly with a potato merchant in Edinburgh and he and I bought this place in Glasgow for a potato business. And, unfortunately, he went on holiday on a ship, got into the pool and died in the pool. So I was left with the potato business. I was a wee bit lucky there maybe, but it was a terrible thing.

At the end of the War I can remember potatoes were rationed. How did that affect you?

JMcC: On the farm we had pigs and the local butcher would kill a pig, make ham and that would feed the family for the year. We were never really affected by shortage of food on the farm during the War.

But did you not have certain regulations you had to abide by?

JMcC: [*laughter*] We could always get by the regulations in one way or another.

Did you not have Government Inspectors?

BG: Very seldom. Very seldom. I don't think that I was ever bothered with them.

Your potatoes were never requisitioned?

BG: No. As John says, we had a lot of pigs and they were killed the same. And always one was kept, and you had some of your own milk, turnips, potatoes. … We were always very lucky.

When the same howkers came over during the War, have you any idea what they did about ration books?

BG: I couldn't answer that.

JMcC: No, I don't know what happened there.

You would have ration books, everybody had ration books?

BG: It didn't seem to affect the farm because there was always something on ...

I was just thinking of things like ... butter, cheese.

BG: Well, we always had plenty of butter because we had our own milk. [Mr McColm is holding a kind of brochure which advertises the Cairndale Hotel in Dumfries, the George Hotel in Stranraer, the Douglas Arms Hotel in Castle Douglas and the front of it is a picture of two women lifting tatties at Cairngarroch.]

Can you tell me more about it please?

JMcC: Yes. This hotel was very keen to publicise local food. And in the hotel, during the tattie season, most of the potato merchants lived in the hotel. And the owners, Jarotti, were very keen to publicise the local food. It would help their trade. And we have this photograph here of Rita, an Irish colleen, and her mother from County Donegal. And, I remember the mother. I don't remember the daughter, but they were lovely people. And when the Inspector came to look at the premises it was the local, what we call the Sanitary Inspector, Ian McMillan ...

Was this after the War?

JMcC: It would be during the War. I left Cairngarroch in 1945, just at the end of the War. So anything I'm talking about is before 1945. The local Sanitary Inspector came every year to hae a look at the premises and how we had them laid out. And we had to have pails of water and sand in case of fire, and we weren't always in agreement with him. The local people weren't too happy about having these inspectors. After we stopped keepin the workers on the farm, my brother and Bob Lammie [at] Low Drummore, bought what were the billets at Drummore. These billets were built for the War. The lads who lived in them were being trained for the Air Sea Rescue. And these lads would train for six weeks and then they would go to Norfolk to man the Air Sea Rescue boats off the East coast o England. Many o these lads lost their lives when they went to do this work. They rescued British fliers, and German. It didn't matter which nationality they were, these boys rescued them. And they were all trained in Luce Bay, and they lived in the billets at Drummore. And after the War these billets were redundant, and Bob Lammie and ma brother bought them. And from then on the Irish potato diggers lived in these billets, and this was a big improvement to what the conditions were on the farm.

Would they have running water and stuff?

BG: They had water into them then.

Mr Grierson and Mr McColm, on behalf of Stranraer and District Local History Society thank you very much.

Jim Wallace

The potato workers in them days had to stay at the farm, so we had to do a bit of alterations to the steading for them to stay in. Bedding and cooking accommodation, toilets, hot and cold water, all these things had to be done and was passed by the Sanitary Inspector. These workers started about six in the morning and finished up about four in the afternoon so the potato lorries could get up to Glasgow with the potatoes for the early market in the morning.

3

Tramps and Travellers

Many contributors recalled a time when tramps and travellers were a part of everyday life in the region. There were many different reasons why people took to the road and some of these are explored in the extracts which follow. In the first extract Andrew Love recalls some of the travellers that he remembers from his childhood. He tells how they came from all walks of life, with some providing services to the rural community such as the cobbler who came round with his barrow and mended shoes. Andrew also speaks about those, like Mary and John Fullerton, who came about the farms selling nick-nacks from a basket. In another extract in this selection Mrs Brownlee also recalls travelling merchants coming into The Glasgow House to stock up on small haberdashery items. One might assume that these 'wheelers' would be picking up farm work along the way, as was common in other parts of Scotland, but none of the Stranraer interviewee's referred to this practice.

However, there were many others who had their own reasons for travelling about. In his interview with Jack Hunter in 1999, Bill McCaig said that many of the tramps came from a military background and that they had simply found it impossible to settle back into normal civilian life. These were 'people who didn't fit into the system and walked the roads'.

Travellers often sought a bed for the night at the farms they were passing by and the interview extracts also shed light on some of the temporary residences they took advantage of. Andrew Love's father was happy for people to stay in the barn and simply locked them in at night, matches and all, while Bill McCaig remembered that his own father 'lived in constant fear of them setting fire to the stackyard'.

Bill McCaig also explained that many of the people who squatted in the RAF huts on his father's land were families who were leaving the land and for whom the huts offered the best accommodation they could hope for at a time when no new houses were being built.

Mr Andrew Love

As a child, Mr Love lived at Bridge of Aird Farm, Stranraer. He recalled the characters who would be at the farm of an evening. When asked about why they came,
Andrew said, 'it was just a place tae stay for the night'. The farm was the nearest to
the town, and folk would often just turn up, often soon after 9pm, when the pubs
closed.

Well, alright then, Andy, on you go and tell me about all these [people].
Well … A've scribbled this doon yesterday, and it is that long as I have
written anything, I can hardly read it.

Now that I am retired, I often think of the past and the folks that I
knew. My memory takes me back to the many tramps that used to stay at
Bridge of Aird. Up until the War the pubs shut at nine o'clock and just
after that the door would go, and this would be men and women asking
to get into the barn or sheds for the night. On one particular morning
there was 13 of them in the shed. We never knew what circumstances or
tragedies forced them into this way of life. One of the best of them was
Scotch Jimmy. Many of the older people in Stranraer may remember
him. He spent most of his life in and out of jail. When drunk, if anyone
spoke to him, he took his stick and broke the nearest shop window.
When he appeared in court, he was usually given seven days in jail. A
small man with a grey beard, he was given the cast off clothing by John
Chalmers of the neighbouring farm, and went about in plus fours, spats
and a bowler hat. [*laughter*] He was later found in Girvan harbour.
You don't know what happened?
No.
And your father didn't mind somebody that had been in the jail in your barn?
No, no, no. He just opened the door and let them in and that was them
for the night … . Now, there used to be a sandpit here, just where the link
road is. And in it there was a caravan where Mary and John Fullerton
stayed. Mary was a small woman with a bad limp and used to lead John
about, who was blind. Mary sold buttons, safety pins and leather laces,
called whangs: a word you never hear now. In 1940, they were walking on
the Limekiln Road when an army truck struck them. Mary was killed and
John was badly injured … . It wid be dark, uh huh. This accident
happened just where Palmer's House is and it used to be called the Red
Barn. Now, several years after this, a man walked into the yard one day
and said, 'Hello Andy'. An A looked up, and this was John Fullerton.
And he had neither glasses nor stick with him, and A often wondered was
this Mary leading him, was he just kiddin – a sympathy thing?
They weren't try[ing] to con people out of money or something?

33

No, no, no. But she had more sympathy, you know, if she wis leading him about.

On the other side of the sandpit was a hut in which Minnie and Charlie Fox lived. Charlie wis a piper. An ex-Army piper. Now both took a good drink, an one night they set the hut on fire. Minnie was burned to death, but Charlie survived. Minnie sold dishes. These goods were all supplied to them by the Farroll family, who'd a rag and bone store in Hanover Square. It amazes me now to think how many of these men were tradesmen, and they just upped their jobs and took to the road. At one time, we had a blacksmith, Ned McWilliam, who stayed with us for several years. A believe he belonged to Wigtown. Sanny Davies, a tinsmith, and a cobbler used to come round with a barrow to mend shoes or boots.

… when you say 'stayed with you for several years', did your mother and father feed them?

No. They usually got a cup a tea and a scone in the mornin … they sorted their own food. They went away to the town after that, spend the day in town just. … Yes, just wandering … [they] used to stand often at McHarrie's garage … [they] would get pennies and that.

And this was during the War … did they get much, do you think, from the soldiers?

Och, I don't think it. No. You see, and then, in those days, even getting a penny that was something to them. They worked in pennies.

On you go then.

There was a cobbler who used to come round with a barrow and mend shoes and boots. Quite a few of these men played the fiddle and A often wondered where they learned, or were they self-taught?

So they obviously carried their fiddles round?

They carried their fiddles with them. An, there was one man, Murphy, he was a ships' engineer who never lost his love of the sea. He used to make his way to Glasgow docks an then steal ontae a boat that was getting ready to sail. An he would appear in the morning after the boat sailed an he's usually given his breakfast and sent down to shovel coals. The boat usually went to Southampton to load up. Now, one night, he had too much to drink an he got on the wrong boat an spent the next six weeks shovelling coal to Australia. During that time he was not allowed off the ship, so illegal immigrants are not a new thing. Jamie O'Neil, he collected rabbit skins and made paper flowers. He spent his time between here and McCullochs o Port O' Spittal. Now, Lisa Docherty, or Dundee Annie as some folk called her, rumour had it that she had murdered her man in Glasgow. These people all had a drink problem, but A'm sure they caused less bother than the present yobs of today.

And what brought them to Stranraer?

They were called 'wheelers'. They went round the country lik a wheel, an all had special places to stay at, and they just kept going round and round.

So, they were true tramps?

Aye.

And when they came here, they knew they could come …

They knew that they would get in here. An, they maybe just stayed a day or two an away again an you'd maybe see them, maybe twice a year.

And did they ever do any work on the farm?

No, no.

They never gave you any payment?

No, no …

That was very kind of your father and mother.

So, no, they just moved round the country and they knew their special places to stay at. Wheelers they called them.

And how did you, as children, look upon them?

We were going to the school an you saw them in the morning an then at night again.

And they were people that had no family connections?

No, no.

And did you know the history of them?

Well, a few of them, aha … . Weel, Charlie Fox, he was an ex-Army piper an I think he belonged to Annan. An there was a man from that way told me, that – this would be the First World War – when Charlie came home on leave to Annan, they drafted in two extra policemen, in from Dumfries. Cause a couple of days of drinkin an he was back in the jail, just to his leave was up, and then they put him back on the train.

But they never gave your family any trouble?

No, not a bit. No …

And you said something about them giving up their matches when they came to stay?

Ah. There was one man came to the door one night to get in, and A went to open the door for him. An he offered me cigarettes an matches, and, 'Och,' I says, 'I don't want them. When you get in there, the door is locked an if you set fire to the place you will go up with it'. So he turned an went away again. Wouldnae go in …

But you never had any trouble?

We never had any fires or any trouble whatever … . Mind, they all sold safety pins and laces and buttons, an that kind of thing. Minnie, she sold dishes …

And how did she carry them around?

In a big basket, jist.

… And did they get much sale?

Well, they seemed, they always made a livin, and I mean things were jist pennies …

These are only a few of the ones that passed through. Many more were here for the one night only and we never knew their names. They passed on to good knows where, but that was their way of life and they seemed to enjoy it, and it never seemed to do them any harm.

Anne Brownhill

Regarding the merchandise the 'wheelers' took about with them Mrs Brownhill, talking about the family business, The Glasgow House, noted that:

Towards the back there was various boxes, and the gaun folks as we say, the folks that went round with the pack, Sunny Allison, the Kings from Sandhead, they could go round and get stocked up with hooks and eyes and buttons and so on that they sold from their pack.

Bill McCaig

The RAF built huts to provide dispersed accommodation for the RAF population working from Wig Bay and this included two sites on Challoch Farm. The accommodation consisted of insubstantial huts with corrugated roofs. As Mr McCaig explained, these were problematic from the start:

Well, of course, it was all very well in theory, but in practice, it didn't work. Because no airman was going to live in a hut and then get all his washing stuff together to walk to Wig Bay, or march to Wig Bay, which was two miles away, and stay there all day and then come back at night into a cold hut, with no catering facilities [and only] a picket post somewhere with a cold water tap. So, of course, the airman hated it, and did everything they could to get out of staying in these huts and hied back to Wig Bay whenever they could. After the War we were left with these huts, and if my father had had any sense, he would have bought them from the Air Ministry. But he thought his arm was being twisted, and he wouldn't buy. When the people who were leaving the farms saw these huts, they were much better than some of the houses they had been in, so they came down and squatted in the huts. And we hadn't bought our huts, they belonged to the Air Ministry and [so] it meant they squatted with us. We would have … five huts on one side that were occupied, and maybe six on the other side that were occupied. So we had a little village round us, of uninvited guests. And they were there for several years until the houses were built at the different villages and … the authorities managed to get them out of them eventually. Obviously, there had been no building done for years and these people were desperate for housing, and there was [these] huts. So you couldn't blame them for going and living in them, because they were free. But it caused a lot [of] problems for us. It was not a good arrangement at all. I think my father must have many times regretted the fact that he hadn't put his hand in his pocket and bought the huts. It was done and that was that. We had to live with it. Oh, some of them we were on good terms with, but some of them we would have been even better without. So, we were surrounded with 30 or 40 people for quite a few years after the War.

…

Later on the stable became the resort of tramps because tramps were universal in the twenties and thirties and here they were with little apartments all done with the best Scotch pine and straw. Quite often a gangin body would come in and ask for a battle of straw, which he would carry up to the stables. And we could see from where we were that occasionally a fire was lit and they would have a happy hour if they had any bottle at all. In the late 1930s, I think, my uncle to whom the stables had then belonged went up one night when there was no tramps about and set fire to it and, boy, that place fairly blazed because it was the best of Scotch pine. That stopped the tramps. That was another thing we had to bear, because practically daily we would have someone at the door. There was a lot of people on the road then. People who didn't fit into the system and walked the roads. Maybe not every day, but quite often we would have them coming in. Well, of course, [our farm] was on the road to the stables and we would have them in wanting tea or pieces and things like that. Some were independent enough, just to ask for hot water for their billy cans.

Were they offering to do any work?

No, they were just people who were displaced and had no place to go. My father lived in constant fear of them setting fire to the stackyard. He wouldn't let them stay in the buildings at all because there was so much flammable stuff there. It was too risky. They just vanished eventually, once the stables weren't on their route. Once the stables were down they didn't pester us.

Vivien Delf

Mrs Delf was interviewed by Nancy McLucas in 2013 and recalled her early visits to rural Wigtownshire. As well as speaking about the tattie harvesters and tramps and travellers, Vivien also recalled a time when horses were an integral part of farm work and when large numbers of rabbits, along with salmon and lobster, were sent off daily, by train, to the London markets.

Right Vivien, tell me what your connection is with the area?

My mother was born and brought up in Ayrshire, in the Irvine Valley .... .
When her eldest brother, Johnny, came back from the First World War
grandpa wanted him to get a farm of his own, but he said no, 'We'll all
move'. And they decided to come down to Wigtownshire. They were in
touch with the Findlay family, who had been in Crofthead before them,
and I think they were influential in getting them into Auchness.

Where is Crofthead?

Crofthead is at the Priestland, just outside Darvel in the Irvine Valley. [They
came down to Auchness]. That was in 1920. My mother was 16 at that time.
She'd been going to Kilmarnock Academy before she left the Valley and
intended going on to Stranraer Academy when she came down here, but it
meant a very long day and granny persuaded her to give up school and help
in the house instead. Granny was very interested in the dairy in particular, so
ma mother did most of the cooking in the house. After my grandfather
retired, Uncle Johnny took over Auchness. In the meantime my Aunt Aggie
had married, and she and her husband were in Balgowan. Uncle Robert also
married and he, I think with the help of the family, bought Auchneight –
near the Mull .... . Ma mother stayed in touch with the Valley because one of
her sisters had married before the family came down, so she used to go back
to dances up there. And [then] she married ma father, who came from the
Valley. So I was born and brought up in Newmilns. But most of my holidays
were spent down in Wigtownshire, staying either at Auchness or Balgowan
or Auchneight. Virtually all my school holidays were down here, and even
before [I went to] school. To begin with it was mainly at Auchness, on my
own. And, I would either wander around on my own or follow Uncle
Johnny around, if he was at home, although he was often away lobbying for
the Farmers' Union ...

Tell my about your uncle and the NFU.

He was Vice President for 13 years. He was also one of the founders of the
Scottish Milk Marketing Board. So he spent quite a lot of the time away at
meetings up in Edinburgh, or lobbying down in London. He was also a
great Burns man and about the middle of January to about the end
of March he was often speaking at Burns' suppers all over the country.
Nevertheless, he would work on the farm whenever he was at home, and
would be up for morning milking, etc. If he wasn't around, then I would
often tag onto some of the workers, either helping in the dairy by my way
of it, or helping thin turnips or something like that. Some of the cows
were still hand milked at that stage because they wouldn't take to the
milking machines. And that was always fascinating watching that.

A lot of the ploughing and harrowing was still done by horses at that
stage and of course I used to love being with the horses, out in the field.

One time it proved rather dangerous to me, a horse turned away – I didn't expect – and it hit me on the ankle. Thankfully, it had already shod its shoe on that hoof, so no permanent damage was done. There was the stables in the courtyard at the farm. Also, there were three parts of the byre, and above the middle section there was a loft where the tatties were stored and where, at the harvest time, the tattie howkers used to live when they came to stay for that. You could walk right through from the hayloft above the byres and come down into the kitchen at the house. Part of the loft at the kitchen end was partitioned off, and … that's where the Land Army girl lived.

How many Land Army girls were there?

I just remember one at a time. There may have been more during the War but this was just after the War. We had a generator for working the milking machines, and in the evening they were able to run electricity off that for the house. There was an old range in the kitchen … . The house had its own well and the water was pumped into the house for that. So that we had running water, but during the summer it often ran dry and we had to take milk butts down to Longrigg, to the spring there, and fill them up to top up the tank. The dairy house had another well which was out in the garden, and I think it was used until relatively recently … . Later on I tended to spend more time at Balgowan, and often my cousin would come and join me there. She was the youngest of the Auchneight family, Yvonne. At Balgowan we learned to feed the hens and collect eggs, and at tattie harvesting we would go out and help in the fields. And at lunchtime we would bring back just newly dug tatties and wash them and boil them up and they would be put in a great big tureen in the centre of the table, with chives and lots of butter, and that would be our meal. At harvest time for, the oats it was then, or corn, we used to follow the binder and try and catch the rabbits as they came out from underneath the binder. We weren't very good at that, but some of the men were. And I remember the rabbit-trapper, who got his rabbits from the traps as well but also from that, stringing them up along the fence. It seemed like hundreds of pairs of rabbits, and they went off on the train that night to go down to the markets in London. Sometimes I would go out with the trapper early in the morning and that was exciting … . Sometimes if the rabbit holes were fairly near to a hen house there might be rats in the trap, and we had to be careful of that. I also remember sometimes seagulls were caught in the traps, because they'd come down to get a rabbit. They were enormous, I was surprised how big they were. And the only way to tackle them then was to hit them with a spade, and it often took several blows before they could be killed. But they were too dangerous to get any closer to … . When I stayed at Balgowan, well, when I stayed anywhere, we went to church regularly.

But my Aunt Aggie, from Balgowan, used to play at Ardwell Church. She played there for 30-odd years. In fact, she had a little organ in the house that she used to play. Originally, the Ardwell organ had to be pumped, and there was somebody employed to do that every Sunday, but they didn't always turn up so often one of my cousins ended up doing it. My aunt also played once a month at St Agnes' Church, which belonged to Logan, and the Laird liked to have a service there once a month.

It's no longer a church of course.

No. It fell derelict, oh some time ago … . I didn't go to that church at all though I remember going to arrange flowers before services. Sanny Muir from the *Daily* was the beadle there, or church officer. He was also in the choir at Ardwell. In those days the choir at Ardwell consisted of two people, Sanny Muir and Lezzie Service.

It couldn't have been a very big choir?

… No, it wasn't … . Regarding Lezzie Service, she and her husband, Johnny, for a long time – or it seemed a long time – lived in a Nissen hut that was left in the wood opposite Balgowan road end. They had a daughter, Millie, who was around my age and we often used to play together. I sometimes went out in the fishing boat with a chap, Gibson, I think it was Johnny Gibson, who lived down close to Logan Mill. He used to go out for salmon and lobster, he'd a lot of lobster creels. I was very frightened when he went out for lobsters even though they were tied up, I didn't like them. The salmon were much nicer. But all these used to go off on the train to London, ready for the markets the following morning. There were a lot of fishermen around the Mull in those days, but they're so few now.

… At Balgowan there was no electricity in the farmhouse at all. It was all oil lamps. Though we did have running water, it came from a spring which was down near the shore, and when there was a storm, or a high tide, the water was brackish … . In Balgowan, it was a dry toilet underneath the stair. My Uncle Willie an my cousin, Ian, built the bathroom themselves. And the mirrors that they used in the new bathroom came from very large mirrors that had been in Logan House when it was the extended Victorian building that was pulled down about that time. And that gave a huge mirror in the hallway, a huge mirror in the lounge and two pretty decent-sized mirrors in the bathroom as well.

And where did they bring the water from?

… It must've come from the spring. But I do remember that when we washed hair we used buckets from the rain trough at the back door to wash our hair and rinse it, and [we] used soft soap as well.

On behalf of Stranraer and District Local History Trust Mrs Delf, thank you very much for your interesting reminiscences.

Hugh Reid

Mr Reid was interviewed by Nancy McLucas in January 2006 and during their time together he shared many stories with her about the adventures he had when he was a poacher. This light-hearted account also includes a great deal of detail about the methods and practices used in poaching as well as information relating to the relationship between the poacher, the law and the game merchant.

Mr Reid, you had some experiences with poaching when you were younger. Tell me about it?

> Yes. Well, when I was a boy in [Lowe] Street the old men came back from the First World War. They came back to nothin, but they were poachers before they went tae the War and I used to go the messages for these three brothers, who were poachers. And through time I grew up, I was 14 and we shifted up to Murrayfield Gardens and the same men moved up into the new houses, and one was called Pat Halliday. He was a great poacher, and the other brothers were poachers. So, I thought I would start the poaching too. So, I asked Pat if he would learn me the poaching and he said, 'Certainly, I'll take you out tonight …'. So I went with Pat out that night and he showed my how to run a net out. The net was 120 yards long.

Was this in the loch?

> No, no, in the fields, rabbiting … . Aye, we run the net out 120 yards long, and he showed me how to put the gibs in and how to put the pins in. And after we had it all pinned up we went down into the field an we chased the rabbits in. And Pat showed me how, when the rabbits was in the net, how to take them out, how to keep their heads clear … and then break their necks and then take them out and lay them down with their bellies turned up white. So I went in … and I had the bag and I was carrying the rabbits and putting them in the bag, and then Pat showed me how to take the pins out after we got the rabbits out. So we went on to the next set and we did the same again … . We got about 60 rabbits anyway, for the night. He showed me how to gut them, and we hid them. You see Pat couldn't ride a bicycle, he had to walk. Well, but I had a bicycle, and I fetched the net in and I went down to … the butcher in the mornin and I told him I had so many rabbits. And then he run me out in the van and we lifted the rabbits up and came into town wi them. [The butcher] weighed them and he gave me the money for them, an a list what they come to. So I went up to Pat, and Pat was in his bed, and I told him, 'That's the money for the rabbits, Pat'. Well Pat would count the money out, he would give me 7/6d and he kept 2/- off for his nets. And I would go home and give my mother five shillings and I kept the other because I wanted to buy a net of my own, for I'd get a fair share then. So at the finish up I got a net of my own, and Pat

and me would work on the two nets then, and [so] we're getting more
rabbits. And things were going fine there, and I was doing well with a
night's poaching, because there wis no work. I wis always handin in money
to the house, to keep the house going. To keep us living. But the risk was
with being caught. You knew you were going to get the jail.

Where did you do this?

In the [Mark] road. After we got the two nets we were hunting in the
[Mark] road and then wherever the winds took us. Maybe inside the Inch
there, inside Balker hills there, or the Cairn hills, or the Chlenrie hills, or
Dunskey at the Port. After that Pat took ill, Pat died. So I got in tow with
another two chaps, George McMillan and Tommy Cope. So these fellows
weren't caring where they went. So this night we went on to Dunskey with
the three nets, and we had the three nets. I knew all the ground, with Pat
showing me where we were working. So, we put the nets out that night,
three nets, and we had the most rabbits I've had. We'd nearly 400 rabbits
that night. We were getting 60 and 70 in each set, that was wi three nets,
of course.

Did you sell them?, to the butcher?

Yes, … the butcher got them.

He must have known they were poached?

Oh, he knew they were poached. He knew they were poached rabbits. But
he wouldn't care, as long as he got the rabbits, what way they come.
Because he was buying all the poachers' rabbits. … The farmers in them
days, they knew a poacher wouldn't touch their hens. If ever you stole the
hens from the farmer that was a blot against you with the poachers. They
knew if poachers were round about the farm they never lost anything. A
poacher would never kill a man's hens, or [steal] from him. They were
honest in that way. They got what they wanted, the rabbits. The farmers
knew that from poachers [then]. In a way they were happy too, because
round the [rigs] the rabbits were eating an awful lot of the corn … .
But, what we used to do then, maybe I'd hae went to maybe some place to
harvest . … . A big estate, the likes of Dunskey. I went up there, and my
brothers would have went to some other place. And we got to know the lay
of the ground, you see. But if we'd ave went ourselves, on a bicycle through
the day, the keepers [would have] seen us and they [would] know we were
spotting the ground. But when we were harvesting there, then they would
expect that. We knew all the ground, we knew how to get in and how to
come out. At the turn there that's up at the Chlenrie, we were up there one
night – poachers with three nets – and we had nearly 400 off it too.

Did you get rid of all 400?

Yes, they couldn't get enough rabbits in those days. You only got … about
6d a piece for a rabbit, a shilling a couple. That's all they gave you, but still

it was a lot of money. Because in them days, when you were working the fields there, you were only getting about 5/- a day. But you see, if you had ten rabbits there that was always a days' pay for you. But we never went to the extent to go too far. We got what done us and we always had the risk of getting off the ground quick you see. If you had waited too long on the ground, you coudave been caught.

Were you ever caught?

No, never caught, I was lucky. I was running clear the whole time.

Did you ever go for things other than rabbits?

Yes, we went for fish and everything, salmon. And we went for pheasants, but you had to hae a gun. But I was never inclined to go with these men with guns, because [there] were desperate men with guns. And they would have shot people and thought nothin o it. Because they were wild men. [Anonymous] there was a wild man. [Anonymous] there was a man with a gun, he was a gun man. And he always carried it in his jacket, a sawn-off shotgun. And he had been at the Port, Portpatrick, at a plooin match. And [Anonymous] was a well-known man, and [a] desperate man. An the farmer's told [Anonymous] this day at the plooin match, '[Anonymous], you had better watch today because there is a man coming down here … he's from the north of Scotland, and he's goin to take you … in bits'. [Anonymous] said, 'No keeper'll ever take me'. So, my father told me this, the plooin match started and any hares that caught under the ploo, [Anonymous] shot them. Well, as he did this, this keeper stepped out, 'Ha, Ha,' he says, 'I've got you at last, boy'. 'Got me? Get out of the road or I'll shoot you too,' [Anonymous] said. My Uncle Joe said, 'For God's sake … don't touch him. If you dae shoot him, you'll be took for murder. You'd be hung'. 'Alright,' he says, 'you've saved him'. But [Anonymous] turned round and got the butt o the rifle, and he smashed the keeper's head in with it … . He nearly killed the man! And the man came out after about six months in the hospital, and he was coming down past The Cross and most of the poachers were standin there. They knew him. And he came down – [Anonymous] got 18 months of the jail for that – an when the man come down past he seen ma Uncle Joe and he said, 'Boys, I must thank you for saving my life … I never thought he was a man like that,' he said. … He sat down and he thanked them, and he said, 'If that's the kind of man you've got in Stranraer poaching I'm going back home to where I come from'. And the man cleared out. But the thing that [Anonymous] did there, was desperate …

So you didn't want to be involved with the shooters?

No, not wi guns, because I got entangled wi a fella, [Anonymous], an I was out wi him. We were goin tae shoot something anyway, rabbits or pheasants, whatever you could get your hands on. So we went oot an it wis at the Red Brig out there, and here there was a peewit or something in the field. And who came down the road but the gamekeeper ... Allison the gamekeeper, on a bicycle. And he knew [Anonymous]. And, he said, 'Right [Anonymous] I'm taking the gun off you'. And [Anonymous] held the gun up at him. And this chap, McMillan, came doon past [then], with his horse and cart and his wife. He was a dealer – a hawker, and he knew me. He said, 'Right boy jump into this cart come on, come away out of that'. He thought [Anonymous] was going to shoot the gamekeeper. But I don't think he shot the gamekeeper, because I was away. But it could have been murder, he would have shot him. He was a tailor to Provost Dyer, this man. He'd one leg, he was on crutches, an he used tae poach with dogs. He never poached wi long nets, but he poached with dogs. Catchin rabbits. He done it more or less just for sport, ken, he had a good job.

What was the difference between nets and dogs?

Och, well, they just kept the dogs, well mibby tae get a rabbit there for the pot. You kept a good dog there, maybe on a Sunday or that, for a bit of sport. But you couldn't make a living off a dog. Some of them just kept them to get a rabbit for the pot, something to eat you see ...

Tell me about the salmon poaching?

Aye, well, the salmon poaching was a different thing altogether there. I was only there three times but when you were caught at it you knew you were going to get a long stretch in the jail. And there was no excuse if you were caught, because the gamekeepers there, they weren't caring what they done. And if you put up a fight there, they could have killed you. But, John there he was a great man for the salmon, my brother John. And, John, I remember, he went too far. He's away down in England now. They went out and they never stopped. When they maybe got ten or 12 salmon, they wanted 100 salmon, greed. And then they come and ... handed one into the house and he would tell me how many he got, and these other three chaps along with him. But, you see, with the salmon, you had to go into the water and you had to get across there, and it was a risky business too.

Where did they do this?

At New Luce. There was the Minister's Pool. And that big pool at the viaduct at Glenluce, in there too. John knew all the holes right up that bank there. And some of the chaps went down as far as Ballantrae, to the rivers Stinchar an that. John and them, they went oot o place with it because they got in tow with these men and, here, they were away out this night and they got about 24 or 30 salmon that night. And here, they had them in the house, and they set off to go in to ... Newton Stewart [to sell them]. And their wives and aa in the car. And when they got to the viaduct, somebody had seen them carryin the salmon out of the house, and when they got the length of Glenluce the police was waiting on them, and they were all caught.

What happened to them?

I just forget how they got on but I knew they were all caught, an they lost the lot.

Did your father ever do anything like that?

My father, no. He wouldn't go in to the poaching. He worked on the boat. He was a seafaring man, but he always told me, 'If ever you are caught mind you boy, don't look to me for help'. He said, 'You don't need to do that'. But I was daen alright at it, and getting a shillin or two. And I just kept at it, because there was no work.

How long did you carry on doing this?

I carried right on till the War started, and then I was called up for the War. And after I came back from Burma I started back up again at the poaching, an that was with [Anonymous] and [Anonymous]. ... We just carried on then till myxomatosis came in and we had to stop.

Is that what stopped you poaching eventually?

Aye. We would never have stopped poaching, because it was easy money for us, ye ken. An when I started at first it was very strict, the gamekeepers watched a lot. But at the last, they hadn't many keepers on the estate. They wouldn't pay them to do the work.

So, tell me, and without giving anything away, are there people still poaching?

No ... I don't think there will be anybody poaching now. Because, if there is anybody at the salmon the now, they know what's in front of them. It's a severe stretch in the jail. It's two year or three year. So I don't think that they bother doing it now.

And they don't poach rabbits any more?

No ... but I know, I don't want to go into details, but I knew people that wis poaching salmon. And I could have got them all the jail, ... [But] they werenae worried aboot rabbits, as long as you didn't touch the pheasants or the salmon. It still went on in the country.

So you did the salmon two or three times but you just didn't like it?

No, the only thing in its favour was getting a stretch in the jail, you could get about two year. Oh, no ... . The men that tried you there was most of the men that was buying the rabbits. ... In my opinion they didn't want you in the jail. They wanted you out working for them. You got more out working for them, because they were buying the rabbits.

Was it not very dangerous?

No it wasnae dangerous. The only danger ever I seen was the chap, I wasn't there, an ... there was three of them. And they mostly worked about the Inch poachin, but never worked about the Portpatrick side. And they'd begun to do this set anyway with the nets, there was three of them. And they always used to carry this big pin pocket, for your pins for your net, inside there [close to the body]. Well, this night this chap, it was a high bank, and he jumped over, and the pin went right up through there … through his neck and the side of his face. The pin was all pointed, and it went right up through his chin. And they had to rush him back to the Garrick Hospital to get the pin taen oot … . He survived it, he got over it. [But] you had to be careful with the pins. You couldnae [be] jumpin here or jumpin there wi them in your pocket. If they'd gone out through you they could ave killed you.

Where did you get the stuff to poach with? [The nets and the pins.]

We went out there tae a wee place at Cairnryan, the glen there. It wis hazel pins we used, you cut them the length of your arm. We measured them and cut. And then after we cut them, we pointed them. And you always had plenty of pins and then you put them up the side of the chimley and it hardened them. And they never broke, these hazel pins, but you always had plenty of pins. Plenty of pins to put in the nets.

So you made your own?

Yes, we made our own, but the nets that we bought came from Kilburnie [*sic*]. … 30/- it was then for a net, a long rabbit net. Setting 120 yards, so that would give you ten yards for slack, the slack to run it back in again. If the rabbit net was tight the rabbits hit it an just bounce back off it, but when the slack was regulated right they got entangled in it and just lay there till you took them out, ye see. [*laughter*] It wis a great life, the poaching.

… These poachers … they all stuck together. They were loyal tae one another. An when one got the jail – there was no such thing as handouts. And when he got the jail his wife and his children was punished too. There was no food for them, only the poorhouse. But the other poachers always stood by one another. And the wives would have took over pots of soup, and maybe potatoes, different things. They never starved. But they were all loyal to one another. And what they had they were quite willing to share. And maybe for coal, the poachers went oot an stole the coal, they would have got the coal … . They wouldn't have cared. They made them comfortable. They never regretted when their husbands was in the jail, because their husbands knew that they were bein looked efter. That was one thing. There was nothing, but what they had they halved. And they were very loyal to one another. When Christmas time came round and night come on they would say, 'Right'. Well, two of the poachers went out there, and they would maybe have killed about 40 or 50 rabbits. And they came round the doors handin a pair of rabbits to this woman and a pair of rabbits to that woman, and never charged them anything for it. They always seen they had a Christmas dinner. And if you were out with the van there, lifting the rabbits, I won't tell you the man's name in the van, but if you were near the place where there was potatoes or turnips, we always made sure we got two bags o turnips, and put them in the van. Then, maybe before Christmas, we would get two bags o potatoes, an we would have had them in the van. And the man liftin the rabbits wasn't too pleased about it because then if he was caught, he would be caught for stealing turnips an all. We had them all in the shed, and when it come Christmas time they all come with their basins and they got to have a basin of potatoes and a turnip and a pair of rabbits. They all got that .... And we helped one another, and it never cost them anything. They were never hungry. That was one thing, they were all loyal to one another. If they had nothing, we would have given them somethin. And that's the way they worked. If ever they got into trouble they knew their wives and their children was safe, they'd always help them. So that was the loyalty of the poachers ...

This chap that I poached wi .... Well, it was a very severe winter .... They used to call him Ton Halliday, for a nickname, they called him Ton. So Ton got a job wi a man called Tom Johnston, workin the horse and cart. Cartin coal from the station down to the gas works. And, here, Ton would be coming down Rose Street and folk would be complaining about the coal, they'd no fire, an they'd no money to buy coal. And Ton said, 'Don't worry ladies, I'll get ye coal. Dinnae worry'. The first cart o coal he fetched down, he fetched it down to Rose Street, and he tipped it up in the middle of the street. And the folk were runnin with bags and cans gettin it. Ton got 60 days in the jail for it. That's how he was cried that name. He dumped a ton of coal right in the middle of the street for the folk. That belonged to the gas works, and he got the jail for it. But he was a poacher too, and that was the way they helped one another. ... He said, 'I'll get your coal today'. And then he dumped the ton of coal off, in Rose Street. And that's how he got his name?

That's his name, Ton. He was called after a ton of coal ...

4

Agriculture and Farming

The period covered by the interviews is marked as one of tremendous upheaval in farming, and many interviewees reflected on the changes which they had observed. Key among these was increased mechanisation which caused a rapid decline in the number of people living on farms. In this selection of extracts we learn of the impact of change across the agricultural community.

The extract from Barbara Hannay recalled a time when the necessary hard physical endeavour of bringing in the harvest was celebrated at the final carting-in (in October) when the whole community came together to sing and dance and tell stories. From others, such as Bill McCaig, we learn of the impact of mechanisation on farm communities. The reduction in the number of people living and working on the farms as a result of mechanisation also had an impact on the social structure which that population supported. For example, the demise of participation in local agricultural shows. As John McColm said, as a result of reducing farm populations 'only dedicated showmen are left to present their animals at the [Stranraer Agricultural] Show'.

Increasing mechanisation was not the only factor for change, however, and in the extended extract from the interview with Andrew Hannay we learn how outside factors – such as changing consumer demand and the availability of cheaper grain from abroad – impacted on his family's milling firm.

Margaret McColm

When Mrs McColm was interviewed by Nancy McLucas in 2004, she spoke about the changes she had seen during her life in farming. By the age of 14 Margaret was helping to look after 140 dairy cows, with all the milking done by hand. She recalled one occasion when, in the interwar period, the family farm lost three lads at once when they put in for a scheme for farm workers to emigrate to Canada. In this extract, Margaret talked about agricultural shows and about her husband's work with Clydesdale horses: work which started at Whiteleys where Mr McColm was grieve for Mr Hunter.

… Tell me about your husband's work at Whiteleys.

Mr Hunter had two stallions, and in these days you went round the farms where you know were booked, where the mare was, and [that] was what my husband did. He went round and he looked after Mr Hunter's horses. He had quite a lot of mares and had foals and he looked after them, sat up at nights waiting on a mare foaling and that.

Were they all Clydesdales?

Yes, oh, aye. Pure bred pedigree Clydesdales.

And so your husband would know a lot about that?

Oh, aye, that was his work …

And did your husband go to sales with Mr Hunter?

Whiles, yes … . Oh, not that often. There wasnae so many horse sales in these days. But there was always like maybe a month afore, they started going out with the stallions. There was a display in the town, I mean, there was other folk, Bernie Marshall at Bridgebank had stallions, and they came in and they paraded in Stranraer.

Whereabouts?

I think it was doon where the Breastwork is now. Farmers came in and saw the stallions and said, 'Well, will you call on me?' This is where they picked their stallions.

And did this happen every year?

Oh aye. There was a lot of Clydesdales and a lot of breeding of foals in these days in the district.

And whenabouts would this be?

Oh, I don't know. It certainly was in the twenties …

… When did the breeding of the horses actually stop? How long did this go on?

Oh, it went on for quite a long while, but there was still Clydesdales at Whiteleys when we left, but not nearly so many.

When was that? After the War?

Oh aye. Aye, after the War a bit … . About 40 years ago.

What was it like during the War with the horses?

Oh, it was aaright. They grew corn and they had it for feeding and that.

And what did they do with the horses? Did they do all the farmwork?

Oh, aye. Until the tractors came. They did the ploughing and aw the rest of it. Everything. There would be aboot six pairs. Six ploughmen.

What else did the horses do? I mean, they would draw carts? Did you breed them for pulling, like coal lorries, and things like that?

Yes, and showed at the shows.

Now, your husband did very well at the shows. Tell me about that?

Oh, aye. They did well. And there was a show in Glasgow of horses and I remember one time, this young horse won, I think it was Championship at this show … but they always had them at the cattle shows, and

especially Stranraer and Wigtown. They always did well … the horses were
at the grass then, and anither ploughman … [who] lived next door to us at
Whiteleys, they were up at three o'clock, him and my husband, getting the
horse in to get them ready. They were washed the day before but they were
put back in the field, and this was to get them in when the float came.
They walked them into Stranraer show, oh aye, they walked them.
That must have been quite a sight.

Barbara Hannay

Well then Mrs Hannay, would you like to begin please?
I was born at Colfin Farm on 30th March 1920. An only child of John and
Marian Tulley. I went to Lochans school with other children from the six
cottages on the farm, walking about a mile and a half. The school was two
teacher, Mr and Mrs Miles. Mrs Miles was the head and managed to cope
with two classes in the same room. Everyone took advantage of the soup
kitchen at the school. Mrs Miles was an excellent teacher who also loved
music and pantomime and plays. She put on … pantos in the little theatre
in Stranraer, the pupils loved preparing for this. I can't remember the
names of the plays but I remember being dressed up as [a jolly] stick in a
yellow and green costume which had bells jingling as I moved. Life on the
farm was good and I enjoyed the company of the other children because I
was an only child.
Was your farm a rented farm?
Yes, off Stair Estates. Harvest time was the best. And as I grew older I
realised just how hard the women worked. They ran a home, cooked,
baked and went to the milking, thinned turnips and at harvest time, with
the men, they went to the fields following the reaper and tying the sheaves
of corn.

… during the harvest time, mother fed both the men and women at
lunch time in the farm kitchen. In the afternoons we took cans of tea, and
fresh scones, and we sat in the cart to go up the hills. I loved the tea times,
because supping out of a bowl tasted much better than in a cup … . The
final carting-in, [well] into October sometimes, was celebrated in the loft
of a huge barn. There was singing and dancing to fiddlers. There was a
dairyman called John and he had a very long story. Sometimes we got a bit
fidgety, and it was about 15 verses I think and we were all very pleased he
done it, but glad when he was finished.
And did he do this every year?
Every year. He was there most of my life. In fact all the people, my father
had no changes in those days. Perhaps he was lucky with the people that

worked for us, because they actually didn't move on the 28th ... term day [which was] 28th November. We never seemed to have anybody moving. People stayed with my father. [He seemed to be a good boss.]

At this point in my life we did not have electricity. Aladdin lamps and smaller lamps (wicks checked), oil filled paraffin heaters and, of course, open fires. And, I remember the big black range, which was a task to black lead. My parents loved company and we had lots of friends who came to stay summertime from the cities. It seemed like a hotel quite often. Mother went to the Rural and there were whist drives and concerts. Children had Brownies and Guides and I personally joined the Brownies aged five, then Guides.

Bill McCaig

You have been involved in farming for the greater part of this century, and you must have seen a tremendous number of changes during that time. And, I remember you saying to me once that one of the biggest changes you have noticed is the reduction in the number of people living and working on a farm since you became involved in farming. Is that correct?

Oh, well, yes. When I was a boy there was a very large number of people about the farm. We had seven cottages and each cottage produced a large number of children, as well as workers, and a perfect army of people went to work. Certainly, in the summertime, there was work in the fields for them. There was a large contingent of people. But, when I started, there would be three horse ploughmen and an odd man, and maybe six outside workers who snedded, and scaled dung, and did the different jobs on the farm. And, of course, there was the dairyman an his staff. So there was generally about a dozen people going about the farm.

A farm would be a wee community on its own.

It was a wee community. Each farm had its staff and there was a bit of rivalry, you know, between Challoch and Kirkland, Balwhirry and similar sized farms. We always had a football team – well, the children had a football team. There was ... more than 11 and, of course, one or two people from Leswalt too.

But most of these folks actually lived on the farm then?

Yes, because the cottages were quite often let to women for milking and working. And these women milked, and they had the cottage.

The fact that they were all living on the farm would add to the community?

The community spirit, yes, of course. You never went down to the steading but what you met several people. And, of course, there was so much hand work then, so much actual physical work. Working with the oat harvest, and then with turnips, snedding, lifting, picking, carting into the house, and then, eventually too the cattle, that needed a lot of hand work.

You were saying 'carting', that would be horse and carting, of course. That would make for a long day for the workers, having to get the horses ready?

In the mornings the men came down and fed the horse. I can't remember, I think it was half-past six. Then they went back for their breakfast, and then we came down. And in the winter, we threshed two loads of corn for the byre, and then, when it was daylight, the men would go and yoke up and go to the plough, or go carting turnips or whatever job was on for that particular day.

You mentioned the women earlier on and I think, again, you told me once that on a dairy farm, in particular, you said that women played a very key role and you also said that women had a very, very demanding and exhausting life.

Oh, yes. It was hard work for anyone. Because she'd ten cows to milk in the morning, and ten cows in the early evening. And inbetween times she sometimes had to work out in the fields as well. So that she could start about five o'clock in the morning. She made herself a cup of tea, then she went down to the farm and milked her ten cows, came back up and would have to get her children ready for school. Feed them and prepare something for the dinner, and then go out to the work maybe at half-past nine. She worked from then till 12, came in and snatched a bite to eat and … back out and work till maybe four o'clock in the afternoon, when she would have another cup of tea. Then go to the milking and then, as the old song said, the rest of the day's her own.

You said the cottages were let to women. Was that in recognition of the fact that they were important?

You had to. In those days, before the days of automatic milking, you had to have milkers too. That's why they's so many. But some of the cottages were let to men, but generally it was let to a ploughman with the women able to milk and work.

In some ways the women were more important than men on a dairy farm?

Women were as important as men, and if you had a good woman worker and a good milker, well, you didn't want to lose her, because she could make all the difference.

What are the other sort of major changes, obviously there have been a great many changes. What do you see as the particularly major ones, significant ones?

Mechanisation, of course – the fact that the horses was eventually superseded by tractors. My father held on to the horse as long as he could, because he was fond of horses and his father had been a successful breeder of horses. And he valued the horse as it was his means of locomotion and he didn't want to shift to tractors. Of course, but eventually he just had to. Once that happened, of course, you didn't need so much staff with the

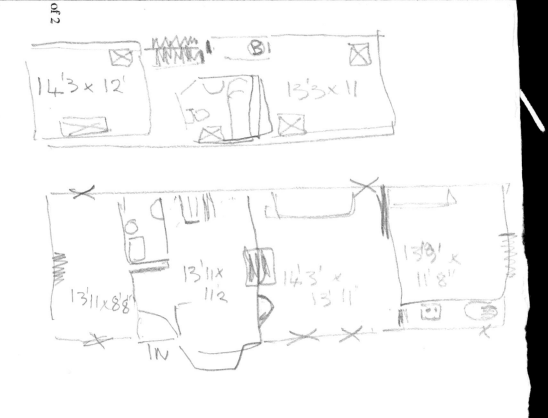

14'3 × 12'

B1

13'3 × 11

13'11 × 8'8'

13'11 x
11'2

14'3' x
13'11'

13'3' x
11'8''

IN

tractor and, of course, now with the implements they've got you can plough a field in a couple of days whereas once a man would plough for weeks, with a single plough. Backwards and forwards, ploughing a field, with horse, oh aye. [The tractor] speeded things up and it dispensed with a tremendous amount of labour.

… In your particular case, from horse to tractor, are we talking 1930 or 40s, or 50s?
After the Second War. There wasn't much change between the wars. Things stayed pretty much the same. But after the War people started to buy tractors and they were finding it more convenient. They used to say about the tractor that when you werenae workin, it wasnae eatin, and with a horse, even if it wasnae workin, it was eatin. It was after the War tractors came in, and progression got quicker and tractors became universal. And then implements became larger, and that was happening in my last years of my farming. Then the younger sons of farmers who weren't needed at home were buying tractors for themselves, and going out and contracting. And that's what has really happened now. There are very few people on the farm now. You can go to a farm and hardly know it was inhabited, because if the cows are out in the fields there is no one about the steading the way there was in the old days.

There is a kind of loss of human contact?
Yes, aye. After I put the cows off and was in beef, I used to go down to the steading and there wasn't a soul about. It was a kind a lonely place.

Later, Mr McCaig returned again to talk about the population change on the farms:

… There were larger families then … . I got people coming in with five and six children, quite common, into the cottages [and] that was happening all over the area. The farms were carrying quite big populations. I mean, it was said that when Mr and Mrs Findlay of Drumbreddan came home from their honeymoon, of course it's a big farm, they were met by 110 people. Of course, it was a big farm, there was a lot of labour on it. I would have, what? If you count ourselves as seven and five of the dairy houses, 12, and one cottage had three, that's 15 and 11, is 26, and four is 30, and three and three is 36. That's 36 folk at Challoch.

John McColm

When Nancy McLucas interviewed Mr McColm in 2006 he talked about many aspects of farming, including the annual Stranraer Agricultural Show, which was an important part of his life. John's comments on rural depopulation illustrate another consequence of the falling farm population:

There are not many agricultural workers left on the farms since the decline in dairying. This means that the farmer and his family are doing the work. Many farmhouses and cottages are now becoming holiday and retirement homes. Rural depopulation is now a major issue. This leads to the farmers having less time to prepare animals for showing. Only the dedicated showmen are left to present their animals at the Show.

Andrew Hannay

In 1999, Jack Hunter interviewed Mr Hannay about his life and family. The whole interview, the latter part of which concentrated on Andrew's own professional life in banking, is rich in detail. The extract given here is taken from the earlier part of the interview in which Andrew talked about the family milling business and history and the changes he had seen over his lifetime. Andrew could trace a continuous line of millers in his family back, at least, to 1695 and the area around Kirkcowan village. We pick up the narrative at the point where the family had moved from Kirkcowan:

> They moved from Kirkcowan to Portpartick, to Dinvin Mill, which again would be a rented mill, just at the entrance to Portpatrick where there was a good fall of water.

Is that where the Old Mill Restaurant is?

> The old mill used to be there. It is now a restaurant. It was said that they rolled the millstones, they put a tree trunk through the millstones, and rolled them over to Stranraer and then over the old road to Portpatrick. I don't know how long they took and it must have been a pretty hazardous journey because the old roads were very rough. My great-great grandfather moved, about 1750, to Portpatrick, Dinvin Mill, and his son, my great grandfather, was born there in 1799. He moved, in 1820, to Corsewall Mill, again a rented mill. He lived there, married a girl from [a farm] outside Girvan, and had 11 children. She must have been a wonderful lady, my great grandmother. Father used to say when he met his granny [she said] 'I was born in the year one dear … 1801'. Having had 11 children, she lived to the age of 92. I wish I had met her.

That was kind of long-distance courting for those days, if he was in Corsewall and she was near Girvan?

> Yes, I just wonder. I think it would probably go back how he would meet her, it may have been, and certainly my great grandfather – I don't know about his father – but my great grandfather, who came to Corsewall in 1820, travelled up the coast selling oatmeal and bringing back dried fish and slates.

This was travelling by boat?

Yes, sailing ship, steam ship. He did take his wife on one journey because the tale goes that she fell into the harbour at Girvan and was saved by her sealskin tippet …

I think you mentioned once before that relics of his selling oatmeal were still to be found some time afterwards up the west coast …

I remember when I was a boy, that would be just after the First World War, they were still using white bags and on them was written 'R & A Hannay', 'Hannay's Oatmeal' or 'Hannay's Flake Oats', and they were taken up in bags. And I have heard from an old sea captain who lives in Oban, that the children on Islay had no hesitation in using them as a sort of dress. They were made of good stuff.

So [to go back for a moment] the Hannays were in Kirkcowan and then they were in Dinvin at Portpatrick and then they were in Corsewall Mill and they moved again, didn't they?

They moved again. Two of the 11 children, Robert who was the third son, and Alex, my grandfather – who was number 11 – went into partnership. That must have been when they changed the name to R & A Hannay. Alex Hannay, my grandfather was born in 1846. So it must have been around 1870 that they changed it to R & A Hannay. They remained in Corsewall Mill, the two of them, with various brothers. Alex … never met two of his brothers, they had gone off to the Crimea War over 20 years before he was born. There was 25 years between them. They both fought in the Crimea and went on to India where they took various jobs there. … One joined the army, the other joined the police. So, eventually, they came down, R and A, from Corsewall Mill to Stranraer, in the 1890s.

Did they build the mill there?

No. There was a mill there, Sheuchan Mill, and it was burnt to the ground towards the end of the century. And I don't know whether the Hannays were actually in it then but it was rebuilt by them. There certainly was a mill there, because there was a dam.

That was another water-powered mill then, was it?

Yes. There was a small dam at the mill and there was a field called the Dam Fields. It must have been the main dam. The dam road ran up, past what is now Seabank. It has a different name now, but when I was a boy it was called the Dam Road, but the dam had gone. There is a dam up Auchneel way and the water cames down that way. My father used to say, many years later, the water was more a nuisance than of any use when they went over to steam and the water part went out. I don't think they had water power in the new rebuilt mill at the end of the century, after the old one was demolished and the new one built, but it ran underneath the mill and it used to flood it.

That would be the burn that flooded not so long ago, last winter? Same trouble, same burn. I think you said also that your family were inventors in the field of milling?

Well, my father was always a very able chap, a pity that he never went to university because I'm sure my grandfather could afford to send him. He took a great interest in the machinery ... he did invent a machine which was very high powered grinding, used for making oats. And they probably made five different kinds of oatmeal going from flaked oatmeal, called flaked oats, which eventually were packaged, to pinhead oatmeal, which was very large. Then there was a medium oatmeal, and then there was a fine oatmeal and then they made something which was fit for babies – a sort of porridge ...

... They formed a partnership with a firm, or they took shares in a firm in Bristol, which was Groaten Ltd. The flaked oats in the early days were taken down by train. Sometimes they were shipped in a small type of vessel, like a small tugboat. I can't remember what it was called. Some-times they were shipped down there, because it was much cheaper than sending by rail down to Bristol. They were packed into cardboard containers in Bristol and sold throughout the south-west of England by Groaten Ltd. I myself, after the Second World War, I had been 12 years in the bank and six years in the army, my father wondered if I'd like to go down and take a job with Groaten Ltd, who was actually two firms together who made biscuits and had a small flour mill and sold the Groaten. I can remember they had about 20 vans and they toured the south-west and on the back of the van it had, 'It's that van again'. However, I decided against it ...

I think you said your father patented this grinder?

I didn't know the chap, Higgins, but Higgins would be the millwright, and my father, who was really a self-taught engineer, [and] I suppose [together they] came upon this thing and had it made by a firm called, at that time, Henry Simons later Simon Engineering, who were worldwide engineers. It was patented, and I have the patent in my house. ... It was sold by Simon Engineering all over the world and I got various stories from him about that, but it did make a very good income ...

And the business of selling oatmeal up the west coast by ship, did that cease when they moved to Stranraer, or was that a side of the business for quite a long time?

I don't know whether they would be able to load the oatmeal at Wig Bay. I know that when I was a boy that I remember farmers coming in to Wig Bay and this steamship coming in. It was very, very small, and [it would be] unloading coal, and farmers coming down with carts and filling up with coal, so it might have been.

So, when they were at Kirkcolm, the oats went out by Wig Bay probably?

They may have done that. It was a sailing ship and I think it could be quite possible if they could come in. The tide would go out, of course, and leave it high and dry, and then the carts could go out and load, and then it would float off …

… When did the firm actually close down then? It's not that long ago, is it?

They were very busy, certainly, during World War I. There was no difficulty, and I was just a youngster about six or seven years old when the First World War ended. They must have had a method then of packing oatmeal which then went off to army places. Whether it was in tins or bags, I wouldn't know. That kept them busy, but between the wars they had built up a very good business, mostly in England. I can remember that one of the biggest customers was the Co-operative Wholesale Society around Manchester, and by that time Robert's son and Alex's son, my father and his cousin, William, were running the business. William used to travel down extensively to England, and sold a lot of oatmeal. I can remember, vaguely, one monthly cheque from the Co-operative Society for £13,000 and that was a great deal of money in those days. They also, between the wars, worked overtime up until 11 or 12 at night in the wintertime, for the demand was so high. The oats that made the meal were grown locally. It was a very profitable business.

It was a kind of a seasonal business? There was bigger demand in the cold weather, people wanting porridge?

Yes, a bigger demand in the winter. So the mill was a busy place, and employed probably up to 20 people. It was, by that time, fairly well mechanised and, even when the firm closed down, they were still using H & H Hannay and Higgins' showers, and eventually they built silos, which they could store oats in. They say that when the oats came in from the farmer they had to be tested for water content, because sometimes, if it had been a wet summer, you could find that it was as high as 30 per cent moisture in them. To keep it in the silo you had to put it through a kiln and dry it down to 16 per cent moisture and oats would keep – they had four silos holding so many tonnes, I couldn't tell you. Quite a number of them would keep at 16 per cent, but when it had to be milled it was taken out of the silos, put into the drying plant and it had to be dried down to 5 per cent moisture before they could mill it. So there was quite a lot of work in that.

In the old days, going back to Corsewall Mill, you would wonder how they found out when it was fit for milling. They had a metal floor in the drying compartment and my father used to say – there was no such thing as a thermometer – that they used to spit on it, and if it sizzled to a certain amount it was fit for milling. I hope he cleaned up the spittle first! It was a fairly complex business.

Did the Second World War bring difficulties or bring increased business as the First World War [had]?

They were able to cope at that time with any amount. I don't think they would sell as much in the Second World War as in the First World War. There were such luxuries as Spam [by then].

The forces wouldn't be such a good customer, I don't imagine?

No. Certainly, one could get porridge by oatmeal [in the forces]. Having been in the War myself, I don't think there was as much consumed.

You said originally all the oats which they used were home grown?

Well, this is what happened. After the Second World War the demand started to fall away. In the fifties, breakfast foods, some of which had arrived possibly from America, Quaker Oats and things like that, packaged, were not made from oats. Gradually, the housewife didn't fancy this [oatmeal, for] one part – cleaning the pot. It was much easier to take it out of a packet and just add water to it. So the demand slipped, and by the end of the fifties had almost dried up. The other thing that made [it] more expensive and less profitable after the War, it may have been before it, farmers were starting to move from growing oats to growing barley. This was largely, I think there was something like three times the number of milking cows in Wigtownshire as to population, and they grew barley instead of oats. They started buying oats from the north of Scotland to begin with, which was adding a lot to the cost. I can remember my father saying that they actually bought oats from Australia, Russia and Canada – imported. So that really started hitting the profitability on the head. There was the cost of milling it, and the price they could get for selling it. So that, by 1961, they stopped milling oatmeal.

Before that, and towards the end or during the 1930s, they had started going into animal feeding stuffs, and they had put in a provender[3] mill. This was all electric, mixing up various ingredients, of what a farmer would call dairy nuts. They could make these, or various mixtures. Sometimes they put as many as 15 different ingredients into a thing for feeding dairy cows.

… they were buying the raw materials from outside the area, but making their own mixes?

There would be maize and things like that. Maize coming from South America. That was a completely new plant … . By then two of my brothers were working in the mill and my father, sadly, died in 1961. My brother often said that [my father] couldn't really relinquish making oatmeal and he had put in, possibly after the Second World War, too much machinery than was needed, really. From 1961 onwards, my brothers developed a fairly reasonable business. It was highly competitive. There were at least four other people in Stranraer, certainly Wyllies had the manufacturing capacity. They were very big. They were all over Dumfries and Galloway. So that in the late 1970s, they were starting to look round.

My eldest brother, he was about retiring. My younger brother – the family were all shareholders and it was too much for him to carry on. They looked around and eventually, in 1974, they sold out to a subsidiary of Unilever. And, by that time, my eldest brother was away in New Zealand and my younger brother retired, and […] stayed on with the firm that took over. But, I think in his mind he thought they were really taking it over to close it down, which they eventually did about five years after he had been with them – about 1980. And that was the end of the milling at Sheuchan Mill.

John Barr

… things have changed so much in the past. Agriculture has changed out of all recognition. There's practically nobody employed on the farms and everything's gettin bigger, not for the better. And what the future holds, I do not know. The price of milk is still going down. When I left Auchneel, the price of milk was 18p a litre and the present price today is 16p a litre so you can take from that that things are not good. So in conclusion, just what does the future hold? …

5

Rural and Urban Living Conditions

The selection presented in this chapter looks at changing urban and rural living conditions and includes interviewee transcriptions relating to the introduction of electricity, indoor toilets, telephones and the provision of new housing. One might assume that the introduction of services such as electricity would have been subject to a systematic implementation plan that would have progressed without outside hindrance. However, the short extracts in this selection illustrate a more complex pattern of change.

We can readily appreciate the excitement that accompanied the arrival of the first flush toilet in Drummore, recalled by Isabelle Shaw, especially when we also hear about the outside toilet from Agnes Lamb and the shared facilities experienced by George McClymont in Portpatrick.

The impact of people moving into the towns from the countryside, and the constraints on building due to World War II, are illustrated here in extracts from John Carruth and Nancy McLucas. Nancy's account of Bishopburn, known locally as 'Little Whitehall' is rich in detail and provides an interesting account of how new communities were formed in an urban setting, just as they were being lost in the rural landscape.

John Barr

The electricity didn't come in until 1939. I just can remember, just before the outbreak of war, the line went over the back of Auchneel. There was one at the bottom end of Auchneel that went to Kirkcolm … it was the first line to go to Kirkcolm. The one that we got our power off went in on 1939. And I can still remember the Aladdin lamp in the dining room at Auchneel, for the light. It just shows you how things have changed. Also, it must be remembered there was very, very few telephones in they days. There was … very, very few. McCormick's was 21, we were 211. There was very few telephones. And all the wires, of course, the poles went up the side o the road. There were poles all over the countryside with … 20 or 30

1. William Simpson's delivery van, *c.*1935. Vans like this one were once a common sight in the region and were an important part of the local economy.

2. Steam-powered machine powering a travelling mill, 1920s. Equipment such as this would have been a common sight on farms at harvest time.

3. The Baird-Jardine family tattie riddling. REF: 026.

(WITH KIND PERMISSION OF THE DUMFRIES AND GALLOWAY LIBRARY AND ARCHIVE SERVICE)

4. Travellers at camp, Galloway. C0014320.
(WITH KIND PERMISSION OF THE DUMFRIES
AND GALLOWAY LIBRARY AND ARCHIVE SERVICE)

5. Worthie with rabbit skins, Galloway. C0014357.
(WITH KIND PERMISSION OF THE DUMFRIES
AND GALLOWAY LIBRARY AND ARCHIVE SERVICE)

6. Hannay Mill and the Lairey Burn. The Lairey Burn, shown in the foreground, has since been covered over.

7. A steam wagon by Corsewall Mill, Kirkcolm c.1912.

8. This building, on the High Street in Stranraer, was occupied by a man who ran a shoe repair workshop (the door and window on the right). The nearer door down was occupied by a family of 13 prior to its demolition. Housing developments at Dicks Hill and Murrayfield were built to replace housing like this.

9. Auction Mart, Thistle Street/ Bellevilla Road junction. The Auction Mart housed sales of everything from livestock to furniture.

10. An early photograph of Portpatrick showing the railway bridge.

11. Lochnaw Castle. C0290007.

12. Portpatrick School.

13. Stranraer Butchers, 1897.

14. Staff lined up outside the Stranraer slaughterhouse, 1920s.

15. Staff at McHarrie's Forge, Harbour Street, 1907–08.

16. Caldwell Grocers, Hanover Street, Stranraer *c.*1920.

17. F. Bonugli's Ice Cream Saloon at the corner of Charlotte Street and Harbour Street, *c.*1920.

18. The Georgian, a McHaffie business, refurbished in the 1930s.

19. The Glasgow House.

20. Trades Parade, 1937.

21. Richard Keir, Apothecaries Hall, interior of the shop, late 1920s.

22. Stranraer Gasworks from the shore. The timber yard can be seen on the right and the slaughter house on the left.

23. Stranraer Gasworks, after the 1946 rebuild.

wires on each line going out to Kirkcolm. And, of course, you know it was the call girl, you phoned up the exchange. And the old exchange, of course, was in Charlotte Street just above the present Hugh Aitken's, new shop. On the top side of it, there is a narrow entrance there, and that was the telephone exchange for the whole of Stranraer.

Barbara Hannay

There was no electricity?

No, just Aladdin lamps. We still hadn't electricity. There was a reason for that because there was three farms, Cairnpat and another one in the middle. And it would have made life easier if one of the farms, I won't mention which one, had taken the leads through. Two of the farmers agreed – one agreed with my father – because it was to get transformers, it was going to be a lot cheaper, naturally, because things like that didn't just come in your rents you know. You couldn't expect Stair Estates to pay for everything. So this other farm, it took ages for them to decide to join us to get the one transformer, and that was why we had [no electricity] at that time.

John McColm

In May 1946 my Aunt Jenny came to be my housekeeper [at Garthland Mains]. We had very little furniture and it was quite a cold big house, but fortunately we got an Aga cooker for our kitchen and that made quite a difference. There was no electricity on the farm when I arrived, and we didn't get electricity until Christmas 1946. This was quite a change for me, having to live with paraffin lamps, because we had had electricity at Cairngarroch by a homemade plant when I was four years old, so it was quite a change to go back to paraffin lamps.

… there were eight cottages … . Those eight cottages had no toilet facilities and the first thing I did was have them made dry loos for all those cottages.

Agnes Lamb

And this is laugh, which might be funny. When we went to live at the Drums, and there is still a burn that goes down past there, the toilet was built over this burn. And you had to go out at night in the dark if you want to go to the toilet. An my sister, she wasn't that long there because she got married and went away to Canada – her husband and her – but she would [be] out this night, I believe, and there was an owl in the tree an it hooted. An she was so scared, she was frightened to come back in, she didnae know what it was. All these things are quite funny. But no, and you didnae have a bathroom. But you were clean, because I can remember, when I was quite young, the boiler where we boiled the water to wash the clothes. It had to be put on, and you had a big tin bath an you had running water. We had a … motor pump, pumped the water intae a tank …

Isabelle Shaw

Aunt Annie [in Drummore] had paraffin lamps as well, but along came electric light … . This man that came from the town to put it up – but he did it so quickly. He never bothered much about the wires. He just went along the top of the skirting, and up like that and your light was on. That was in the late thirties …

Then the next thing they did was, she had a flush toilet. That was the first flush toilet in the village, so everybody had to come and see this. Jessie Turnbull and Maggie. Maggie had to sit on it and somebody pulled the great big long chain. And she said, 'Oh, you've wet all my bum!' It was an unheard of thing, because they all had to go out to this little place at the back, in their courtyard.

George McClymont

I was born in Portpatrick on the 8th of April 1931. I was the youngest member of a family of nine, and Hill Street houses were a room and kitchen, more or less. It was quite a squeeze, although when I was born the elder members of my family had moved on so there were nine of us in the house at one time, but it was quite a squeeze.

And tell me, did you have an inside toilet?

No. We shared an outside toilet with our next door neighbour. It was upstairs and downstairs. There was two families up the stairs and two families down the stairs. There was toilets top and bottom, so we shared with another family – the MacKenzie family.

It must have been difficult for your mother to bath you and to wash?

I can always remember there was a big tin tub that was kept below the bed in those days. The girls were washed and then the boys were washed.

You had water in the house?

Yes, running water and a big white sink, I can always remember it. Sometimes we were chucked into it … and sat on the end of the board and washed our feet and got a wash before we went to bed at night. But bath night was a big night, kettles were boiled to fill the tub.

Mother and father shared one room and there were two beds in a back bedroom. And probably there were five or six of us at home and five or six of us got squeezed onto the two beds in the bedroom. There was happy times and Hill Street was very busy. There was something like sixty kids in Hill Street. And I think 16 houses for something like 60 children reared in Hill Street – filled half their school!

John Carruth

There were some quite dreadful slums in the town. In off Dalrymple Street was Rankin's Close, which the local people called the Pritty Mill Close, pritty being Irish for potato. The houses there were in a row opposite the town burn which was open, and the houses and the burn was infested with rats because the people threw their slops etc. into the burn. And they just had earthen floors and in a wet period, as far as I can remember, the water ran into their houses and their floors were soaking wet, dreadful conditions. There were also quite bad housing in Fisher Street and Rose Street and St John Street wasn't very good either, and neither was Glen Street. In about 1936 the council decided to have a slum clearance and started to build houses on Murrayfleld and Dicks Hill. It proceeded very slowly because the scheme was not finished by the time the War started so it was suspended, and restarted again after the War. Mr Goudie was the architect for that scheme and unfortunately he gave the people tremendous size of gardens which they had never been used to in their lives. They had never had a garden either front or back of their premises and I'm sure they just didn't know what to do and the gardens became just dumps for rubbish, terrible sight.

Nancy McLucas

In 2007 Nancy recorded her own interview and in it she spoke about moving to Bishopburn in August 1956 after her husband got a job in the area.

Now Bishopburn in those days, like the McMasters Road scheme too, was plonked down right in the middle of the country … there would be about 50 families perhaps in Bishopburn at that time. It was known locally, well politely, as little Whitehall (maybe it was known less politely by a name that we never heard). And it was called that because most of the houses were given to local county employees, what would now be called the public sector. There were lots of teachers; there was the assistant medical officer of health, the assistant director of education, the assistant county clerk, the assistant librarian, the weights and measures inspector and the postmaster, as well as all the other teachers in the various departments of the Academy or the High School. There was also a water engineer, a road engineer, two country architects and just generally employees of Wigtown County Council. ... most of us were incomers; young people who were quite happy to get a Council house which gave them a start and most of us, as I say, with young families. It was a very, very friendly place ... . We had all sorts of things in common and really it was a kind of Scottish village in miniature.

...

We started off in Burnside Terrace and we were fortunate in a way in as much as the people who had been in the house before us had installed an immersion heater so we weren't dependent, as most other people were, on our local coal fire for heating the water. They also had the telephone [which] had been installed for them so we were able to take over their telephone which again was quite an asset because not every house had a telephone. The people who did have a telephone in those days, you had to have a thing called a party line. You couldn't have a line all to yourself. It never really bothered us and our party line was with neighbours, people we knew in Redhap Crescent and I can only think of one or two occassions when we actually tried to phone and they were already on the line.

...

Bishopburn was virtually, I would think, a paradise for children – it was safe, everybody kept an eye on everybody else's child and we were all of an age; our children were all of an age and really they seemed to have a very enjoyable time ... . Another thing, in those days when we arrived in Bishopburn was that the schools did not actually start till half-past nine. So you could look out at eight o'clock in the morning and there would be hardly a curtain open ... . Round about nine o'clock people began to more around in Bishopburn.

Bobby Gemmell (i)

In this transcript, of the first part of the interview which Nancy McLucas recorded in June 2003, Mr Gemmell recalled his early life on the Lochnaw Estate. At that time, Lochnaw was leased by the Pollock family and supported a substantial community of workers who looked after the household and surrounding areas. This is a fascinating account of a way of life which, as Bobby himself observed, had changed little since Victorian times, but which was changed irrevocably by the onset of World War II. Lochnaw was requisitioned by the Air Ministry and the American military established a field hospital (which arrived prefabricated from the USA) in the grounds. The Pollock family moved out of the big house and, although they remained on the estate for a while, they subsequently gave up Lochnaw.

Tell me about your family background please, Mr Gemmell.

Well Nancy, A wis born in Kirkcowan, my father and mother were both people who were brought up and who lived all their life in Kirkcowan and ma father served his apprenticeship at Craighlaw Estate. And when he was a young man, a journeyman, he left Kirkcowan an moved to Dunragit and he went to be the foreman gardener on Dunragit Estate. An we were there a few years, I just don't remember, maybe four or five years at Dunragit and the sisters were born at Dunragit. An … this opportunity came for Lochnaw Estate and he applied for the head gardener's job at Lochnaw and got it, so the five of us moved to Lochnaw.

And when would this be?

That would be 1930. And I can remember well, though I would be six years old then, arriving there and this big house, this enormous – to me – big wall round the place and not another house in sight. That was the first thing that struck me, not another house in sight, after leavin a village where we had, what, eight houses in a row plus the station and the creamery. A thought we'd arrived in at an absolute wilderness. But, however … we got settled in and, there wis houses within 150 or 300 yards of us. The head keeper and one of the other gardeners. And it turned out that it wasn't as bad as A first thought. But the schuil was goin to be the problem right away for me personally. Because I was the only one schuil age so I went to Larbrax schuil to the Miss Withers, they were the teachers there. A went there for mibby, A'm not sure, about a couple of years and my sister went with me and then there was a kind of turnaround in the schuil programme and they decided that there were too many children at Larbrax and not enough at Leswalt. And all the estate children that went to Larbrax were transferred to Leswalt schuil and that's where we went right up til we left Leswalt schuil. But we were very fortunate, in a way, because the lady that owned [Lochnaw] Castle picked us up one morning an we were very wet and she was quite perturbed that we'd be sitting all day in wet clothes, so we were very privileged an the shooting bus from then on took us to schuil in the morning.

And who had the estate at that time?

It was owned, well it was leased at that time, by a Mr Pollock, he was called Oliver William Pollock, OWP. I can remember that well because it was stamped on all the garden tools. All the tools were stamped OWP and he leased the estate until the War broke out … . But we spent all the thirties and most of the forties on the estate. I grew up there and … ma father was the head gardener, there were two under gardeners with him that actually worked in the walled garden and there was a third man, he looked after the horse and cart and he did all the hauling up and down and round about the estate. Plus ye'd the head keeper, Mr William Murray, and two under-keepers, plus a groom. There would [be] … four mibby five ponies there. He was a Yorkshire man. I can't tell you [his surname] but his first name was George. We used to call him the cowboy because he was a bendy-legged guy. And there was a chauffeur an he was a local fella, he came from Stranraer, by the name o Gilmour, James Gilmour … . Now that was what looked after the estate on the outside, but on the inside, at what we would call the Castle, now [there were] quite a lot of people in there. There was a cook in the kitchen … an assistant cook, a kitchen maid, a scullery maid an sometimes a pantry maid. But there were definitely always four, but sometimes there were five. Plus a butler, a footman, and I think they caed him a boots boy. Plus, again, the chamber maids – there was Mrs Pollock's personal maid, and then there'd be one, or two, probably three other chamber maids. And that roughly would be the staff … . Sometimes maybe one or two more, you know. People shifted around a lot in those days. But in thinking back, that wid be the steady number o people, up til the War, that worked on the estate. The fella, Mr McColm they called him, looked after the horse and cart. He wasn't so much involved in the garden because there was a lot, there was grass cutting and all the grass cuttings were hauled down to the garden and the leaves had to be cleared. And all these jobs, he would be responsible for that. In the garden you had quite a range of greenhouses, much more that you wid have in any other garden in the south of Scotland.

And why was that?

Well, we just had this big range of greenhouses, more than you would have at Lochinch and Dunragit definitely, and there was three vineries and a […]house and a greenhouse an a carnation house and melon pit. That was the names [of] the glass.

And, your father must have known how to work all these?

Oh yes … looking back, he would be probably one o the last o the old-style gardeners. If you ever watch the television, there was a programme on it, it ran for quite a long time and I watched it every week, the 'Victorian Garden'. Well, we werenae many steps ahead o that at Lochnaw in our time there. Well, up tae the War anyway … . I can remember, seeing, in that same programme, the horse going over the lawns and I was tickled pink at them puttin these leather shoes on it so that the steel … the horse shoes didnae mark [the lawn]. The same thing happened at Lochnaw. I can remember them lifting its feet up and putting these big leather shoes on an it goin over the grass to get the thing it pulled. They had a mower, that they didn't use … very much, but it did work. And the scales that they weighed the stuff on, the tomatoes and the fruit that the garden grew. The ones on the telly an the ones in the potting shed at the Lochnaw were identical [and I noticed a lot of things]. So, as I said, we werenae that far ahead o that particular era either. But the garden produced all the fruit and vegetables that was necessary fir the Castle. And at the end of the summer everything was stored … . [There was a] great big shed at the back that was the potting shed, there was the mushroom house and there was the outhouses where all the vegetables were stored. Everything was stored in sand. There wis carrots, beetroot, parsnips, turnips, onions … . And then, in Lochnaw gardens, we had in one corner … whit they caed the round house, an in the opposite corner ye had whit they caed the square house. An the square house, [that wis] the fruit room in our time. Beautiful big cases, all drawers, and the peaches and the pears and the plums, everything was kept [in there]. Every Saturday mornin [the fruit was] lifted out, inspected and put back in an anything that was bad pit out. So … you had fruit a long time, you know. And in the garden, you had strawberries, blackcurrants, redcurrants and gooseberries, cherries, Victoria plums and a host of different apple trees. Absolutely the whole inside o the garden wall was lined with fruit trees. The whole distance round. Plus, the gardens were divided into two. There wis the east garden. Now in it was fruit trees. Plus, Mr Pollock was friendly, I suppose he'd business interests in Holland and he was very friendly with a Dutch family and bulbs came from Holland [and these were planted] in between the fruit trees. I remember them planting these, just when I was a very young boy. I can remember carryin them up to my father an the gardeners and these bulbs wis all planted in mibby, oh, about three-foot-wide strips up between the fruit trees. An then, when they grew up, they were picked and sent away to a place in Manchester to be sold around there. Now, also, Lochnaw wis covered in snowdrops in those days, an still is today. There's quite a lot of areas where there's thousands and thousands of snowdrops. They were pulled, what, from the end o January into February. They lasted about, I think, three weeks and they pulled an average of 500 bunches a day.

And did you help with this?

Later on, when A left schuil, I started in the gardens with ma father. They thought, the family, thought that I wid carry on but I'm afraid it was no a job I liked, and I don't think I had the education anyway. Never [to be] a head gardener, anyway. But even when we were at schuil … if we came home early, we would maybe give a wee hand. But the gardeners, plus maybe one or two of the keepers, depending on how things were, they would go out after they got the morning chores done in the garden, the watering, and seen to the boilers for the heatin. They would go out with their trogs, that's what they were called in those days, and [they] would pull snowdrops, 50 in a bunch and they would set them down, one beside the other. And my father came along behind them, and he would put an ivy leaf or some stalks of the snowdrops an they would tie them into bunches, cut them neatly an put them in these trogs. And then they were carried – everything had to be carried, there was no transport, no fancy motor bikes the way they have today, tae drive about. They were carried intae the garden an they were packed intae big cardboard boxes [wi] what we caed tissue paper in those days. And they were all put in there and the shootin bus would arrive down about five o'clock, because it wis dark then. That was stoppin time. And they would be put [the boxes] onto the shootin bus an one of the keepers could drive … and he took them into the station and they went to, I can even tell you the name of the firm they vent to, J L Forbes of Manchester and they were sold for sixpence a bunch … the following morning. So transport in those days wasnae so slow as probably we think it is today. Now, the surplus stuff in the garden, there wis quite a lot surplus fruit. Not so much o the vegetables, but definitely the fruit and the tomatoes, [an] the tomatoes were sold in the town in Peter Davidson's, Lochnaw tomatoes were sold in there. But the fruit was sold locally, to farmers and to people who worked on the farms – an they would order their blackcurrants an their rasps for jam making.

So it was a business as well?

Oh, it was a wee business. There wasnae a lot a money in it. There would only be a few pence a pound. There wouldn't be a lot of money made. But I can always tell you a lovely wee story about that part of it. In our time at Lochnaw, there wis three days in the year that you treasured. There wis Christmas Day, there wis the Cattle Show day and the October Fair day. Those were the three highlights. The reason I said Christmas Day was again very privileged being where we were … we were treated to a Christmas do in the Castle. Now the things we got wir unbelievable …

Do you mean the children or all the estate workers?

Just the children on the estate. Your mother an father went with you. The whole estate was there, but the children were the only ones that got the presents. I can remember getting a Mickey Mouse watch in the box, you know, and I remember getting, [an] it wis funny I should get this, a box about two foot six square an it was a buildin game. And it was made, in those days there wis no plastic or anything, it was made of what was called Bakelite. And there was two or three bases an wee holes about every half inch over the whole thing, and you put wires into these holes and you had wee bricks that you slid down the wires and made your wee bungalow and the roofs fitted on. An that was in the house til I was in ma early twenties. I don't know, my mother would probably give it away to somebody. And my sisters got dolls' prams.

Oh, these were good presents.

Oh, unbelievable, an stacks of books an boxes o crackers that when you pulled them you got ornaments. My mother had them on the mantelpiece. I can tell you the addresses on some of these things was Marshall Snellgroves … London, so that's where they were bought. And as I say, we were very, very privileged. And this story I'm goin to tell you, wis, there was no money about, Nancy. We'd everything we needed but there was nae money. An I can remember my mother saying to us, 'Well, I'm sorry there's goin to be no October Fair for you. Your father gets a wee retainer for the sales over the year an it hasnae come, so there will be no [fair]'.

Did he not get any pay at all?

Oh, yes, you got your pay. But it was very, very little we got and, as I say, we had a free house, we had as much coal as you could burn, as many logs you could burn. All the fruit and vegetables you could eat. So that way we were very well off. But I can remember going to schuil that morning, kinda down in the dumps because there was goin to be no October Fair. And then, well just about half an hour before we would be leaving anyway, I heard a lady's voice at the door. I says to myself, that's my mother. And, here, the money had arrived and this was them wi a taxi to take us to the October Fair, so we got to the October Fair after all. And those were our highlights. And these people, although, as I say, the wages weren't big, everybody seemed unbelievably happy. And another great thing about them, if you were ill, she was on the doorstop, Mrs Pollock herself. She was well up in the … WVS … and she liked to play a doctor. [*laughter*] She did. If we took ill, you had to go tae the Castle first. In those days, when we got there first, there were no phones, so they had to go in on the shooting bus and deliver whatever messages there was.

Was there not even a phone in the Castle?

There was no phone then. There were no phone lines. The phones hadnae reached Lochnaw til the mid-thirties. I can remember them puttin them up the glen, the telegraph poles with the cups on them, an the wires. I can remember that. So, you had to contact her first. And she came down to the house with her wee Red Cross uniform on and took your temperature. That was the first thing. I remember puttin that thing in below your arm, and sometimes in your mouth. And she decided whether you needed the doctor or not. But, maybe she would have a crack with ma mother and decide what was wrong. And in those days you had chickenpox, whooping cough and the measles an we had all those things at Lochnaw. An maybe about an hour after it there would be a knock on the door and this would be the boots boy down with two suits of pyjamas an a coat, which I thought was a coat, a dressing gown. [I'd] never had seen one before. And a … big jar, you know, the old fashioned stone jar, full of concentrated blackcurrants. The blackcurrants had been taken up and you put it into a glass of hot water. And that was the kind of things she did for you. So we were fortunate, very fortunate.

They were good employers then?

Oh, wonderful, I would say, wonderful. Far better than good, you know, honestly. That didn't only happen to the head gardener, it happened to all the houses on the estate that [had] children there. We weren't privileged because we were the head gardener, no, no, no. And as time went on, I grew up and left schuil and went into the gardens, as an apprentice gardener, 12/6d a week, was your wages and that was for practically seven days. Because there was no time off in those days. My father had to see to the greenhouses, he had to water the plants. They didn't know whether it was Saturday or Sunday. So when the men went away at twelve o'clock on the Saturday, the boilers had to be stoked at nights. And you had to open the ventilators if it was sunny, and close them if it wasn't. And, as I say, you were never ever were free. You couldn't get up in the morning an just walk away. You were tied that way. But, however, I went intae the gardens anyway and started as an apprenticed gardener. An the first job you were taught, I knew it anyway as I had done it while at schuil, was bein the vegetable boy in the morning. You went up to the Castle at seven o'clock in the morning. And the cook would be there, or if not, the assistant cook would mostly be there. The cook wasnae an early bird while I was there. But the assistant cook would give you the order for the day. So you picked your baskets up, two great big baskets – sometimes three – and walked back down to the gardens and filled them with whatever was required for the day. And in the summertime, you went back up again at three-thirty and they decided what kind of fresh fruit they would have … maybe strawberries or plums or peaches or pears or whatever [and] they were taken up. Dinner was in the evening, at seven o'clock, for them. Of course, that year I started was the year War broke out and within a very, very short space of time things were changing rapidly. That particular year, their eldest daughter Wendy, Miss Wendy we call her. They had three of a family, Miss Wendy, Miss Olive and Master Billy. That was the way we addressed these people. She, Miss Wendy, ran off in July of that year, that would be 1939.

Before the War?

Yes, the War hadn't started then. She ... had a boyfriend who was a squadron leader at the Freugh, West Freugh. And he used tae fly over the Castle. You knew, because he used to come down gey low. And it was rumoured that he dropped sweets one time ontae the tennis courts. But I was up and had a bit look and didn't find any. But that was one of the rumours anyway. And this particular morning the post[man] came into the gardens – which was unusual. I don't know where my mother would be and [he] shouted to my father, 'Headlines in the papers – wealthy mill owner's daughter weds at Gretna'. She had took off an got married at Gretna. But there was a bit o tragedy to that. This was July, War broke out in September. Well, this fella was posted missing in November o that year. He was shot down over Germany. So, it turned out that she had been pregnant, she had a wee girl and unfortunately he never saw her. As I say, he was killed in the first months of the War. And, of course, at the Castle then there was a lot o staff took off. As a matter of fact, there was a Norwegian cook there at that particular time. They didn't stay very long, then they were off. They went back to Norway, her and her assistant. And I think my mother stood in for a wee while until they got another cook. And then there was talk o the Castle being requisitioned, if that's the right word. I think it was going to be turned into a hospital. But this took a bit of time, you know, we're getting well into 1940 by the time that happened. And the Air Ministry, I believe, started this ... . They were going to take it over and make it into a hospital. And they were busy making some of the rooms [ready] and it was turned intae a hospital. And, of course the Pollocks, they stayed in the house over in where the garage, the coach houses was. They stayed there for a wee while and then they disappeared and we never ever heard of them again. That was the end o it. And, my father was took over by the, I think it would be the ... Air Ministry, and he was kept in the gardens. But he was only himself and ... at that stage there was camps started up, North Cairn, for instance, the radar station. So I went there and ... left the garden and got a job as a tea boy. And the Castle, it was started as a hospital but I don't think really there was ever very many patients in the actual Castle itself. When the Americans came into the War that was a different kettle of fish. They built a hospital.

Built a hospital?

Built a hospital, independent from the Castle, maybe about 250 yards away, in a field belonging to the Home Farm.

A prefabricated hospital?

A prefabricated [hospital] which came all the way from America, in packing cases almost half the size of where you are sitting. And they were all in the one field. I can remember cycling back and forward past it,

morning and night. There was an enormous amount of these packing
cases and all this red writing on them [an] this wis [a] hospital. They were
American Nissen huts and everything was there that was required. All of a
sudden there was Americans in the War, they were running around in
jeeps and organising. And there were local firms employed and this
hospital was built .... The huts were put up facing one another, an end
and an end, an end and an end. And then at the end of the day all these
packing cases was turned into a corridor and a half sheet at the curve o the
Nissen hut put on the top, and all the hospital wards opened into this
corridor. And there was more doctors there than there was in the town.
There wis eight doctors there that I knew very well indeed. That came
about the house, you know. And there was WAAF quarters built, and
you're talking about a couple of hundred WAAFs maybe.

And how did your father and mother adjust to this?

Well, ma father, it didn't make a lot of difference to my father in actual
fact, he was still in the gardens, but my mother got a job. The Castle,
instead of a hospital, it was turned into an officers' mess. All the doctors
stayed there and she got a job in there, as cook. The Squadron Leader was
a man by the name of Pimlet. He was a Harley Street specialist and the
doctor was a Dr Grant, he was another Harley Street specialist. And there
were another five doctors over and above that, plus a lot of top women
that had been in the hospitals right round the country. Matrons, there
were one or two matrons there and they were all ranked. I don't know their
ranks, but they were all officers. They all got the rank of officer. And when
you think about it, in this area at that particular time, this was an RAF
hospital ... Wig Bay was starting to open up, North Cairn, Castle
Kennedy, the Freugh was always there, but it had grown immensely,
Baldoon, and all the other wee places, you're maybe thinking about eight
or ten thousand RAF personnel. So the place changed, in months, fae
what we were used [to] – it just changed completely, in months.

And did your father still provide the veg?

... All the produce that was grown in the garden went up to the Castle and
to the hospital and it was all used up there. And he got help. They sent
him down a couple of airmen, or maybe three if he needed them, you
know. The workers just disappeared into other jobs.

He wouldn't be growing peaches and plums?

Oh, just the same Nancy, just the same. They were there and ... even the
grapes were still growing. The vegetables wis just sent up tae the
cookhouse as they called it then. And, I think maybe if there wis any
surplus they were sent to wherever. As I say, I was gone then, and I ... went
to North Cairn as ... a tea boy and A remember the foreman saying to me
one day, 'What are you gonna do with your life?' I said, 'Well, if this war

lasts long enough …'. 'Oh,' he said, 'That's a long road away. You're only a kid yet,' he says. 'Och,' I said, 'You never know'. But I was making tea for the bricklayers and I said to him I wouldnae mind a go at that bricklaying. 'Well,' he says, 'Get yourself some tools and you can start on Monday as an apprentice bricklayer'. …

A few more questions, Bobby, tell me what your home was like at Lochnaw?

Well, the home, it was a fairly big house. There wis four bedrooms up the stairs an downstairs we had a front room. And in those days, we werenae sae posh, we had what we would call the kitchen, and the back kitchen. Now, it's a fair big kitchen an there's a wee passageway, and then down two steps into the back kitchen. That's where my mother did all the cooking. But we lived in what we called the kitchen. And then, of course, there was the front room. It was a nice big room too, and we werenae very often in it. You know, just at kind o special [times]. It was always there, if people came you could show them into it.

Did you have running water?

No, nothing like that. Oh no, the water, there was a wee tap about, oh, roughly 50 yards from the house – an just a lead pipe. It jist trickled anyway, an there was a tub sat in below it and it was always full. An there was a little overflow an it just ran four or five yards into the burn. And when you went down, in those days they were enamelled buckets … . You got two buckets of water and carried them up. And on wash day, we were quite fortunate. We had a water barrel, belonged to the gardens. It was just like a big bin mounted on wheels. So we could take that down an fill it up an bring it up for my mother and she would have all the wood gathered. There was plenty o wood to gather up because we were surrounded in it. And it was piled up outside beside a sep pot, what we called a sep pot in those days, with a wee chimney stack, jist a three foot length of pipe. And it had to be stoked up an the fire lit, an that boiled the water.

So you wouldn't have a flushing toilet?

No, no, no, we had a loo about, what, 30 yards from the house. We had to go up a wee ash path to what we caed the dry closet. And then we got a wee bit more modern and we got one of those, it was the Nelson we called it. We got one of those, and that was it.

And obviously no electricity?

No electricity.

No gas?

No gas. The three burner, was it a Valor stove? I think so, and that's where all the cooking was done, in this back kitchen. And I could tell you a very funny story about it. Every Saturday night at Lochnaw, about tea time, five o'clock, it was a fry. Without fail, it was a fry. And in the kitchen the table sat right in the middle of the floor. My father sat at the head of the table, my mother and myself and my two sisters, an we were eating away at our tea and all of a sudden the cat came flying up the lobby, right up onto the middle of the table, over my father's shoulders and right through the window … . Oh, what a fright everybody got, and nobody could think why. That was on a Saturday night. No sign o the cat at all on the Sunday but on the Monday morning, we heard the cat. And it could hardly walk, and my sister picked it up and brought it in and we discovered what had happened. My mother had set the frying pan down and the cat had jumped into the fat and, of course, that was the story about that.

But, it was a fairly happy home … . We had a lot of people visited, even from the town, you know. It was difficult to get there … transport in those days wasn't easy, but we had [quite a lot of] friends came up at weekends.

Did the big house have electricity?

Yes, they had a generator and made their own electricity. But, I would say they got the power in from the late thirties. It would be some time like that. There was no electricity on the estate at all. None of the houses had electricity. We had paraffin lamps and, of course, we used our candles. We all went to bed with our own candlestick and our candle. But sometimes, when things got modernised in the Castle, they would dish the stuff out to the people. I can remember the most beautiful lamps, big long stands and the glass bowl, and lovely big kind of like crystal bowls sat over the globe. And we would have two or three of those at one time. And then, of course, the Aladdin lamps came into go, and with the mantles, which were never very popular in the house [as] they were always getting broken. But they were a better light and that was how we managed, you know, we managed fine.

And the cook in the big house would have a big, big stove?

Oh, a great big thing. I'm not sure of the name of it … but oh, it was a very big one, And there was, I can always remember, it was a greeny-coloured thing and the brass bits in it, how they shone out. I can always remember that as they did all the cooking on that, I would assume. And they had a pantry. That's where I would go in the morning when I started in the gardens at seven o'clock [to] get the order in. It was a fair-sized room, and it was all marble shelves. I would assume that was to keep things cool. And that was where all the vegetables was taken to.

Bobby Gemmell (ii)

In the second part of the 2003 interview, Mr Gemmell recalled his apprenticeship as a bricklayer and his subsequent life in the building trade. Again, this account is rich in detail and includes fascinating information about his apprenticeship during World War II. He was often working at Wig Bay where security was tight and special passes were needed for workers to get onto the site. Later in the interview Mr Gemmell described the way in which his trade has changed over time and talked about some of the many building projects around Stranraer that he has been involved in. This included his greatest challenge, setting out Portpatrick School, which he describes here as his 'pride and joy'.

Now Bobby tell us about starting your apprenticeship.

Well Nancy, I started ma apprenticeship at North Cairn. Now North Cairn wid be one o the top secret sites in this area, if not the one. I am quite sure of that …

And it was a proper apprenticeship?

Oh yes. I did sign the forms and everything … it was a proper apprenticeship.

Even although the War was on?

Even although the War was on. And the firm was called Gerrards, they came frae Manchester and there would be four or maybe five busloads o men. [Murray's buses] would take the men up in the morning, plus one or two lorries. So there was a lot of men working there and as you can imagine there was an awful rush to get these radar stations built, and they were built right round the coast I believe.

And did you know what you were building?

No. No idea. We never heard what they were to be honest. But we knew there was something odd because of these masts. There was a firm there building these masts. There were two steel masts, and they were over the 367 feet high plus two wooden masts and they would be a couple of hundred, maybe 250 feet high too. And I was fascinated watching them actually building them. And being a wee country boy, everything fascinated me as we were busy building. I started building with the bricklayers, for the first time, on the wall. And there were quite a lot of local bricklayers there, but they were being called up every week, one away and one away, you know. And in no time at all they were running short of men. And I think that would be one of the reasons that they started two or three boys as apprentices and I … worked for some time and then, of course, Wig Bay started up and the same firm got the contract at Wig Bay and we were [all transferred] to Wig Bay.

And how did you get to your work?

Cycled to Leswalt and the bus picked me up at what they call the Kirk Corner in Leswalt. But when it was at Wig Bay I just cycled on, it wasnae all that far to Wig Bay. But there was a hiccup there for the simple reason the firm wasnae gettin on quick enough and they lost the contract and Wimpey took over. Now the excuse was that they could produce plenty

75

men, the English firm Gerrards couldn't seem to get enough men to satisfy these people that were wanting this job to get on. And how they overcome it, they built, oh, maybe five or six huts quickly, prefabricated things and they filled them with Irish labourers.

And where was this?

At Wig Bay. They were up maybe – the road that you would travel up and down now maybe 200 or 300 yards up into the Salchrie fields. And they made this workers camp, and that is where these Irish men came. And there was a big, big squad of them. But as it turned out, in those days there was a man here called the NSO, a National Services Officer, everybody called him God because he ruled the roost and he controlled the labourers. And he could send you to the Freugh or anywhere, didnae matter where, he could just come and say, 'Look, they're needin men desperate here … . We will send men there'. [And] so I was shifted back to North Cairn. And by this time the job was well on and for the first time there was Air Force personnel there. But things, in a couple or three month I was away, had changed, with the result that when we went down to get into this side of the bottom where the masts were, no way were we allowed in. So we had to go and they issued special passes out and I got one of these passes as a bricklayer and a joiner. And from then on any work to do in those build-ings in that line was done by us, it didnae matter where, we were, we were just transferred back there.

That … must have caused a lot of talk having a special pass?

Well, it did, and of course everybody had a pass for the site. But to get into this bottom site, not so much to get into the site, but to get into this building they called the Ardblock. I assume it was [a] receiving [block]. There were two blocks, one to the left and one to the right. One was the receiving block and one was the transmission block – it wasnae sae busy. And then there was another big block which was called the Standby [and there] was a big generator in there for the electricity. And, as I say, always under armed escort … when you went to that particular site – and I can remember it well. It was a block that was built three brick thick – that's 14 inches – thick. Plus, a metre away from it was a blast concrete wall round it, covered, and the whole thing was covered in wire netting with grass all twined through it and it was sprayed to look like hills. And they altered it: as the season changed they would come back and give it a brown or a green spray to blend in with the hills round about it.

You must have wondered what it was?

I did wonder, because I tell you … I never saw anything in it. Every time you went in these machines that these girls, these WAAFs were sitting at, wis covered in black sheets. And there was a wee buzzer went [off and] it doesnae matter what you were doing, 'Out!' [What people don't realise is how much the trade has changed over the years.] Say, for instance, they were wanting port holes, holes put in the wall. Nowadays you would stick a mason master into a drill and drill it. [In these days] you had to do this wi a wee hammer and chisel, [an] jump it round and there was a lot of mistakes made. I remember spending days fixing this sea gantry up so that they could bolt these machines and fix them to it. But then it didn't work for some reason, I don't know [whether] it was the steam or whatever. But then a month [after] we were there [again] taking it back out and had they had to figure some other way to do it. But as I say, we never saw anything – not a thing did we see. They just had these sheets and put them over [everything] and then maybe [we were sent out, and] we maybe sat there for three or four hours and did nothing.

And were you never asked at home what was happening?

Oh aye, everybody was questioning you, 'What's going on up there?' you know, 'What's radar?' And I said I didnae know … . There wasnae that many people had radios. They were nae very good in those days. The one we had, we got it from the Castle and you had cracklin on it, and you had to cycle away to Leswalt to get the battery charged and one thing and another … . [So] you didn't really know what was going on round about you. But I can always remember one of the officers letting us know and telling us, 'Ye're working in a top secret place,' he says. 'If anybody asks what you are doing, just say you are working there and that is all you have to say.' But we never thought too much of it. I can remember going back one time we were working, I think I was back at Lochnaw working at the hospital. And all of a sudden there's a lorry [to take us] back to North Cairn. And we had a different labourer with us, there was a bricklayer, this guy and myself. As I say, I was quite young and he was a man in his … thirties, and not in very good health, and that was why he wasnae called up. And when we got back, they wouldnae let this fellow in because he was Irish. So that lets you know how secretive it was and how particular they were. Whenever we went down and whenever he spoke, 'Let us see your pass. That pass is no good'. They could have phoned up and cleared him, but because he was Irish they wouldn't have him.

He was Southern Irish?

He was Southern Irish. Yes … . There were hundreds of them here.

[It] must have made a lot of difference to life in the town, and round about, all these people?

Oh, it was unbelievable. I mean to get them digs you know … . As I say, Wig Bay, they had a good idea having this worker's camp. And there was another out the town here, just at the golf course, you know where the repeater station is? There was workers there, stayed in huts there and build a road … . We were transferred to Brown's about that time. Once North

Cairn had got completed it had to be maintained, and they got the maintenance of the site. And right away a bricklayer, Jackie Wilson, they called him, and myself and a couple of joiners, we were transferred to them immediately – so they had us to get into North Cairn … . And, as I say, we were back and forward there for the whole of the War, plenty of times. And some of other things, mistakes were made. And I suppose the architects they maybe wouldnae know what they were maybe designing. And I can remember the entrance into these blocks were built were what we called baffle walls. They had one wall to the left, then there would be a gap and there would another wall built to the right so that if there was a blast it would nae hit the doors. And I can remember this machinery came and they couldnae get it in, so we had to cut [the wall] down, hammer and chisel you know, and then rebuild them and then cut them down a second time, and then rebuild them again. I can remember that. But, as I say, [then] the War ended and we [were] back and forth.

But before that, tell me about the building of Wig Bay and the Flying Boats.

Wig Bay was an enormous site, Nancy. There was a lot people there. Just baffling, how big a site would be, [when you] think about it. There would be hundreds and hundreds of men working at Wig Bay … . And, as I say, I was back there back and forward many times. And they built these pens up the side of the road – they were called pens – I don't know how many they built, maybe eight or ten of them. And they were to bring the flying boats up the slipway. There was a firm building the slipway, and once [this] wis completed [the boats] were brought up and towed down the road and towed into these pens, and that's where the mechanics worked on them.

Do you remember the first flying boat arriving?

Well, there'd have been flying boats, of course, on the loch prior to the War, at times. But I remember them, and quite a lot of them got sunk in the storms, they were badly moored. And local fishermen, I believe, that towed them – their moorings were too short. And another thing … you would know when a change in the weather [was coming]. You would see them taxiing up from Stranraer up to Wig Bay or vice versa and you knew that a storm was coming.

There was boats moored there from time to time. I can't remember but these were Sunderlands and then the American ones … Catalinas, they came in and you're talking about, over and above that, you're talking maybe about a couple of dozen big RAF launches running up and down there. That was where they trained the airmen. These guys were stationed at the Freugh, but they were still part of Wig Bay if you understand what I mean. They had the slipway and then maybe just 100 yards [an] they had a wee pier, a wee jetty built, and this where they trained these guys for Air

Sea Rescue, for the pilots in the channel. They were all trained up here in Wig Bay. And they were stationed at Corsewall, and there was quite a lot of them too. And A remember working at Wig Bay, this was an awful tragedy … . You … could see [this] Sunderland rising up and then it started to bank round, and that was just up above the Salchrie Farm. There was [a] workers' canteen there and I had been sent up … . [It was] very difficult to get cigarettes [and] fortunately I didn't smoke, but most of the men did. And they would send you away to the town, you could spend as long as you liked just as long as you came back with the cigarettes. And I was up at the canteen, because they [often] had [cigarettes] in the morning, but they were sold out in no time. And I was watching this Sunderland coming up and it was banking very steeply. I thought to myself, this guy is going back into the water – just thinking – and all of a sudden I heard this [noise] and saw it disappearing. And the big floats that hung below the wings, it [had] hit one pen and crashed into the next pen. And it was loaded up with the fuel, it was going away for a long, long trip, it just burst into flames. And I could see all the men running but they just had to stand and look, a tremendous heat. You could see the girders starting to buckle with the heat, and you were unable to do anything …

These camps must have had electricity?

They had electricity. A big lot of them had generators of course, big generating plants.

And they didn't bring anything up to Lochnaw?

No, they got electricity there for the camp, plus a generator. Because, if they were operating and there was a cut, they had to have the electricity back on. But they came to the camp, they never came to the houses. There was never any electricity there at that time … . But, the size of these camps, and the amount of bricklayers that we had at Wig Bay … . Just to let you know, we had a wee brass disk, every one of the workers had a brass disk and there was a big board put ootside at night, outside the office. And as you went out you hung your disk on it an … there was a guy watchin that you hadnae two or three mens disks, you see. And my number was 81, and that was the bricklayers. But, if you think about it, the amount of bricklayers that were there. And, I mean, the hangar was all brickwork and all the buildings were brickwork up on the hill, the communal site.

There is a lot still there.

Well, there is but there is an awful lot of them gone. I think the first aid place is still there, the sick bay, along the top road. I think most of it's still there. But all the top site there was the cookhouse, it was a colossal dining room and ablution block. You're talking about maybe a row of 30 or 40 toilets on each site [and] showers, which I had never seen before. That was where I had my first shower. One day I was in and there was naebody aboot, so I tried it. Two chains hung down with wee handles on them, you could pull them hot or cold, and there was nothing like that in the houses roundabout the place. And we were absolutely fascinated by this. And up there you had the cookhouses and all the paraphernalia that was round the ablution blocks, and there wasn't too many billets, because they built the billets away on what they called dispersal sites. And they built them beside the wee woods, and round Leswalt, and all round there were these huts, in case of air raids. And then they realised that the officers' mess and the work quarters, they were quite close to one another. And then, as you came down to the farm, that was where all the stores, workshops and goodness knows what all was there. There was everything.

And [did you] have to do anything with Cairnryan?

Nothing at all to do with Cairnryan. It was military. Cairnryan was built by the army.

And you were RAF?

This was RAF. All that side of the loch – the Kirkcolm side of the loch, was RAF. The other side was the Army. And, of course, what we didn't know then was what they were [building] harbours and things like that ... out there, but it was a place I never ever worked [at] ... . As I say, [as] the War got over very shortly after that, we started to get sent back out to work on farms ...

And who were you working for?

The [McLeods] of Goatend, and I was with them up until 1948. [Then I] went for a couple of year with my brother-in-law, he'd a plumbing business. And I went with him purely for the simple reason that I would get a lot of different jobs to do, you know. People were starting to work [at] their houses – do a bit of slatin, a wee bit of tilin ... . I think I was maybe nearly three years [there], until 1953. That's how long I was there, from '48 to '53. And then I decided I had been long enough at that, and I went and got a job with Mr Iredale.

If I can go back a little. Were your mother and father still at Lochnaw at this time?

No, no, no. They had moved. My father had got the option of taking the gardens on.

On his own behalf?

Yes, but he said to me, 'What about it?' And I had no interest in it whatsoever, and I liked the job I was doing. So, I said to father I wasnae interested in it. There is no point of me going an getting miserable. And I don't think – my own opinion Nancy, was [that] none of us could drive, [so] how were [we] going to get rid of [the] stuff. And I pointed aa this out tae my father. And he knew this as well as I did, probably better than I did. [So] he took the job as head gardener at Corsewall, in at the Buchanans, but he didnae settle there at all. And then he got a house in the town, in Station Street,

and moved into Station Street. And he got the parks superintendent's job
and that was him tae he retired. But in the meantime, as I say, I went to
McKenzie Partners and Mr Iredale, just as a bricklayer, intae the squad ...

You didn't have anything to do with Bishopburn then?

No, I didn't. It was up then, in '53. A lot of houses were up there then. I tell
you where I went, Ashwood Drive. There was houses built, in behind
which is the labour exchange now, I went to four or five houses in there.
That was the time the boat went down – it was just after that, and [I] then
went to Castle Kennedy housing scheme and I wasn't very long there. Oh,
let me think, I think two or three months. And he came to me one day and
said to me, 'We have a lot of houses to build. There is the Lochans, Portpatrick and Dunragit and Kirkcolm'. All these places ... these wee villages
housing schemes were going up then [and] he offered me a job as a
foreman. And I wasnae very keen on takin it but he talked me into it, and
it was probably the best move I ever made. So I was there for 20-odd years.
I was general foreman as a matter of fact. It was a job I liked doing ...

So you were at the building of most of these house in the villages?

Oh yes, well, I worked in Castle Kennedy, Dunragit, Kirkcowan, Portpatrick, the Lochans, Kirkcolm. Went down to the Grange of Bladnoch,
and built houses there, and probably others I have forgotten ... . Years
were getting on now, and bigger jobs started to come in ... and I went to
build the new broo, the labour exchange. That was my first big job really –
the new labour exchange in Ashwood Drive. [Then I] went to Brookfield
Crescent and did all the bungalows in Brookfield Crescent, and I enjoyed
it. Again, in 1963, I ended up in charge of the new post office in Stranraer,
and that is when the new school started. Because the fella that was a good
friend of mine – and had taught me a lot – he was the foreman in the post
office and he was moved out to the new schools. And I took over the post
office and I was with McKenzie Partners right up until they finished up.
And then Mr Iredale took it on on his own, and I was with him until he
finished up 1972, or '73 ...

So you must have seen a lot of changes?

Tremendous changes. When you think about [it], in those days these big
big houses scheme like Knockcullie you know, and compare it today
[when] there is not one going up. There is not a council house being built
in the town, or anywhere around.

I mean with tools and circumstances?

Well, in the building trade, when I started – for instance a wet day was a
wet day and you sat in the hut and you got no pay. If you didnae work –
no pay. And [I was] very fortunate, being a foreman it didnae affect me,
because we got our pay. But it used to worry me something terrible to
think that these men were sitting there and did not get paid. Then a new

law came out that you got paid half the time you sat, so if it was a wet day where you could do nothing, you would get four hours pay. But we progressed again, and then we got what they called the 8-hours guarantee that if you went out in the morning and it rained all day, you got your 8 hours pay and that was a tremendous boost to the workers.

But when you started as an apprentice what were the conditions then? Did you work in the rain during the War?

Well, being a bricklayer, it's difficult. Because when you think – along a wall you maybe have eight, ten, 12 mortar boards sitting full of mortar – the more water gets on to them, the wetter it gets. So bricklayers can't really work in the rain. The mortar does not allow you. But you could be sent inside and, if it was possible you know, [you] were sent inside to work.

If you were doing three layers of brick and the thing was built in a hurry, you must have worked during awful weather?

Oh, we did. If it was possible at all, you worked, you know. They tried one or two schemes [like] putting sheets and tarpaulins over, but here you got rain and wind and it wasnae worth it really. And another thing, it was difficult to keep things like bricks and mortar dry and that, it was very difficult. The joiners, I have seen them working out, you know, and water running out of them. Especially when things were being rushed, you know, during the War. They were very strict that if you could do it, do it. But it was difficult for a bricklayer, as I say, [with] the water problem on the mortar boards, [if] it was too soft ... you could nothing about it.

Have there been many changes in equipment?

Well, there has. If you think today for instance, if you are going to cut a slab today, you just pick up a Stihl saw and pull the string and a diamond tip blade cuts it in minutes. In my day, I didn't have any of these things. You did it with a hammer and [chisel which was] four inches wide and marked along it. And that is just one instance, you know. To drill a hole, you had to get a hammer and chisel and cut it out. Nowadays you just pick up an electric drill, or a Kango hammer or any of these tools, and you know ... in minutes the job is done. For instance, just across the road from where you are living, they cut a wall down. I don't know if you noticed it. They just cut it the way you would cut a piece of wood. [They] put the Stihl saw into it and cut it dead straight down. But when I was a bricklayer, we had to that with hammer and chisel, no other way. ... You did it as neat as you could, but nothing like what they're doing today.

Tell me about the first things you did [when] you started your apprenticeship.

Well, the first thing, I said to my father, 'A've got a chance o a trade. A think I'll start this bricklaying, [and I] need to get some tools'. And he cycled into Stranraer to McHarrie's and brought me a hammer and trowel and foot-rule and ... that is what I took off with on the Monday morning.

You didn't get them given to you?

Oh, no, you had to supply your own tools. Nothing like that given to you. And one of the bricklayers was a local man, and a very well-known name, it was McMillan, Andrew McMillan. [A] big, tall guy. The same McMillan that started up the Empire. And I can remember this as well as I can remember eating my breakfast this morning. He had a look at the trowel and he said, 'That's too big'. And he went to his tool bag and he gave me a smaller one. And he showed me how to put this mortar on. I already knew, but I watched him doing it. But it's a lot more difficult when you picked it up, and picked the brick up and jointed it, and I can remember [him saying], 'No, no that way'. And he was showing me how to joint it, and I set it on the wall. And the first thing I did I cut the line, there was a line goes from end to end, you know, what they call a William Peacock … Line. And that was the first thing I did, I cut it when I hit the brick. 'Oh, dinnae cut my line. It's just awfy if you cut the line.' So I was going to tie a knot in it. 'Oh,' he says, 'You cannae dae that. It will catch the brickwork and stick out'. And he put a buckle in the wall. And I thought it cannae be that much in it, to maself, and he showed me how to splice it. That was the first thing I actually learned. He showed me how to splice the line – putting the two pieces together. And it was just a wee brick building we were on, I don't even know what it was for now, and single brickwork. And that is where I started, and it was something I picked up very easily. In no time at all I was able to manage, and no to cut the line anyway. And, as I say, it was something I enjoyed. I worked hard at, and I enjoyed [it].

How long was your apprenticeship?

Five years apprenticeship. I think I only did about four years and a couple of months … . I would say about five years was [the] standard thing in those days, I don't think it is near as much today, but all my apprentices served five years.

So what else did you do after you found out how to put on the mortar?

Well, you just had to just learn to joint the brick. It was difficult for a beginner, because when you watch a bricklayer doing it, it looked so easy. But when you put it on and by the time you got it over to set it on the wall, it had fell off. And, of course, you tried it again [until] you got quite adept at it. And then you wid progress from there, this is after a good few months mind, onto building a corner. Now the corners were built first, and then the line was stretched from end to end and you filled in between. But the corner fellows were the main guys on the jobs. And then you were put ontae a corner, and by that time you had acquired a club rule … [plumb line] … . There were about 18 courses and … then you stuck the line pin in at each end of the line course. But, as I say, in those days and compare it with today – it's an awful lot easier today for one simple reason, the mortar. In those days a lot of the mortar was mixed by men with shovels. They put a great big board down and they mixed, with men with shovels, even well into the War. We saw the first mixers coming [in at that time], but then you couldn't get them. They were crying out for them everywhere. And these men would just mix it by hand and it was brought forward to you. Some of them carried and hauled it on their shoulders, but mostly with barras. An it was dumped onto your board, and you generally had an empty paint tin sitting on the end of your board – full of water – and you had to soften [the mortar] up to suit yourself. But nowadays it's mixed in a mixer, and there's what you call plasticer put in, and it comes out like butter, you know, like cream. And it cuts all that extra work out. And that was a tremendous boon to the bricklayer, the plasticer. When they brought it out, it was just soap. I have seen us just using squeezy [liquid], putting it into the water barrel. That's all it is. To me, that was one of the big pluses, plus the pre-stress lintels – that was always heavy work. Imagine a window just … a five-foot window, and you would need roughly a seven-foot lintel, nine inches deep, four inches wide. And some of them had what you call a boot on them, to close the cavity. Nowadays they're just made four-by-three, these lintels.

If you knew it had been so hard would you still have gone for it?

Well, now that's a hard question. Wasnae much good at much else, I don't think. I was not very good at school, and never made high school, never passed my 11-plus, so I had no other option to tell you the truth …

You must have been using maths all the time you were building?

Well, I was quite fortunate when I went, as I told you, I went to Wig Bay. And [they] were just setting the site out and they said to me this morning, 'Hey apprentice, come here. See that gentleman over there, he is wanting you for a week or two'. Now, what was he wantin me for? 'Well,' he says, 'I don't know. But you're going and that is it'. I went over to the big fella, 'Ah,' he says, 'I want you with me young fella,' he says, 'For two or three weeks. We are going to be setting out all the buildings on this site and I need somebody to hold the end of the tape and hold the staff for the levels'. 'And,' he says, 'I believe you are an apprentice bricklayer?' And I told him that I was, so [he said] 'This will do you the world of good'. The first thing that jumped into my head was, I hope they don't ask me too much here, or I will let myself down. Because that was what worried me. Because, as I say, I wasnae very good at school. But, however, we set off up to this communal site and [we had] this old van thing loaded with pegs, hammer […]. [They would be] checking the sizes and putting these pegs in and I was holding the staff on it, and they were reading it … and putting all those sizes on the pegs, you see. This is for the guys [to] come and put the foundations in. So, he said to me one day, 'Are you paying attention to this?' 'Well,' I says, 'I am'. And I worried about this [because it was tricky]. Now the secret of setting something out is, if you know the diagonals it makes it an awfy lot simpler when you're squaring the building out. And these fellas were talking about diagonals – and I didnae know a thing about it. But he said to me he would teach me how to do this, I said, 'That will be something, I am no very good at that type of thing'. 'Oh,' he says, 'It's quite simple. I'll teach you how to do it'. The next day he brought me out this book and gave me a lot of tables, and one thing and another, and told me study them out. 'And,' he says, 'Have they taught you about the three-four-five system, the very simple system?' I told him I had heard the bricklayers talking about it, but none of them seem to have it off pat. They seem[ed] to be arguing between one and another about what they were doing. And what happens is they get the joiner to make them a great big square, maybe 6 feet by 5 feet, and they put it down and they stripe the line one way and stripe it the other and that is the way to do it. And I said to him, 'I see your fellas don't use the square', which absolutely fascinated me. So he taught me how to do diagonals after that, using [Pythagoras]. After a struggle, I managed to get the basics of it. 'And,' he says, 'The three-four-five system … is the simple way for you. If you measure four feet one way, three feet the other way, it should be five feet across.' … . On a big building like this, that is no good, because you have to get nearer the corners. So the simple thing was just multiply by any given number … . Say you use seven. Seven times three is 21, seven times four is 28 the square, seven times five, etc. It looked that simple I just couldnae believe it, and by the time I left these guys I had it off pat, and I worked hard at it every night at [home at] Lochnaw. Left alone I worked them out, and that was a great boon to me.

And that was because you could see the point of it, but you couldn't see the point at school?

No, never would have got it at school. But, as I say, that set me. And the wee guy that was the foreman at the post office, a man called Willie Murdoch, I had tremendous faith in him. … he taught me quite a lot too about the setting out, that was what I would say. At the end of the day, looking back on 50 years – without boasting – I would probably be as good as anybody in the district. I built Portpatrick school, which ended up my pride and joy. You will have seen Portpatrick school?

Oh yes.

Well I set that school out. That was the hardest and most difficult thing I've every attempted.

Because it is a peculiar shape?

Well, a shape of all angles. All the toilets, teachers' room, the headmaster's room, they were all outside and they all blended one into the other and three different floor levels of four foot, as you probably know. And one the architects was a lady, Miss Dale, and there was another architect, I forget his name now … . I remember them coming saying [they would] give [us] a hand to set this out, but they didn't have any idea [of] the difficulty in setting it out on a slope, you know. Because, if you can imagine working on a slope, if your tape is not level, if you lower it down [you] shorten [the measurement] you know. And [we] had to get great long pegs in, and what a job it was. But at the end of the day A was quite proud of it.

So you were quite a mathematician really?

Well, [as] I say [I] got that past early in my life, and it didnae bother me at all to measure and to work out the diagonals and use two tapes, which I never saw bricklayers doing up to that particular [time]. I had never seen all that much of it … . [One time] they were setting out this square, and it was just a square brick tank, a static water tank. And it was going to be filled with water in case of an air raid, [so] there was water handy. [This was] for one of the main stores at Wig Bay. And these two bricklayers, they werenae local fellows, were arguing about squaring it out and I was watching … . I said I would square it out for [them] … and they told me [the sizes]. And I just sat down and worked out the diagonals, and got another tape. And just with that, one of the foremen drew up and he [gave me] another tape … and [so] we had the two tapes. And these guys were watching me, and I put these pegs in with the two tapes and set it out. 'Now,' I says 'The check is that measurement there'. … [and if] it was the same as the first measurement … then that is a dead square. I remember these two guys, and that was it. They didnae like it, but that was the way.

And it was a tremendous boost, that six weeks with these guys at Wig Bay.

So you reckon that meeting all these different things at the beginning of the War helped you with your work?

No question at all. Because you have to think, Nancy, up until the War, a lot of the bricklayers here, probably more than half of them, werenae bricklayers. They were stonemasons. A lot of them had served their time working. A big lot of them, were good stonemasons, so they were not as adept as these city guys they brought in at actually laying bricks. I noticed that. And another thing I did notice, I used tae wonder how one man could build his corner quicker than another man. And I used to watch … like a hawk, and when I saw the technique [of] one [I] compared it with the other, and that was what I worked on. All through that, [when] I saw one guy very good at something … I said, there was a reason for that, and [so I] studied that and immediately I got it, I used it.

What was your first job on your own, as a foreman?

Castle Kennedy housing scheme, that was my first when I took over at Castle Kennedy and I did the right hand side of the road at Castle

Kennedy as you drive in, the houses on the right, the ones on the left were someone else. And I went from there to the Lochans and I moved around a lot of the sites. And then I can remember, Mr Iredale saying to me one time about the fireplaces in a lot of them were having problems with them. And I followed them round after that and did a lot of that type of work, and the steps and the retaining walls and I enjoyed that too. That was another handy thing for me.

Thank you very much Bobby, that was very interesting.

Ian Jack (butcher)

Mr Jack was interviewed in 2007 by Nancy McLucas. The interview, which covered the history of the family firm, highlighted many of the challenges which small local businesses have faced over recent decades.

When was the firm actually started?
> The firm was started in 1914 by ma grandfather, who arrived here from Falkirk. Prior to that he'd worked in Stranraer as a butcher for a few years and then he acquired the shop in Bridge Street.

Can I ask what brought him to Stranraer in the first place?
> That, I don't know. I don't know.

Was your ... grandfather a married man when he came to Stranraer?
> ... I never knew him and it was never talked about. That's why I don't know a lot about it. Father and my grandfather didn't get on at all.

Not an unusual thing ... in families. Have you any idea then how many men he would employ?
> Probably he'd have about ten or 12 employed in the shop at that time.

Why so many?
> Because things were a lot busier in these days. There was no supermarkets. Even though there was probably eight or nine butcher shops in Stranraer. But, of course, we had chaps that done the deliverin as well, so that increased the staff as well. But, that would be at its peak, ten to 12 people. And, then, of course, as years rolled on ... we had to decrease staff because we put a lot of the vans off the road. And we ended up with just one solitary van, and then we done away with it.

So your grandfather would start with vans, now would they be horse-drawn?
> No, no. The vans actually had American V8 engines in them, believe it or not.

In 1914?
> No, this ... would be in the thirties then.

But in 1914 what would his vans be like?

We've got photos of them. Very old basic vans, much the same as Ian Gillespie has. Have you seen Ian Gillespie's old vans? Much the same as that …

Motor driven vans?

Yep.

Did they go out selling in the country?

They went out selling, and they went out with their wee money bag to give out the change, etc. And it was all done on trust. … They called all over, even up to Ballantrae and all the distant parts, Wigtown, away down that area, Drummore … oh, … Whithorn.

They didn't go in to the Stewartry?

No, they didn't, I don't think. But I know they went up as far as Ballantrae and Girvan.

It must have been a very good business, because if there were all these other butcher shops in Stranraer they couldn't all have been sending vans all over the county?

No, we were about the biggest one at the time, I can remember. Some of them maybe put out one van but that was about it. Most of them concentrated just on their business in Stranraer. But, I think my grandfather was trying to get it all, if you know what I mean, because he moved in and he decided to go for it.

Did he, at that time, live above the shop?

He had property in Sun Street and that is where they stayed, 57 Sun Street, where my late aunt [lived].

I remember Miss Jack. Your grandfather, when did he stop actually working in the business?

… He died in 1944.

So, your grandfather actually saw two World Wars? … Have you ever heard any stories of what it was like in the First World War, for instance as regards shortages or things like that?

Just what it was like in the Second World War. And the rationing, etc, and the misdemeanours that went on.

Yes, of course. Now tell me, who supplied his meat?

He bought it from the farms and they drove it in from Kirkcolm, early in the morning, [to] bring all the cattle in tae the local slaughter house. My father would have to do that. And it was all locally sourced. There was nothing brought in to the area in these days. They were all killed in Stranraer. The pigs actually were killed at the back door in Sun Street, believe it or not … the back of the family home. And, I've still got what they call the mell, in fact it is up the loft there, that was used to kill these pigs … . A mell is a green bowl, what bowlers use and there is a hole drilled in it and a big shaft put in. They are actually illegal now, but that's what was used to kill the pigs. And you had to hit it on the right spot first time or you could hit it all day and you would never have killed it. It's a work of art.

Have you ever attempted it yourself… and would you be allowed to?

Never attempted … . No it's got to be humane, etc [now].

So how did they kill the cows then and the sheep? … I'm talking about your grandfather's day.

I don't know if they would have the humane killer then, the humane gun, pistol. Either that or they would just cut their throats, and that was it.

Once your grandfather had brought the cattle in, he killed them, and then what did he do?

They used to hang down there in the slaughter house, and in these days there was no refrigeration, or very little. And then, probably after two or three days, [you'd] be sent down with a wheelbarrow, which James and me used. And [you] brought them up [to] hang them … in the front shop, without refrigeration, all the rails – some of them are still in the shop yet – covered up mind ye, and that's the way it was. Completely different. As it is now.

Your grandfather carried on in business until 1940, when did you father take over?

Immediately. His father died [an] he was already in the business, so he automatically [took over].

When did your father go into the business?

He would go in … well, that's a difficult one.

Did your father willingly go into the business?

No, he hated it, never liked it. … That's why he bought other things like the Quay […], which is being demolished at the moment, which used to be the Chinese restaurant – remember the Seaview Chinese restaurant? He bought it and turned it into a hairdresser's and a café and a restaurant, because he wanted out and he wanted something better for my sister and myself. But I really enjoy what I'm doing, and I'm glad in a way it didn't work out, because I'm happy where I am. I like doing what I'm doing.

Did your father talk about what things were like during the War?

Oh, great fun at times. And the ration books, which I have still got, it's so interesting to see the names at the top of the ration books. Like the local minister, or Miss Thorburn that was next door … and they all seemed to get maybe a little bit of priority, I'm not sure about that. But I've still got the books there, and it's really interesting to look at what they got, but it wasn't a lot.

I can remember that though, it was about 1/2d.

That's right. And, of course, in these days there was a lot of rabbits and hares, which he was in to dealing with in big time. And we used to send them off in the train loads down to Manchester … . Rabbits and hares, during the War, and after the War. And also poultry, as well, found its way into the Manchester market from here.

How did you send them? Were they refrigerated?

No, they werenae refrigerated. Just sent down. And we never got paid for them, the last lot we sent we never got paid for. Normally we did.

But you never sent them after you didn't get paid for them?

No, that was that finished.

It was a big market then?

Oh, it was a big market, aye. But that's where aa the poachers and that came in, in these days. That was the different ball game. I continued on with the game, but obviously now we cannae do it because we've got to have separate premises for everything. But we've still got a game licence, and we've still got the sign above the door, [and the licence is] checked every year by the police ... very much so ... . We can still accept game, and if we do we've got to write everything in a book. The name and address, the vehicle registration number. If it's a bicycle I need to know all the details of the bicycle and put it down in this book so that the police can come and check ... . That's just because of the poaching situation, to make sure everything is legit, and everybody is doing it properly. It's interesting, even though we don't do it now, that the police still come round and ask for the book.

When I came to the town at first I can remember, if you went in for a chicken you could actually hear them down in the cellar, is that right?

That's right ... . Sometimes ower the festive season there would be around about 200 turkeys, 300 chickens, 20 or 30 ducks in the cellar that's in below. And it wasn't very big, it wasn't pleasant ... . The staff killed them. My father's killed them, I've killed them, everybody had to do it. And it wasn't a nice job, and you would go home at night with the lice crawling off you. You had to take your clothes off at the foot of the stair, well I did, and upstair and jump into the bath ...

What did you do with the feathers?

The feathers, we used to make money out of them. Especially the feathers out of the ducks, for making, you know, pillows, etc. And, they commanded quite a bit of money in these days.

You must have had some kind of person you supplied it to?

Well, we used to [take them] down to Mr Farrell ... the bone man. And he took them and he took all the rabbit skins, the bones, etc. What a place! What a place! It was quite good money we got, and we split it among the staff, and everybody was happy ... . Most of [the butchers] done it.

Did most of them have a cellar like yours?

No, they would have an outhouse, somewhere but not a cellar ... as such. Tommy Jesson, he had a bit at the back specially for that, so that was a different ball game. They were still good days and happy days wi the staff. I think it was a better environment to work in, even though it was maybe unhealthy and probably not as hygienic as it should have been ... . But I've spoken to old butchers who say exactly the same, that these were the best days. They all clubbed together and all the butchers met in The Grapes at night time for a drink … and it was really good. And everybody helped everybody out.

I can remember sawdust [on the floor of the shop], you … quite liked it?

Oh, yes, we liked it, and we used it. I would be about 22 years old when we stopped using sawdust in the shop. And what we done, we went round to the local joiners, got the bags of sawdust – and then we would put it down fresh in the morning. And every night there would be a rake and we raked through it to get all the bits of string and bits and pieces off. And that usually done for maybe a day or two and then after that we'd sweep it all up and put fresh sawdust down. And it really stopped people from slipping on the floor, which is a big thing in the shop. When we went to new linoleum, etc, and tiles, people were slipping all over the place.

Did you have to stop?

It was recommended that we stopped using it. It wasn't banned but it was recommended.

On Government regulations … how do they work and when did they start, and how often do they come round?

It used to be once a year as far as A remember. We always got one visit per year from Environmental Health. And they basically looked at your nails and looked at your hands and had a quick look at things, and that was it. The years have progressed [and] now we get visits … four, five, six times a year. We get samples taken o our products that we make in the shop … cooked meats, etc. They're taken about every month now and analysed and brought back. All the results are given back to us, and fortunately we've been A1, and everything okay. But, oh, how it's changed, and it's going to get worse.

So you will have a lot of paperwork?

Paperwork is now the killer. That's the same with every business. It's totally overpowering.

In what respect? Thinking back to your father's time and your grandfather's time what kind of things did they not have to do?

Nothin, they did nothin at all. No paperwork. Just the basic books and that was it. Now, of course, you've got to start with the products you sell in the shop, you've got to make labels for them, you've got to do equations to work out the percentage of meat, what colouring is in it, all [these] things. Which takes a long, long time. And then you start printing new labels, which takes a lot of time. And then you get that done and they'll maybe say there is a change is the regulation – which is what I'm doing tonight – there is a change in one of the colourings which has been banned completely, and we've got to change all our recipes for certain [products as a result].

So there is a lot of room for error here, because you could overlook something?

Oh, absolutely. There is only so much we can do. But we try our best to do it. And in fairness Environmental Health are very helpful if you go and ask them. And they'll help you rather than just say, 'Look, we are shutting you down for this'. They're pretty good that way.

Have you ever known of a butcher in Stranraer that was shut down?

No, no, never. There is very few have been shut down. Because once these chaps come in, and if they spot something's not right, you do get a chance to get it right. And I'm sure 100 per cent of butchers nowadays will adhere to what's to be done.

Obviously from your grandfather and your father's day you now have to contend with supermarkets. Has that affected the business very much?

Without question. Supermarkets – William Low came to Stranraer ... 20 years ago, they opened up where the electrician's shop was. Well, when William Low's arrived that's when the trouble started. And I had to really think ahead, because I knew there would be more to follow. And everything just changed overnight with the supermarkets. They took a phenomenal money in their butcher counter in these days, which meant the six or seven butchers that were left were having a big chunk taken out of their turnover ... . So I decided, probably the best way to go was to stick to the top end and buy the best I possibly could, in everything. Don't cut corners, and do it that way. That's what I've done, and continue to do to this day.

These supermarkets, was the meat brought in or did they have a butcher on the premises?

To start with they had their own butcher on the premises and then they diversified and got it all pre-packed and brought in. Which, I think, Low's is now Tesco, I think that's the way they still work. I think that's a mistake they made, to be quite honest. But, now with the arrival of Morrisons, they've got their own meat counter. And that hasn't helped either, but we're still holding our own.

So presumably the meat counter at Morrisons has a proper butcher?

It's got a proper butcher. They've got two butchers, I think, going there. But all the stuff is brought in pre-packed, some that they butcher themselves, and some is brought in. We won't go into that.

How long did it take you to learn to butcher?

Eh, I'm still learning. That's being quite honest. And I was never taught. I've been self-taught ... . My father did try his best to teach me, I maybe wasnae as interested as I should have been. I was away doing other things in these days. But then, when he passed away, I realised I had to do something and I got help. I went to every possible meeting up and down the country. I went to all the courses I could possibly go tae, and I still do to this day, and that's why I'm still learnin.

I can remember Miss Jack working in the shop. How long did she actually work? Did she work for her father and then for her brother?

She worked for her father, then her brother. And she was there tae she was ... 82, something like that, in the shop.

Did she start as a school girl?

Straight from the school, and into the shop. And she didnae get on with her father either, in fact they never spoke!

That must have been very awkward?

Very awkward indeed. But she got on with her bookwork, and everything was done ... meticulously, in triplicate. And you couldn't change her ways, or she went absolutely ballistic. Believe it or not! She remained doing that till she managed to get retired, at 82.

She worked in a horrid, cold little corner, I can remember.

And walked up and down the hill every day and night, probably worked till about seven o'clock at night and started early in the morning. And it was a bare existence. But that's what she liked doing, and she done it that way. And I tried to change things, which was a bad mistake because that didn't really work out. She wasnae happy at that, so we just kind of let her get on in her own way.

Pardon me for asking, but, if she didn't talk to the boss how did she know what she had to do with the accounts?

She was in total control of that ... . He knew that it was being done right.

She would be 14 when she started?

That's right. She just got on with it and done it her own way, and got into the bookwork as well.

That means that during the War would Miss Jack be the one who dealt with the ration books?

Yes, she was the one that done it all, the rationin.

Have you any idea how they actually worked it?

No ... I don't know how they worked it at all. That's being quite honest.

Any idea how many people were actually registered with Alex Jack?

... Somewhere about 1200 customers registered.

... Did your father ever talk about, did he, for instance have to supply any of the many camps that were round this area during the War, soldiers and airmen and stuff like that?

They had to supply some of the camps. That I don't know a lot about, but I think it was work that all the butchers got an equal turn, to supply such and such with things. ... And I'm quite sure in these days they all helped each other out. If one butcher hadnae got what he needed he could go to the other butcher and he would loan him the stuff. That went on in these days, not nowadays, it doesn't happen. There was a lot of people about this area at that time needing fed, out at Wig Bay, West Freugh, etc, so there was a lot o stuff shifted, a lot o stuff.

The shopkeepers would obviously get extra supplies. Have you any idea where these came from?

... That, again I don't know, I never discussed it wi my father at all ...

It's quite interesting because you would wonder if there would be enough cattle locally.

Well, there was definitely no wagons bringing ready-killed meat into this area in these days, not as there is now. ... I don't think there was anybody came into this area at all, during the War that I know of. In fact, I'm sure of that, it was all done locally.

So when did this local sourcing stop?

Well, when the slaughter house shut, that put the kybosh on slaughtering local meat. We had no other option but to move to other places. The first port o call for me was to go to Dumfries, and there was an abattoir there. And they sent a wagon up to us wi all the stuff we required. As so often happens, they went bankrupt. And then, as time went on, we got involved with a chap called Peter. And Peter has been my buyer of meat for around 22 years now. [He] opened up a factory in Inverurie ... that's where him and his partner started, [but then] they went bust. So, they got a job in what is now Millers of Speyside and they are now partners in it, and running a very successful business. But as I only deal with Aberdeen Angus beef, we've had this great relationship, because very, very few butchers go totally Aberdeen Angus. And, once again I decided, if I'm going to do it, it's the whole hog. It's Aberdeen Angus or nothing. And that's the decision I made about 20 years ago, and stuck to it.

And you don't regret it, and neither do your customers?

Definitely not. And I think it's been my saviour to be quite honest. There's so many dubious people about nowadays in our trade, I can see what is happening.

What do you think is the future for individual private businesses like yours?

A think it's got to a stage now you can't stop. You've got to keep improving, an keep ahead of the game. I think there is a future left for the butchers that are dedicated to quality. But anybody that's just putting any old thing over their counter, they are not gonna survive. Things are going to get very difficult in the future, because increases are already starting to bite hard on everythin. Every single item that we use in the shop is goin tae skyrocket in the next two to three months. It's already started, which makes life very awkward, but I've always been optimistic about things and said, 'Well, I think we'll be here for a long time yet'.

There is a growing interest in vegetarianism. Has that, like [with] the supermarkets, have you noticed anything from that?

No, no, definitely not vegetarianism. That has not affected us, definitely not. The one thing that is coming in ... is organic. I tried organic and was told by Peter, he said, 'I'll let you try it, Ian, but I want your honest opinion'. So we bought a full body o beef, organic, with a register where it come from, etc. We matured it and left it hung for the usual length of time. And we tried it, and it was very disappointing. When I phoned my supplier back and I said to Peter, 'I was bitterly disappointed in that'. 'Well,' he said, 'I could have told you that'.

Why do you think that was?

That I don't know. I've spoken to other butchers that went along the same lines, and they have tried organic. Some of it has been okay, but the bulk of them, no. It's got this name, and you pay way over the odds for it. And as Peter said, 'It ain't any better than Angus that you're selling anyway, that's for sure'.

Do you think a lot of the attraction is because people feel the animals are better treated? And are they?

… They are just handled the exact same way as any other cattle, just the same.

They're not happier cows in happier fields?

I don't think so. I definitely don't think so.

So you think there is still a future for your son is now in the business?

I think so. My son is now in the business, so that is the fourth generation. And I always said that if you get by the third generation the fourth is a doddle – I could argue with that, mind you.

So you have only actually got another seven years to go to your centenary? Are you thinking of doing anything special?

I'd love to do something special. That, we'll have to think about.

It certainly would be something you would want publicity for.

That's right. If we were going to do it we would do it. Seven years is a long way off … . It soon passes, but we'll certainly do something for that.

Mr Jack, on behalf of Stranraer and District History Trust, thank you very much for your time and assistance.

Agnes McClymont

Mrs McClymont was interviewed by Nancy McLucas in 2008 about the time she spent working with the Scottish Gas Board (SGB) in the 1960s and early 1970s. This interview described in detail the day-to-day work with the SGB and also looked at how gas provision has changed over time. It is interesting to learn of the impact this industry had on the physical environment in Stranraer and about how, for example, emergencies were dealt with.

Right, Agnes, tell me when you started …

I started in the Scottish Gas Board in 1963, straight from college in
Edinburgh. It was ma first job. The manager of the Scottish Gas Board at
that time was Mr Gray. In the office we had Eliza Jeffson. Liza, who's now
90, ... actually she was the meter lady. She was the lady who went out and
emptied all the coin meters. She did this in a six-week cycle. When she
finished the coin meters she then went round and read the credit meters.
She had a boy with her at that time, Brian McLean, who carried the coins
– an these were shillings. Now she did about between 40 an 50 per day so
there was quite a lot o shillings and the first job in the morning was
actually to count all the shillings that Liza and Brian had brought in the
night before.

Was it your job to count the shillings?

Yes. Jimmy Gray usually helped actually, but at the end of the day it was
my responsibility to count the shillings. Jimmy Gray was the manager of
the whole works. He was the overseer of the actual coal-making, and the
office. We had a showroom at that time as well ... mainly in those days we
sold cookers. In fact, we didn't really sell them, we rented them out at
14/6d a quarter. We also rented out gas boilers at 6/6d a quarter. This had
to be billed to the customers every three months so it was quite a busy job,
and not always just every three months. It usually wis spread out over the
three months, so that was quite busy. We also did a good trade in hire-
purchase, an at that time probably a payment would be about 15 or 16
shillings a month.

During the sixties actually gas fires became vogue in Stranraer,
around about 1965–66. People then started to think not coal, but gas, as a
means of heating. So during the sixties into the early seventies, actually gas
fires in Stranraer were a big thing. And we did a roaring trade in all sorts of
fires. One of the first ones was a metal-cased gold fire called the Sunbeam.
Then they kind o came up in the world, and we got a wood-framed fire
called the Flavel Debonair, and we sold them for fun. We couldn't keep
them on the showroom floor, they were just going out so quick. That was
the start of coal maybe startin to go, when folk realised they had another
source o heating.

Where was the showroom?

The showroom was down in Harbour Street, it's no longer there now. It's
actually a grassed area next to what is now the Information Tourist office.
So that's where the actual showroom was, the office and the actual gas
works. The holder station was across the road [at what] is now the library
car park. So that's actually where we worked – everything happened down
there. ...

Did you work in the showroom as well, or was that a separate ... ?

No, we did the showroom and the office. We did everything actually. As I say, there was Mr Gray, Liza and myself. When Liza was not out doing the meters she was in the office helping out. There was a lot o work, a lot o paperwork. [No] calculators. Everything had to be counted manually, and there was lots and lots of counting. Auditors were very much on your back. We had auditors in probably every two or three months, and you were always guilty until they proved you innocent – an that was their attitude.

Did you actually then serve in the showroom ... [and] when people came in for a fire?
Yes. And we did all the paperwork [and] usually [at] that time it was hire purchase. People very rarely bought cash, it was usually always hire purchase. We had to work that out, yes. And then we billed them every three months ... or every month we reminded them for their payments. Actual works itself – there was George McColm, Bobby Hollis, Andy Snodgrass. George Clegg and Lesley Cuke, and they were stokers, and they worked on a shift rota. Taffy Owen, he was the labourer. An then we had staff of Willie Downie, John Rankin and Arthur Cowan, they were gas fitters. They were the ones that went out and fitting the fires, serviced fires, cookers, boilers. They also fitted central heatin. We did central heating as well. We fitted the whole systems an did a lot around the town in the 1960s as well.

Coal, for the works, was a horizontal works, meaning that coal went in one end and came out the other and the by-products you got were coke and tar, which was sold to the public as well. Coal came from the Ayrshire mines. A lot of characters delivered daily. Usually two or three loads o coal came in. That went on probably tae the late sixties, early seventies, when we then turned to liquid natural gas, an a new holder station was built up in Commerce Road. The actual gas works closed down in 1973, when we moved up to Commerce Road. We then did liquid natural gas which was a whole new ball game. Stranraer did not have gas in every street. There wis a lot of streets in the town that didn't have gas, and couldn't get gas, but mainly we were not outside the burgh boundary. We were contained tae in Stranraer, but not everyone got gas. At that time, we were classed as an independent undertaking. And there was Newton Stewart ... Campbeltown, Oban, Stranraer, Girvan. Muirkirk and Millport – all coal-making plants, and classed as independent undertakings.

And what does that mean?
We were solely responsible for the gas-making plant. We were separate from the rest of, the Scottish Gas Board it was at that time. The Scottish Gas Board had, I don't know how many different names over the years. It evolved intae what it is today, British Gas, but we were the Scottish Gas Board. We were Scottish Gas. We've had all sorts of different names, but at that time we were The Scottish Gas Board, independent undertaking. We were solely responsible for wir own plant. We had to work it. We hid

everything to do ourselves. We had a liaison officer who was based in
Kilmarnock, and he went out to each one to make sure everything was
running properly, [and that] there was no problems and whatever.

So, does that mean it was the person in Stranraer who actually ordered the coal?

Yes, Jimmy Gray ordered the coal … . He actually did everything.

So you had a great degree of independence.

We were totally independent [and] that is why we were classed as an
independent undertaking. We were totally independent. We were responsible for wirselves.

Where did the coal actually come from? Could you pick which coalfield it came from?

No. It came from the Ayrshire mines round about Dalmellington,
Waterside – that's basically where all the coal came from.

All the coal for our independent undertaking?

Yes, Herbert Sutherland actually used to come in and do the gas test,
because the calorific value had to be up to a certain standard as well. So,
Mr Sutherland, he was a science teacher at the school, he would come in
and do his checks on the calorific value …

Who determined what the calorific value had to be?

The government would determine that. It had to be a certain calorific
value and don't ask me, Nancy, because I can't remember what it was.

*I know you said you were independent, but you must have had government inspectors,
as well as auditors for the money?*

Yes, because while we were the independent undertakings, the Scottish
Gas Board in the cities were a different ball game again. I don't know how,
actually, they made their gas – or where it came from – but we were
certainly a coal-making plant, and independent in as much as how we ran
the place. But we still had to be controlled and ruled by whatever regulations that were in place in the day.

How often did the government inspector come?

Oh, I don't know how often Mr Sutherland came down but there was a
Mr Little, a Leslie Little. He come down an did his checks, probably once
every two or three months he did his checks. But we always … had to do
our own CV anyway – our own calorific value. We worked that out
ourselves anyway. So we always knew what it was … . Don't ask me how
we did, Nancy, it's a long time ago! But there was a formula for working
out the calorific value of the gas.

And all the people in the office did this?

Mr Gray did that. He had to work out the calorific value.

The men that you mentioned earlier. Tell me about the work that the stokers had to do?

The stokers actually, basically, when the coal came in it came in on one
side of the gas plant …

Which was where?

Which, looking at the plant from the road was on the left-hand side.

Where the Stena place is now?

No … . I'm trying to think, actually … . That would be just to the side, because that used to be the Electricity Board property. So the purifiers were at that side and that's where, actually, [where] the gas had to be purified – it had to be cleaned. So, before it went to the holder … . The process, actually, was the coal came in on one side, right, it went into hoppers and that was discharged into the furnaces, right, which were vertical furnaces. That's where the stokers came in, they stoked the fires. This was all down in Harbour Street. So they stoked the fires, right, and once they burned off … you would get a gas … and by the time all the gases had been taken off, out of the coal, you got it out at the other end as coke. It was a dried coke. And also you get the by-product tar out of it. To purify the gas, now, the gas holder was actually across the street so that was where the gas holder was. But to get to that part it had to be purified, it had to be cleaned.

Did you have pipes underneath the road?

There would be a mains underneath the road to take it to the holder. So we had purifiers to purify the gas. Now that ground is still contaminated, all these years later. That's why it has not been built on at the moment, because it is still classed as contaminated land. Because that's where all the residual dirt [and] whatever, from the gas was at that point.

How long is it likely to be contaminated for?

I don't know. Til somebody does something about it I suppose. But it is still contaminated land as is where the holder station was, that is still classed as contaminated land.

Yes, I can understand that.

So, the purifiers were cleaned out probably once every eight weeks tae mibby three months, 12 weeks. The town would know about it, because it created the most awful stink when they had to clean the purifiers. It was a horrid sweet, sour, smelly – jist a real horrid smell, and it invaded everything. It was the most dirtiest place to work by the way. The coal dust got everywhere in the office. I mean, you could come out at night and your hands, everything was jist black. Even though we worked in the office, we still had this coal dust all over the place. It was a really dirty, dirty place to work.

So, nowadays, I mean, when you think of Health and Safety at Work, I suppose there was nothing …

… No such thing as Health and Safety in 1960, I don't think.

So, the stokers and people like that weren't wearing masks or protective clothing?

No, no. Having said that, they wid pay lip service. There was masks available if they wanted to wear them. It was their choice at that time. They wore steel toe capped boots. I think probably towards the late sixties they were prob-ably issued with work clothes, but I think even when I started in 1963 it was just whatever they wore themselves. And it was black. They were black.

And there were no baths?

There was a shower ... in the place for them.

And was it used?

Not often, not often. But they were all characters, all these guys were real characters, so they were. And they worked on their own at night. They were in the place on their own at night, and the shift pattern I think, if I can remember rightly, was ten o'clock at night tae six in the morning, six in the morning till two in the afternoon and two in the afternoon, till ten at night, and that was the shift pattern. And I think they probably worked five days on, two days off, or whatever.

And how many were on a shift?

Night shift there was only one.

On his own? And what happened if there was an emergency?

Well, it never happened. Not that I know of anyway. We never lost anybody.

No, I don't mean losing anybody, I mean any kind of stopping in the gas?

That was one of the things that you never wanted to happen, was a cessation of gas supply. That would have been a big disaster to have a cessation of gas supply.

And it never happened?

It never happened in my time. We were very, very close [to] it.

How do you mean by that, what happened?

In the winter months you were dependent again on the roads being clear to bring the coal down to us and obviously if there was a shortage of coal, if there was a strike for instance ... . You were very much dependent, actually, on the coal getting here on time. And there were some times, actually, when we wir pretty close to being out. But it never, never happened ... . That was another thing, there was always a stock of coal in the yard. That was for emergencies. That was the standby coal, [and] that was never touched. That was left there until, at some point in the winter you would delve into it, but in most cases we managed ...

And there was never any form of leakage or anything like that?

... There was one or two, in fact, one big one was up in Commerce Road, when it was natural gas. Actually, we really had to draft in men from all over. ... Again, ... the gas that we made was odourless, [and they] had to put a smell in it. So, sometimes, actually, it was overdone and the men had to be nosed. They had to go through and get calibration, I presume you would call it, in their nose – for the smell.

Now, I don't understand that.

Right, well, to put the smell into the gas they had to have their nose calibrated.

What does that mean?

They had to sniff whatever … so that they would know that there was something wrong. On one occasion before I left, that would probably be in the late seventies, early eighties we had one incident where, in the space of about an hour – and I was in the office on my own – I took 150 calls, in the space of an hour. What had happened was they had put – it's a liquid I think they put into the gas for the smell. I don't know what had happened, whether the wind had changed direction as they did it or whatever, but it blew the whole thing over the town and, of course, everybody smelt gas … . The thing at that time was, by this time there was more rules and regulations actually. There was [a code] of practice you had to adhere to. If you got a report of a smell of gas you had to be there within a certain time. Now, at that time we probably had two engineers, and me in the office. And at that time, because the liquid natural gas plant didn't need stokers obviously, so the staff was reduced from what it was in the old days. So, in this particular incidence, actually we had to draft engineers in, from the most parts of Scotland actually, to help us out.

It would be quite difficult if you had 150 calls.

Well, you just couldn't do it. The thing is, because they smelt gas we had to treat it. We knew what was wrong, but the fact is there could have been a genuine one, gas escape, so every one had to be treated. All you could tell them was turn off the meter and do not use it until someone comes from the Gas Board to check it out. So … there was a huge thing after it. It had to be investigated. How did it happen? Why did it happen? What did we learn from it? The usual things.

Now, were you working in the Gas Board during the three-day week?

That was the early seventies? Actually, no, because I got pregnant round about 1973. No I wasn't actually working at that time. I had left just at the start of that kind of era where the three-day week … left in 1973.

Can you tell me, when did the Gas Board shut down? Is there still a gas holder in Commerce Road? …

No, not any more. There is a gas station now out at the Corner House [at Lochans] … . That's where there's a gas station, and that's where it goes to.

And where is it, underground?

Uhuh, it's at Corner House, in the field on the right-hand side. There's a gas station in there.

It must be camouflaged?

It is camouflaged. But this is, actually, remember when they took the gas over to Ireland – so that is why there is no gas now. The gas actually comes from somewhere else in Scotland. It's probably on the National Grid now … . And that would happen after I left in 1996. … It went on to the National Grid, so there is no gas-making plant actually in the town at all now. It's on the National Grid.

*So, all of us that have gas central heating and stuff like that, it comes in a totally
different form now. The kind of work you did is just no longer existing?*

Yes. When the changeover from the coal gas – that we made – to natural
gas, that was another big exercise they had to do in the town. Because
everybody's gas burners on cookers, any gas appliance that you had, all the
burners had to be changed. They all had to be changed because … natural
gas and coal gas they wouldn't have worked on the same burners. It was a
different rating.

Oh, I hadn't realised [that].

Every gas appliance had to be changed. Now that would be round about
1970, 69–70. Early '70, I think that would happen. That was another big
exercise in the town at that time. Because, again, there was a time when we
had to change over from one gas to the other – so it all had to be co-
ordinated.

*Now, I was always led to believe that certainly up until recently, that there was no gas
at the end of the town – I think you would call it the east end of the town, because …
British Rail wouldn't allow the pipes to go over the railway bridge. Is that true?*

I don't know, actually. Probably right enough at that time. I'm trying to
think. They certainly had gas out London Road. A part of London Road
didn't get gas because Westwood Avenue had no gas, and right out
probably to McMasters Road. That part of London Road did not have gas.
But I can't remember what the reason was.

We were just told the railway objected to the pipes …

One of the reasons, another reason, was the capabilities of the coal-making
plant that we had at that time. It was obviously restricted to where we
could supply to, and how much we could supply. So, that was probably
one [of] the reasons why a lot of the town didn't get gas at that time. But
once we went on to natural gas it opened up to a lot more, but again it was
quite restricted. Again, when it was liquid natural gas it came in tankers as
a liquid [and] we had to make it into a gas at the plant in Commerce
Road. It was made into a gas there.

Did the whole office works and everything move up to Commerce Road?

Everything moved up in 1973 … just about the time I was leaving. I think
I had probably left when they moved up. I left from Harbour Street.

*What happened to that place down at Harbour Street, because I know now it is a grass
covered area?*

It lay empty for a long, long time and then the whole thing was jist demolished … along with everything else. Like the slaughterhouse [that] was
behind us … That's where the slaughterhouse was.

Can you tell me anything about that?

No. The noise when they were killing them was quite disturbing … . It
was behind, towards the shore. Where Ulsterbus is today, behind that was

the slaughterhouse … the abattoir.

How did they get the animals [in]? … That must have been pretty gruesome at times?

    … It probably was. Aye, you could hear them.

Did it bother you?

    Well, of course, I was far, far too busy. Then we had the banana store across the road as well. There was W B Anderson – where Tesco's car park is now. That was W B Anderson, the banana store. They had gas actually, because they needed gas to ripen the bananas, apparently.

I was hearing about that the other day.

    They had gas because, as I say, apparently that's what they needed to ripen the bananas. I don't know if that's true, but that's what they say … . And across the road was the old Downshire, and it was Mr and Mrs Murdoch – they were in the Downshire at that time … . It was a busy street, there was a lot going on. McHarrie's garage was there as well, and then we had Cairnryan Knitwear factory further along the road as well. It was a busy wee bit.

6

Shops and Businesses

This selection of interview extracts offers us a fascinating insight into how shopping provision has changed over the decades and the manner of some of those changes.

The first interview extract presented here is from Isabelle Shaw who provides an affectionate and informative recollection of the shops she remembered from her childhood – a time when very few people had cars and most shopping was done locally. Her transcription includes a detailed description of the store run by her aunt and uncle, McHaffie & Son. Isabelle describes the wide range of items sold in the shop, recalling that bills were often paid only every six months, at term times.

Many interviewees could list the shops which they remembered from their childhood. For example, John Barr named nine grocers and seven butchers in the first two sentences of his response to Nancy's enquiry. John also spoke about the businesses which thrived in Stranraer by providing services to the agricultural community. This included the saddlers, tinsmiths, blacksmiths, cobblers and millwrights as well as the makers of jute bags and dairy equipment.

Shops could be as small as a front room in the shopkeeper's home (as recalled by Catherine Monteith), or as substantial as a city store, such as The Glasgow House. This department store features in a number of the Stranraer interviews, including the extracts given here from Margaret Clark, who worked there as a shop girl while she was at school, and Mrs Brownlee, whose husband inherited the store from his father. Mrs Brownlee's account provides a detailed description of the interior of the business as well as information about staffing levels and merchandise.

The interviews also illustrate the changing patterns of staffing over the decades. Shops such as The Glasgow House had porters or delivery staff, while businesses such as Archie Bell's butcher/baker shop at one time supported a staff of 24.

Other businesses discussed in this selection include the putting green at Portpatrick and the different banks and lawyers which operated in Stranraer.

The final extract presented here is from an interview with Olive Murray and her daughter, Debbie. When they were interviewed in 2014 they spoke about the family firm, Moodies, and reflected on how the business had responded to external pressures. This interview raised many of the points discussed in the interview with Ian Jack and demonstrates how small changes can have an impact on a local business. Such is the case with Moodies, where Debbie reflects on the effect of the decline in footfall past the shop, which started when the post office moved into the Tesco supermarket.

Isabelle Shaw

Mrs Shaw provided this affectionate recollection of shops she remembered from her childhood, including McHaffie & Son, the Drummore business run by her aunt and uncle. The family home was above the shop.

McHaffie & Son

This was a very interesting shop and when I was quite small I used to come down [for] my holidays and it was a shop ... absolutely full of everything. Bicycle tyres, wellingtons, sou'westers hanging up, coats, dresses, and if you opened a drawer there was a whole lot of specs in it. If somebody needed a pair of specs they just opened the drawer and put them all on to see what they could get. Anything you wanted, needles and thread and everything, the lot. Of course, it was paraffin lamps, and they were those huge lamps that came down from the ceiling.

... Next door to it ... was Kerrow McGaw and he had the grocer's and it was a lovely shop. They cured their own hams and the smell ... I love the smell of coffee and all these things – the real smell of the grocer's shop. A great big cheese and he would cut a bit off it you wanted it, and patting the butter, and nothing in packets. They sold hardware like pots, pans and dishes and everything. You see people didn't get away to the town the same because a lot of people didn't have cars. It was only maybe the farmer, the odd farmer, that had a car. Well, with my aunt, people only paid their bills twice a year, like at the term time, and they would come down. This uncle of mine went up and brought them down and they paid their bills and maybe, you know, [picked up items, such as] an overcoat – these days for a man, would cost maybe £2 10s or something like that. They had a whole lot of children, and they all got rigged out. Then Aunt Annie – I usually came down and through this great kitchen – she gave everybody tea and we were pouring out the tea and cutting up the scones, and then he took them away up. He also sold lino and they would choose a piece of lino and he would roll it up and it was sticking out the car window and he had as many kids and people in it, and away they would go. He would lay it for them, and Alex wasn't very fussy, he would just roll it down and cut round the side of the fireplace and it didn't fit, but people never complained. Well, they paid off their bill, for the six month, and then they started over again for another six months. Then at Christmas time – there were nine shops in the village – my aunt had a thing like a funny wee clown and he stood in the middle of the window, and his head nodded and all the kids thought this was great. The shop kept open on a Saturday night till nine o'clock, and there were a lot of people who came down and the young people came down, even Lope Scott. He was the message boy with Kerrow McGaw next door, and I used to be behind the counter and he used to come in and I would be chaffing [away] … and all of a sudden Mr McGaw would come in. And, of course, Lope was standing with his back to him and [Mr McGaw] would give out such a row for wasting time. Then he would be away cycling round the country-side, gathering eggs to bring into the shop and these sorts of things.

… the bike had one of these baskets on the front saying James McGaw … . Then they sold petrol, Shell, at the red pump. I think it was 6d or 9d a gallon, something like that, and they had everything in that shop – hardware, sweets, you name it. James McGaw was very obliging. If he didn't have it, he would say, 'I'll have it tomorrow, phone up by tomorrow', and he had a good business …

Gibson's, the baker's, was up the Sanny Brae and you used to run up there in the morning and get a nice roll for a ha'penny, lovely and hot coming out if you started early in the morning. They baked bread and cakes. They used to use the cochineal – their cakes were almost red. Old Tommy Maxwell … he used to be serving in the bakery for a while, and he was one of the bakers as well. I remember one day my aunt sent me across to get bread and whatever, a cake or something, and when I went in Tommy was busy filling the paraffin lamps – they were huge brass lamps that were on a kind of pulley and they filled them away up. So he had this to do and he was filling it up with paraffin, and then he just (slap, slap, wiping his hands), 'Now, what was it you were wanting, lassie?' Then he would give you cakes and bread. And we used to call them Paraffinos, because you could smell the paraffin. You never thought anything about it, you just had to eat it. And then you would maybe run into McGaw's for half a pound of boiled ham for your tea or whatever.

… old Hughie [Maxwell] was the tailor and he sat crossed-legged on a square bit of wood. I was sent up before the post went out any day at four o'clock. Aunt Annie would have to send packages away and I took them up to the post office. I had to walk right past the pavement [and] Hughie sat chewing tobacco and spat it onto the pavement. And if you didn't watch, you got it! All the young fellas would be in there, they would be telling jokes, so that was what was in that house.

George McClymont

Did your mother do most of her shopping in Portpatrick?

Yes, she did all her shopping in Portpatrick. Maybe once a week, or once a month probably, she would go into Stranraer by train to do her shopping – on a Saturday.

So tell me about the shops in Portpatrick?

Well, there were lots of shops in Portpatrick, if I can just run down the main street for you. At the top of the street there was Gibb Brothers, the baker's, that's just opposite the church. And just below Gibb Brothers there was Ewing's the butcher's. These were both Stranraer shops, branches of Stranraer shops, and Ewing's the butcher's later became Mrs Anderson's chip shop. There was a chip shop there then, and next door to that was Irwin, he'd a sort of cafe and confectioner's shop. And he was a Russian, and he changed his name to Irwin after he came from Russia – probably after the First World War. He was a great character. Then we had Bob Douglas the grocer below that. Then we had Dan Campbell's ice cream and sweetie shop, Nicholas the greengrocer's, Davidson's the grocers and then we had Dobson's the chemist. The same Dobson's as was in Stranraer, another branch. We had Cathy Brooke's sweetie shop, we'd Gillespie's the baker's – who is still there today – and below that we had Young's the grocer's again. Then we had Phamie Brownlee's little gifts and picture postcards. You could buy buckets and spades and little nets for fishing in the pools, she was quite a character. Then we had round the Back Street, Mr McConchie's. He made all his own sweets, homemade sweets, it was boilings mostly. And you could smell his clove balls halfway up the village when he was cooking them. There was restaurant next door, I forget the name of it, it was in Back Street, just up past Blair Terrace, there was a restaurant down there too. So that was the sort of shops and there were lots of them.

And you said there was also a chemist and a bank.

There was a bank, it was in Blair Terrace, it was probably the National Bank or something. It was open about twice a week but everybody done their banking there.

And was it in somebody's front room?

McClure's had a big house, it's the house on the shore front that a cannon sits at the front door [of]. And behind that there is two big pillars and [when] you were at these big pillars that was the bank, to the rear of McClure's house.

How often would your mother go to the bank?

I wouldn't think too often. Most of the money would be spent at the shops. There wouldn't be much banked or taken out. There was a post office, there still is, but it was on the opposite side of the road, next to where the Downshire is now. Mrs Bain, I think, was the name of the postmaster, Mrs Bain, that's correct. It was a busy little post office. Two postmen and a telegraph boy. It was quite a thriving little village with all the shops making a fairly good living.

You talked about the Downshire, but the big Downshire that's there today wouldn't be there then. How many pubs were there?

There was two pubs at one time. There was the Downshire and next door was the Cross Keys. The Downshire belonged to the Blacks, and the Cross Keys belonged to Mrs Laird. And it was only made into one pub maybe 15, 16 years ago. There was two pubs there and there was one further down which was the Railway Inn and there was one at the top side was Alex Brice's, the Commercial Inn.

It's still there, isn't it?

Well, the Commercial's now closed, it closed last year. There was four pubs on the main street.

What about the front?

The front was mostly boarding houses. There was numerous boarding houses all the way down the front shore and then you had the Southcliff Hotel and Mount Stewart Hotel, they were at the top. And then Portpatrick Hotel and Fernhill and Roslyn on the High Road and the remainder of the houses, [along] the seafront in particular, were bed and breakfast. The Crown has always been there. There is now two pubs there too, there's the Waterfront now. But there was only The Crown, which belonged to the Alexander brothers, Bob and Frank Alexander.

Margaret Mitchell

In this extract from an interview recorded by Nancy in 2005, Margaret talked about the Portpatrick putting green which had been established by her father after he secured a lifetime lease from the Laird, Captain Orr Ewing. While the business had provided an adequate living for her father, Margaret explained that she had fared much better, due to the growth of Portpatrick as a holiday destination:

... in those days there wasn't the people. If my father came back today and saw the village packed as it is now, because there is now four caravan sites that did not used to [be there] and a lot of bed and breakfasts, and a lot of boarding houses, a lot of hotels that never used to be. There was just the odd boarding house ... one or two along the front and one or two up the street, that was all really.

...

Now, it must have been pretty seasonal?

Oh, yes, oh yes. It was only from, in those days, from June, July and August. But now, or when I opened it after my father died [1958], I opened at Easter and kept open to the end of September, and then once the caravan sites opened up, which made it busier, we kept open to the caravans closed at the end of October.

John Barr

The trades

There was a tremendous lot of small grocers in Stranraer. There was Latta's, Young's, Coulston's, Davidson's, McDowall's, Lipton's, May's, Carruth and Burnett. There were a lot of butchers, there was Archie Bell, Andrew Bell, Andrew Ewing, Allison's, McConnell's, the Co-op, Waldie. The Co-op was very, very busy and they were actually slaughtering up to nearly 20 cattle a week and they were properly hung and cured, not like today. There were two saddlers in Stranraer. There was Walker's down in … Hanover Square and there was another in Hanover Street. They repaired all leather goods, binder canvases, horse harness, etc. McHarrie's and Reid & Adams were the main garages in the town, and sold all agricultural equipment. They also made trailers for horse-drawn equipment. McHarrie's also had a tinsmith, and there was Shaw in Castle Street. And, if you can remember, there was a small passageway beside Mrs Mercer's shop, a very small passage, and you had to go up that with your dairy equipment to get to Shaw's place – up at the back there. And all the stuff had to go up and down this wee passageway, that was including your churns for the dairy and the … milk coolers, etc. McHarrie's, of course, was a very, very busy place and you had Andrew Leith up the stairs, who you ordered all your implements from and they had the shop and the ironmongers at the front thonder. There was also Henderson & Wither across the street [Charlotte Street] and George Smith was up Sun Street.

There was a tremendous lot of blacksmiths in Stranraer at that time. There was McHarrie's, Reid & Adams, Rankin's – down at the seafront, and McKie's up Sun Street. And there was one at the top of Dalrymple Street, and George Henderson had a garage in Hanover Square, who started with the Fergusson tractor just before the War … . And Reid & Adams was the Ford agent. Hugh Craig had floated cattle and also lifted dead stock. I remember once there was a whale came in down at the seafront, and I remember he had to cut it up and it would be taken up to the station and sent away in a railway wagon. Because that was the way all dead stock was shifted in those days, shifted in railway wagons.

They wouldn't be refrigerated?

No, no … . Down in Hanover Square, it was the hub of the community at that time too. There was Farrell's the bag [rag] and bone merchant, down in Hanover Square. There was Davy Jardine, the joiner, and there was bag [rag] and scrap merchant, King Brothers, McMillans. There was Coulter's lemonade factory, and so it was a very, very … busy place, Hanover Square … . When my father went to Auchneel at first a lot of the potatoes would be taken in to the station in barrels, and then tipped into railway wagons. But that was when the jute bag come in. [I can] remember that. Most stuff going to farms, all the feeding and that stuff, it all went in jute bags. And the likes of King Brothers bought the bags from the farmers, and then they would sell them on to the farmers who were needing them for potatoes. They had to be a certain size. They didn't want big deep pulp bags, they wanted a good bag that held a hundredweight of potatoes. [So] King Brothers sold a tremendous lot of bags, and others as well.

…

There was cobblers in Stranraer and they have all disappeared. Millwrights – I remember when I was at the school, you would go up Dalrymple Street – near the top on the right hand-side just opposite the undertakers – that's where the millwright was. He was a Mr Lang, and he was a great boy for repairing binders and sorting mills. Grain merchants, again is another thing that has disappeared from Stranraer. They're still carrying on but it has all been taken on by bigger conglomerates, if that's the right word … . When you think of the amount of people that were employed in these mills in Stranraer, there was a tremendous lot. And the grain was bruised, and it was mixed with concentrates and made into cubes and sent out to the farms. But that has all disappeared. It all comes from far and wide in big ten-ton lorries and blown into the hoppers above the parlours. Tinsmiths are another thing that has disappeared. I've told you about Mr Shaw in Castle Street but, of course, there was tinsmiths at McHarrie's as well who repaired all the milking equipment.

…

There was a tremendous lot of small shops scattered all over the whole of Stranraer. The goods station in Stranraer, it was the hub of the community.

Catherine Monteith

… Can you tell us about the little shops [in Stranraer] you remember?

We lived in Park Lea Gardens and there were so many shops between us and the town. There was Davidson's shop. Now his name was Ingram Davidson, we called him Inny Davidson, and he had a shop – mostly sweeties … . That was at Orchard View, it's not a shop now. Haining's shop is still there – it was a shop built as a shop, and there was Thorburn's – who was, to me, a very old man but I see on his headstone he was only in his seventies when he died. He had a shop in Glebe Street and you went in the lobby – his shop was to the left and his house was to the right… . One thing I remember that we got there … lemonade bottles were very scarce but he had big bottles of lemonade and tumblers, and he gave us a tumbler of lemonade for the money. Instead of getting it in a bottle you got it in a tumbler. You just drank it in his shop. He had a wee bench where you sat down, and he encouraged the children to go in and just talk. It would be a kind of café I suppose. [*laughter*]

What happened if you wanted a bottle of lemonade?

Oh, well, they were very scarce. I can't really remember much about bottles, small bottles. Big bottles, yes, you could buy a big bottle. But then we didn't really have the money for a big bottle, we just had the money for a little bottle. So that was three shops there in a very short distance. There was another shop which had been there – that was another Davidson. He sold vegetables and it was just round the back at his house – it was in Glebe Street, as well, at the corner of Ashwood Drive. But his house was knocked down when they built the prefabs. They built two prefabs there and that was where his house was. Then the next shop on the way to the town was Miss McAlpine. Now Miss McAlpine had a house in Glebe Street and … when sweet rationing came on she opened a shop and she knocked a door in the side of her house and had this shop where she sold, mostly sweets. And she did a roaring trade with the sweet rationing.

That seems odd. You would have thought [she'd] have sold less?

Well, she must just have had an allocation. Because she did have a good shop, and a good stock. The next shop was also in Glebe Street and that was Jimmy Wilson, his nickname was Kong [and] he sold everything. But he was on the corner next to the shop where the Sheuchan Arms is now.

It was still called King Kong's when I was teaching in Park, all these years afterwards. [*laughter*]

That's right. The next shop on the way to the town was Miss Bell in High Street. It also was at her house, and she had a shop there. That was a minute to the town. My granny lived in Fisher Street and at the bottom of King Street there was Nelson's shop. He was a chimney sweep and he finished his chimney sweeping and he went an served in his shop. I don't think he even washed his hands. [*laughter*] He sold sweeties, everything, mostly sweeties that I knew of. Then the next one at my granny's was Queen Street, that was Sonny McDavitt's in Queen Street. And the next one was Miss Berry at the bottom of Princes Street. Sonny McDavitt's was quite a big shop, but again you went in and the shop was to the left and his house was straight on. And if there was nobody in the shop he would just be in his house. Miss Berry's also was just a room in her house. You went in … and the shop was to the right and the room was to the left. So there was all these wee, wee sweetie shops.

With all these sweet shops, what like was the dental provision in the town?

There wasn't much. Well there was Mr Thomson the dentist, who, Mr Wilson eventually took over that practice and Mr Gare was in between … . That was in Church Street, that was Mr Thomson – that was the one we went to. Of course, there was the school dentist who came to the schools. She used to look at our teeth, I remember biting her finger when she had her hand in ma mouth. [*laughter*]

What other kind of shops did your mother deal with?

… For clothes she was a great Glasgow House body. She had worked in The Glasgow House and she bought our things in The Glasgow House. And The Glasgow House … sold clothes, but before Christmas they always had Christmas toys … the whole windows were covered wi Christmas toys. And immediately, the day after Christmas … they sold all the toys that were left half-price. There was a girl at school wi my sister and she always said … 'Santa doesn't bring us anything at Christmas, he's too busy. He brings us ours at New Year'. … There was Caldow's Bargain Stores but my mother wasn't much of a customer to Caldow's. Although it was a good shop, I always got the impression they were a bit cheaper maybe. That's where the [electricity shop] was, they eventually went in there. Caldow's was a very big shop and he had, well so had The Glasgow House, they both had upstairs as well as downstairs, and had a lot of customers. At Christmas they always had a train running round the window, an electric train ran round in their window display. But that was the clothes shops we went to.

My mother went to Loch's and the Co-operative. Loch's was in Queen Street and of course they are still going now, and the Co – ma mother got clothes in the Co-operative, as well and shoes. They had a shoe department, and upstairs they had a good hardware department and furniture department, in the Co-op. And a butcher's department. We went to Ewing the butcher's – my aunt worked in Ewing the butcher's and we got our milk from Ewing's … . That was in South Strand Street. My uncle was the milkman in Ewing's.

And was there no Stranraer Dairies?

It was the Ivy Leaf Dairy at that time. It wasn't Stranraer Dairies, it was the Ivy Leaf. They had the café and the milk – it was Kilhilt Dairies it was called, because it was the McCaigs of Kilhilt who had it. It was called

Kilhilt Dairies and it was the Ivy Leaf Café they had. A lovely café, with the afternoon tea and high tea, and their cake stands with the three tiers on them. And Miss Allison, she was a kind of head buddy in there.

Margaret Clark

The Glasgow House

… I went to The Glasgow House in 1949, still within school … My job there was sweeping down the stairs with sand to … lay the dust, clean the toilets, carrying the big gates from the back to the front. [The Glasgow House] had three glass frontages, and I used to carry these big gates from one end of the floor to the other right through. I was always terrified I would put the gates through the glass cases, the show cases … . Our bosses there were Mr Willie and Mr James Brownhill and that was the way you addressed them. There are still some Glasgow House girls in Stranraer … . It was a marvellous big shop, you went upstairs, and, [I've] only ever seen these shops in Glasgow, the great … gallery and you're looking right down into the middle of the floor where all your light came from. Because they were bright shops and [in] the glass cases would be rayon stockings for ladies, and the silk. I loved to pull out the drawers, and they had little glass fronts on them. All the things that were for sale were displayed in these drawers, and we had to sort them out and tidy them up every so often. And the bales of Sparva in pale pink, pale blue, lemon, the people bought for nightdresses or pyjamas and I loved the huge counter, not that I ever worked at it, where Mr Willie or Mr James would lay out the bales and measure them against the brass rods for the customers who came in. Oh, these were happy days too, I enjoyed that.

Anne Brownhill

The Glasgow House

My husband's business was a drapery business called The Glasgow House situated in George Street, where Curry's is now, next to the George Hotel. Actually, he'd inherited from his father – he was in the business with his father, Mr William Brownhill, his brother (Willie) and himself. I remember, as a little girl coming up from Kirkcowan, and my mother going to The Glasgow House sales. I recollect that goods, at certain times, were half-price. Quite a number of years before the War, the front was re-modelled. There was a display cabinet in the middle, and then you walked in either side and seemingly, from my husband's views, his father had brought workmen from Italy to lay the terrazzo tiling in the entrance hall. And strangely enough the other night, we were out for a meal and Margaret Clark was sitting next me. And Margaret, before she went into the telephone exchange, had been a message girl in The Glasgow House. And she was saying that her job had been to put up the gates at night time, across the frontage. There were three lots of gates and there was a letterbox in there, and that was Margaret's job – to put the gates up. So it's amazing just how things work round. At Christmas time, before Christmas anyway, the pre-Christmas period that was the only time that they stocked toys. And there were open on Boxing Day, and I remember getting a lovely baby doll. All toys were half-price on Boxing Day, to get rid of them. I also recall that my mother used to get material there. The trade name was Sparva – it was like a sort of linen sheeny material. And the plain material was a 1/- the yard, and the pattern stuff was 1/3d. It really was quite a revelation, really, to think of the prices then and the prices now. ...

Downstairs there was the machinery that you pulled to put the money in, and this floated along a rail along to the office at the bottom of the stairs. [There was a] beautiful staircase up to the millinery department upstairs, and there were mirrors all round there and great big deep, deep drawers, for the hats of course. And then, at the other side, there were the – well, where the dresses and coats and things, and then there was a partition, and through at the front that was where the carpets and the linoleums were. And then, through at the back, there was the sewing room. That was where Maggie Rennie made the curtains, or did the alterations. ... because my husband was 15 years older that I was, that is how I remember the shop as a wee girl, when he would be learning his trade in London. He did a year in London and then he did a year in Glasgow. So actually on my marriage certificate it's, James Brownhill, Master Draper. But, as I say, after I was married, when a consignment of hats [used to come in], I used to go in at night-time because my husband was going down to price them all, and I had a great time trying them on. Oh, wonderful hats, but alright if I just looked in the mirror head and shoulders. If I took a full length, went to the long mirrors, I mean with my height some of the hats were just awful on me. [*laughter*]

Tell me about your husband's trading, Mrs Brownhill. You said he was a master draper.

Well, I think he would be probably 21. He went to London for a year. I don't know what warehouse it would be, but I do remember that he said that he'd been taught how to wear a bowler hat properly, and how to roll an umbrella. [*laughter*] And I managed to get the knack of rolling an umbrella from him. Of course, nowadays that doesn't matter with the collapsible ones. And, I don't know, he used to say about the reading of entries to a tune, or something. So what it involved, I don't know. And they lived in dormitories, I don't think the food was all that good. But he was there for a year.

What firm was he with?

I don't [know] what firm it was, but I think he was at home for a year and then he went to Glasgow, after that. And I think it was Frenchis he was with, in Glasgow. So, he didn't mention much about that ... I really don't know what it involved, but certainly his brother – he didn't do any training, because he was more mechanically minded. And I think he worked in a garage for a wee while – but Mr Brownhill senior, of course, wanted him to come to the shop. But my husband always felt that, you know, Willie didn't know as much about the trade as he did, because he hadn't gone through an apprenticeship.

What kind of an apprenticeship was it? I mean, what did they actually learn?

Well, I suppose it would be buying and selling, and what to stock and probably how to serve customers and so on. [We] never really discussed it. To tell you the truth, I never really thought about it.

I mean he was not obviously learning tailoring?

No, no. It was purely merchandise ... and how to measure up. In fact, I've got a yardstick there, and a set square, because he did the measuring for the carpeting and for the linoleum, and so forth and so on. But, apart from that I really I don't know anything more.

Would this be part of the training in London and Glasgow?

That would be part of the training, yes.

And where did the stock come from?

Probably ... it was Glasgow, probably further south as well. And they used to go up to Glasgow, you see. In days gone by there was also what was known here, now I don't know what Wednesday it was in the month, as the whole holiday. And they went up by train and they went round the warehouses then and if there was any bargains to be had, you know, they could buy them up. I always remember ma husband recalling that this offer come up of stockings. Now, it wouldnae be silk stockings, I don't know what they would be, maybe mercerised cotton. I don't know what they would be. But anyway, he had bought this stock of stockings and the father and Willie really were not happy about him buying them, and said they would never sell. So he had made a display in the display cabinet which was in the middle, as I say, of the frontage of the shop – a glass cabinet – and put them in at 1/11d. Never sold a pair. And, of course, his father and brother said, 'Well, I told you so'. So, he put them away, and about a year later he brought them out and made a display – again in the display cabinet – and put them in at 2/11 1/2d, and he sold every pair. [*laughter*]

My goodness.

But towards the front of the shop there were wooden counters, one on either side as you went in, and then two further back. And, as I say, there was this beautiful staircase up, and that counter in under the stair, that was where the Anchor threaded cottons were, and all the embroidery work, and bias binding, and that kind of thing. At the front of the counters, when you went in on the right-hand side, that was the menswear, the underwear and so forth and so on. And at the other side, that was the ladieswear, and then through at the back opposite where the embroidery counter was, that was the yardage, the material. And then, of course, upstairs was the millinery and carpets.

So it sold practically everything?

Everything, practically. But you see in those days people did not go out of town to do their shopping. They bought in the town. And, of course, there was a big clientele of farmers and they only paid their bills quarterly. And I understand that when they came in to pay their bills, then they were taken next door to The George for a dram, once they had paid their bill. [*laughter*]

And how many people were employed?

Well there would be two, four, six – there'd be about ten probably, altogether, plus a message boy and a message girl. There would be about ten altogether.

And what would a message boy be delivering from a drapers?

Well, maybe a parcel, maybe, that somebody couldn't carry [if] it was too big. You see the folks didn't have cars in those days and so the message boy with his basket, or whatever he had on the front of his bike, would deliver. It could be even maybe that a lady was getting a hat delivered, because they would be put in a box in those days. And [this] was a well-known family, very stylish, very stylish, used to come in on a Saturday night. I'm saying 'used to', not frequently, but now and again. ... [and], try on hats. [They wouldn't be able to chose and so they'd ask] 'Do you think I could take them home to put it against my outfit to see'. 'Oh yes, certainly.' They would maybe take two hats, and bring them back in on a Monday morning, 'Oh, I am sorry. No, it just didn't do with the colour at all'. Having worn one to the church on the Sunday! ... [*laughter*]

Towards the end of the interview, Mrs Brownhill spoke about the closure of The Glasgow House following the death of her husband.

And that was the end of the business?

That was the end of the business. And Fidlers were very interested in buying over at the time, but it wasn't sold as a going concern. ... and everything, old stock and everything [was] brought out in the window ...

old-fashioned combinations and one thing and another which had been in boxes, I think, from the year one. And the stock was sold, and then it was the property was sold after that …

So what happened to the lovely display cabinets and everything?

Oh, that was all knocked down, and the terrazzo tiling was all torn up. I think some of the joiners came and got some of the wood out of it, because it really was a gorgeous staircase, beautiful staircase.

Archie Bell

Butcher shops

My father came to Stranraer in 1933, set up as a butcher shop in Castle Street which is now visible as the left-hand bay in what used to be Alf Walker the chemist's shop. The shop had been a butcher's, but had closed. Father and mother married on the 28th February 1934 in Glasgow and they stayed in an upstairs flat in Princes Street, in the building which had been the old post office. I was born on the 4th October 1935. Alf Walker enlarged his shop about 1937, and my father was put out. Matt Templeton, the optician, was also put out of a shop at the same time. Together they persuaded H P McLaughlin, the joiner and undertaker, to convert two old cottages next to his existing shop. The cottages were number 15 and number 17 Hanover Street and they converted them into matching shops for them.

… Demobbed from the Army, I started with my father in the butcher's shop in December 1956. Our end of Hanover Street was very different in those days, it was almost a shopping centre in its own right. On the other side of the street there was the grocers, McCreadie's, I think which became the Co-op grocers. Then Hugh Wallace the barber; Jack Cowden the electrician; V F Dicks who sold fireplaces and Mrs Sherriff who had a sweetie shop. On our side of the street there was Nestie's Cafe; Jimmy Torbet the florist and nurseryman; Kilhilt Dairy; the fruit and veg shop which became Tilley & McIntyre's newspaper shop; Tommy Fulton the painter; Matt Templeton the optician; father's butcher's shop; H P McLaughlin joiner and undertaker, and then a double-fronted shop, now gone, Hugh McDowall the grocer.

I started baking sausage rolls in a domestic gas oven in the back shop but had to stop after a little while. I was making so many it was interfering with the work of the butcher's business. About this time our neighbours, John McNeill, who had taken over H P McLoughlin's undertakers business, moved round the corner to Mansewood and after a great deal of worry and thought we bought [that] shop in the late 1950s. We started making sausage rolls again and bridies and then scotch pies, pork pies. The shells for the scotch pies were made at first with one hand machine and then two hand machines, then a large automatic pie machine, which turned out about 600 an hour. These products were widely wholesaled in the local area. There was also an automatic apple tart moulding machine and various other bakery machines. Shortly after starting, I started making sponges to my mother's recipe. They were a great success, I couldn't cope the very first Christmas and, in fact, had to lock the baker's front shop door at one point as we just could not cope with the queue. The wall between the butcher's and baker's front shop was then removed. Many more lines were introduced, mostly from domestic recipes. Pancakes, crumpets, scones of various types, tattie scones were very popular. It was an all night job on a Friday, making them, if you were single-handed – gingerbread, fruit loaves, everything right up to three-tier wedding cakes. The only thing we didn't touch was bread, except for a very few fruit loaves. Latterly there were over 80 items being produced between both butcher's and baker's shops, most of them fresh daily. Keeping a check on the costings for this number of products was impossible with paper and pencil, so I went to a computer class and produced DOS programmes to do the costings. This was just before Windows spreadsheets became generally available, and setting up these programmes was a lot of work on its own.

Prior to World War II, the butcher's business had bought cattle from Alex Barr of Auchneel. He bought cattle from David Little of Mahaar after derationing, then from Craig's Market in Ayr after the local slaughterhouse closed. We bought Templeton's shop next door and turned it into a large cold room. Beef arrived by lorry from Ayr, we put up a roller conveyor to the door and the carcasses were hung up on rails and hung for a week to ten days. Stranraer slaughterhouse had produced excellent carcasses but was shut due to modern regulations. The split new slaughterhouse in Dumfries which was right up to regulations did not produce as good quality carcasses. In fact, the first batch of sheep I got from them did not keep and we bought no more there.

The butcher's business won the first Gold Award for Excellence of Product awarded by the Scottish Federation of Meat Traders. This was for our meatloaf. We also won four bronze medals at the same show. In another bakery competition we were awarded second prize for Scotland in scotch pies. Our secret in scotch pies was that we had total control of the meat content and used our own mix of butcher's seasonings rather than the commercially available bakery scotch pie seasoning, which is just a white pepper and salt mix.

For many years we sold poultry at Christmas, there was little demand at other times. At first we plucked by hand then we bought wholesale from

Tommy Jesson the butcher in Castle Street who had plucking machinery. We stopped plucking our own as feathers and bakery do not mix! In later years we sold poultry every week and bought directly from a poultry processor in Dumfriesshire. We were then selling more poultry any week than we had previously done at Christmas, which shows how shopping patterns had changed. After some years we also rented a shop at the corner of George Street and Church Street, which is now part of the museum. This has historically also been a butcher's shop. When we renovated the shop it had both a butcher's and a baker's counter, and at this point we had 24 employees.

Andrew Hannay

National Bank

I had to sit an examination before I got in [to the National Bank in Stranraer] and one of the subjects, I was told and I had to read it up because I knew nothing about it, was Scottish history. I would hate to see my examination papers today, but I was accepted as an apprentice at the salary of £40 a year, and started away. There was intensive competition, there were six banks in Stranraer. At that time there were eight Scottish banks. We didn't have the Bank of Scotland or the North of Scotland, but the other six were all part of the eight, and competition was pretty fierce. As apprentices we had to lift our hats to all the ladies, take on any job we were asked to do, tennis, golf, cricket, you name it. No honorarium or anything, but we enjoyed it.

John Carruth

Lawyers offices

There were, of course, several lawyers in the town [Stranraer]. Starting with Hunter & Murray, who had their offices in at the back of the Union Bank in Church Street. The Union Bank, of course, eventually amalgamated with the Bank of Scotland. The bank agent then was Mr Thomas Hunter, who was also a solicitor. In George Street, where the Bank of Scotland now is, was the British Linen Bank. It was a bank agent in those days, not a bank manager, and the bank agent at the British Linen was Mr McCamon who was a local man, the family being farmers. But Mr William McCamon, he became the agent for the British Linen Bank. And he was always dressed in morning coat, and when he went down town he had on a tile hat. The next bank that I can remember was the National

Bank in North Strand Street which, after it closed, became the offices [of] A F & C D Smith the solicitors. The bank agent there was Mr Jenkins. Then there was the Commercial Bank in Bridge Street which is now the Royal Bank. The agent there was Mr Paton who was succeeded by his son, Mr Ben Paton. And then there was the Clydesdale Bank. It wasn't an agency, it was a manager. And the bank manager was Sandy (can't remember his second name). As far as I remember that was all the banks. There was, of course, no TSB then.

The lawyers that I remember in Church Street was Mr John D Kerr, in an office which is now, I think, a council office. And across the road, of course, was Hunter & Murray in the Union Bank buildings. ... In North Strand Street was Percy Adair who lived in North West Castle before it, of course, was greatly extended into North West Castle Hotel. There was also the Royal Bank on the corner of Bridge Street and South Strand Street which is now ... Thomas Cook, the travel agent.

Olive Murray and daughter, Debbie

Moodies
In October 2014, Mrs Murray and her daughter, Debbie, were interviewed about the family business, Moodies, which Olive's parents had taken on shortly after they married in 1939. At that time, the business was run by Miss Moodie and the couple lived with her, while Mr Murray looked after the printing side of the business. The family lived above the shop, at 56 Hanover Street, until 1961, when they moved out and the shop was extended. The printing side of the business was stopped and they moved into wholesale, and the family later added an area for art supplies, while still continuing to sell all the usual stationery items and greeting cards.

Why did the family move from Hanover Street?
> It wasn't an awful convenient house really. Until Miss Moodie died we were living, the four of us, in one bedroom. Certainly, we got a bedroom back after she died but it wasn't a convenient house. The kitchen was downstairs then you went up quite a big stairs, and then there were two rooms there and then up to the attic [and] bedrooms again. So my mam and dad bought a bungalow in Brookfield Crescent and they moved there. It was much easier for my mother.
> ...

When you say your father went out for orders, what exactly do you mean?
> He went out to the small county shops right down to the other end of the county. It was nearly all stationery of one kind or another, paper, toilet

rolls, pencils and all that sort of stuff. He went round the little shops and then he would deliver the order to the people. It was a different way of them getting different stock that they wouldn't have got otherwise.

...

Why did your father stop supplying these things?

Probably when we moved out of the house of just before it. We moved out in 1961 so it was probably round about 1960s that we stopped doing the wholesale. I think it was getting that we were not making enough from it really, because all the big boys started to come in and we got left behind.

Daughter Debbie joined the firm from school, initially working with her sister in a smaller branch shop in Queen Street. When that shop was closed in 1989, Debbie moved up into Hanover Street which she remembers as a very, very busy shop at that time. As well as Debbie, there were three other full-time workers, her father, and also her grandmother, who helped out in the shop, '... but sadly within the last 20 years the business has gone down dramatically' as the family coped with the impact of the supermarkets and internet.

... The very first thing that hurt Hanover Street was when the Crown post office moved into Tesco's which ... could have been maybe 12, 13 years ago. That was the start of the footfall dropping in Hanover Street and within the last ten years, year on year the business has got worse because of not so many people in Hanover Street.

Alan Smith

A F & C D Smith

In this transcription of an interview Nancy McLucas recorded with lawyer, Alan Smith, in 2007, Alan firstly gave a detailed history of the family firm which was established in 1929 (not presented here) when his father went into partnership with his own father to form A F & C D Smith. The transcription extract given here is from later in the interview, when Alan reflects on the changes he has seen during his time in practice.

I think it is fair to say that there have been very major changes in legal practice since I came to Stranraer in 1968. The law is always changing and whilst we used to be considered in the same vein as general practitioners, we are yes, general practitioners, but we are not masters or experts of all aspects of the law. And more often than not nowadays, when we need to specialise we have seek help from the big firms in Edinburgh or Glasgow. I am also very aware of how, with modern living and modern equipment, the pace of life has increased even in the legal profession. Again, when I came back to Stranraer it was always a pleasure to do business for a client but also to be able to take time and after having done business chat with the client, discuss how families were getting on and taking an interest generally in them. Over the years this has been squeezed out as the modern pace of life and the need to have things done quickly gives little or no time for that more leisurely approach to the law. However, personally now that I am a consultant, I find that I am getting back to that time where I can give more to the elderly clients and indeed find myself doing house visits on a very regular basis, something that I just simply did not have time to do at the busiest part of my legal life. In earlier years, when I returned to Stranraer I became, probably what was known as, the Court partner and I found myself spending a lot of time in the local Sheriff Court. There have been a number of cause celebres but one that sticks in my mind happened in the early 1970s. At that time we represented farmers who were very well-known breeders of black-faced sheep and at the annual tup sales they sold a young ram lamb for a world record price. It was bought by another breeder. That breeder then alleged at the beginning of the next season that the ram lamb had failed to leave any crop of lambs whatsoever and that he was returning it to his clients. I advised my clients that they should not under any circumstances take back the ram lamb but that, for purposes of acknowledgement, the farmer could come to my office with the lamb. I would acknowledge that he had tried to redeliver it to my clients, and he could then take it back. This took place, [and] three years later, after a long court action in Stranraer Sheriff Court, my clients were completely vindicated. It was heard that the ram lamb had indeed worked as it should have worked and, of course, the honour and integrity of my clients was preserved. A matter of great importance to them, particularly in the sheep breeding world.

Did they actually bring the sheep to your premises?

They did, certainly the sheep was parked outside North Strand Street in a trailer, but I went down and acknowledged that they had tried to send it back and that they should now take it back to their own farm until the matter was resolved through the courts by due process of law.

There have been other cases, both civil and criminal, which have drawn me close to clients, although one has to try and stand apart and be objective at all times. It is however very difficult, particularly in a country area where you know your clients and you meet them outwith business. Their case and their problems can become your case and your problems, and it is very difficult to separate oneself from that. I have, for some considerable time now, not been involved in court work except for the fact that I am now an Honorary Sheriff and occasionally sit in judgement on those who have been taken into custody and held overnight in the local police station. In days gone by the bulk of that work consisted in meting out punishment to people who had committed a breach of the peace but significantly that area of work has changed. I often find that I am dealing with illegal immigrants who have tried to come through the Port of Stranraer, have been stopped because they had no documentation, and indeed have no right to be in the United Kingdom. This more often than not means that the next day when they appear in court there will be an interpreter. The interpreter has to be sworn in and then the case is conducted through the interpreter and the outcome on every occasion is usually that the immigration authorities are waiting for the person who has been held in custody, they are removed to a detention centre and ultimately returned to their own land. Then, in more recent times, the type of offences that are dealt with in Stranraer Sheriff Court have involved those involved in drug trafficking, supplying of drugs. We are at a corner of a triangle from England, from Glasgow and the Central belt and from Northern Ireland, and the seizes that have been done either at the Port in Stranraer or at Cairnryan had been of considerable significance. And yet, the sad thing is that as soon as you close up one line of traffic someone else will come on the scene. And I do believe, sadly, that the courts will continue to have a considerable problem with drug traffickers, particularly in the Stranraer area.

One of the benefits of being a consultant and having more time to myself has allowed me to concentrate on a role I have undertaken for some time now as safeguarder of children who appear before the Children's Hearing system. Initially, when the Children's Hearing system was set up, most children who appeared before it were children who had committed offences and because of their age could not be referred to the Sheriff Court. But more recently, the children that are referred to the hearing system are children who are being abused within their own homes. Abuse can take the form of physical abuse, sexual abuse or emotional abuse, and what happens is that a child is referred to the reporter and the reporter decides to bring that child before the hearing. And the hearing may then decide that they want someone independent to look at the best interests of that child, or children, and report back to them. I think this is very important, because more often than not the families who are involved with the hearing system are what, sadly, one would have to describe as problem families. They, therefore, have been involved with the Social Work Department over a long period of time and it is more than likely that relationships between the family and social workers are at their very worst – and there are probably jaundiced views being expressed on both sides. And therefore, the appointment of a safeguarder allows someone who [has] no connection with the family whatsoever to come in, listen to what everyone is saying and then hopefully go before the hearing system and say 'This is what I have found [and] this is what I believe is in the best interests of the child'. And the recommendation may be that that child should remain with the parents, or that child should be removed from the parents care, perhaps for a short time. Or sadly, on some occasions, that that child should not return under any circumstances to the care of their parents and should be placed for permanency, which could be permanent foster care or adoption by another family.

I have enjoyed my time as a lawyer in Stranraer. I think I always wanted to come back to Stranraer. I have indicated that there have been major changes and one of these changes is that banks and building societies have taken over a lot of the conveyancing work. They have also taken over a lot of the executory administration dealing with the estates of dead persons. And, therefore, inroads are being made into what one might describe as the basic work of a country solicitor: and it therefore brings me to wonder what the future may be for the profession in country areas. Personally, I am glad that I am approaching retirement. I would not like to be a lawyer in Stranraer, I think, in the next 20 years. Machines and computers and other things are taking over what was done by a human being, and I am not sure sometimes that it's for the best. I would like to think that there will still be two or three or four firms in Stranraer where people will be able to come along on a daily basis and consult with their solicitors, but I feel that the squeeze is being put on now. And that one might be left with, perhaps two big firms, or even the small firms in Stranraer being taken over by bigger firms outwith the area. It's all very much in the melting pot. The profession, to my mind, is not what it used to be, and I am glad that my time in it is almost at an end.

Betty Findlay

Findlay's

In 2008 Nancy McLucas interviewed Betty Findlay about the history of the family firm, Findlay's drapers in Stranraer. The period covered by this interview is 1896–1981 and includes a great deal of information about how the stock held in the store changed over time, as well as considering issues relating to staffing such as changing staff roles and the introduction of staff holidays.

… Would you tell me how the business started please?

The business started with John Findlay from Port William. He was born in 1871 and served his time in a draper's shop in Port William called, I

24. Findlays the Draper, Hanover Street, Stranraer, late 1920s.
Left to right: Alex Stevenson, John Findlay (proprietor), Mary Nelson,
Mr Balfour and an unidentified young man.

25. Cycling Club, 1912. Mr. Caldow (centre)

26. Bathing at the Creamery diving board, Stranraer 1937. HMS *Spey* can be seen on the right and flying boats on the left.

27. The Miltonians, 1947. Murrayfield Concert Party

28. Simpson Memorial Tower, Stranraer Harbour.

29. Pupils at Stoneykirk School, 1920.
Helen Davies started at Stoneykirk in 1917.

30. LPP&W Railway bus at Stranraer Town station, c.1904–05.
The PP&W was known locally as the 'Poorly Paid and Worried'.

31. Last Coach to the Port, 1910–11. Thought to be the service taking passengers down to the port at Portpatrick. Downshire Arms Hotel in the background

32. John Bell's lorry. John Bell transported farm produce pre-WWI.

33. McCormack's gang unloading a coaster at Stranraer, *c.*1930.

34. Clanachan's Farm Services, *c.*1920. Clanachan's Farm Serices provided engines, wagons and people to help with farm work at busy times. Enfield House, Lochans can be seen on the left.

31

32

33

34

35. St Andrew Street, Harper's Seed Harvest. Private contractors collected and transported farm produce to trains for sending further afield.

36. McCormack's coal delivery at Wig Bay, *c.*1910–11.

37. Stranraer pals, France, Christmas 1915. Mr McCormack is seated front right with Sonny McDavitt just behind.

38. Unveiling the Stranraer War Memorial, 1922. Among those in attendance were the Minister of Sheuchan church, the Provost and Lord Stair.

39. Haunted House, Fisher Street, 1939–40. One of the buildings used by the RAF to house personnel. They painted the sign above the door which depicts a cartoon character, Goofy the Ghost. Bits of aircraft, probably used as bins, are evident on the left of the door.

40. RAF personnel at Stranraer Harbour station during the Second World War.

41. Remains of Braidfell factory. High up in the hills above Stranraer, the RAF used the Braidfell factory buildings for target practice.

42. The war on Kirkcolm Road. A not uncommon sight during the Second World War, here a Sutherland aircraft is being moved by road.

43. A Short Sunderland flying boat patrol bomber landing at Wig Bay Seaplane Base on Loch Ryan, *c.*1937. Flying boats were brought to Wig Bay in great numbers at one time.

think, Kinnear's. Later, he moved to Stranraer to a firm called William Brown, Draper, Hosier and Hatter, at 72–74 George Street, Stranraer. When he left William Brown's shop he moved to 14 Hanover Street and started up his business there [on] 21st November 1896. It seems that the family lived above the shop at that time, from early records and birth certificates from that time.

And why did he go into business for himself?

Well, it's interesting that he choose to go in for drapery and outfitting, because most of the family had been boat builders and joiners, cabinet-makers. There were fleshers further back in the family, and I always wondered why it was that he went in for drapery. However, I find that his mother was a milliner so no doubt she had an interest in clothes. And then, there was somebody, I think a cousin, also had a drapery shop in Port William so it wasn't a completely new idea for him to go off and start up a business on his own in Stranraer.

Why did he choose Stranraer?

I think that one of the reasons he went to Stranraer was that it wouldn't have been fair for him to set up in Port William, where Kinnear's still existed and where he had trained. Also, there was this cousin had this shop there so I think it was a case of going off to pastures new. I think, also, that his mother was rather ambitious for him. The story goes, in family legend that his mother used to walk to Stranraer with clean linen and baking every week. Now, I expect she got many lifts in carts and so on, but the fact that that story existed seems to suggest that part of the thing was her ambition.

When he did start, obviously, he was unmarried and living above the shop, was it easy to get premises do you know?

I don't know that … . But he was married just shortly after he started up in business, and the first baby was born at 14 Hanover Street.

So his mother would be bringing him clean clothes and food when he was still working with the other draper?

That's what I assume, yes.

How did the business go on from then?

Well, it seems that they moved to … 44 Hanover Street … and certainly that had happened … somewhere about the turn of the century. They seemed to have moved along to number 44 Hanover Street. And that was really where the shop existed. The matter of what the business was called is quite interesting. It hasn't always been Findlay's. At one time it was John Findlay Outfitters, and there are other names, on labels and coat hangers and the like, which say Findlay's Drapery Warehouse. So it had different names at its start. Also it wasn't all outfitting to begin with. They used to sell household linen and rugs and linoleum. In fact, one of the ex-employees had said to me recently how he remembers the rolls of linoleum standing up in the street, outside the shop. [There] was household linen, carpets, rugs, bed linen, every kind of sheet and pillowcase you can think of. Haberdashery – endless buttons and reels and so on, some of which were still in the shop when the business finally closed, and some of which are still in my possession.

Was it a successful business from the start?

Yes, I would say it was. I think there was a great need for a shop in a fairly isolated place like Stranraer, because people couldn't get to Ayr or Glasgow for shopping. And Mr Findlay used to go to Glasgow to buy stuff at the warehouses and bring them back down to Stranraer. Stuff used to arrive by rail too, because I have heard that the apprentices used to go with barrows to the station to bring things up to the shop.

When you say apprentices, what were they apprenticed to? Was it the drapery trade?

Yes. I suppose it would be.

What kind of apprenticeship was that?

Well, they weren't all trained in tailoring. Some of them were laying linoleum and learning, generally, about shopkeeping.

So Mr Findlay was a tailor?

No. He didn't make clothes himself, but he would measure people for suits and send the measurements off to manufacturing firms … . He was a business man, he was buying and selling really.

He was also locally quite involved?

Oh, yes, very much so. There are photographs of him standing with the tennis club, with the bowling club … with the town band. Which seems to me to suggest that possibly he was involved in the setting up of these organisations. [He was on the Town Council.] He was what they call a burgess, and he seemed to have been a burgess for a good number of years. He was elected to the Town Council on the 5th November 1924. By this time he was living at 42 Hanover Street, in the flat above the shop. And he retired [from the Town Council] on the 12th June 1946 … although it was about the same time that he retired from the business.

Was he ever Provost or Dean of Guild?

No, not that I know of. But he was very active in the Scottish Retail Drapers' Association and in all sorts of things that were going on in the town, as was his wife. She was a second wife, she was Jessie McCash, and they were married in 1905. By that time they were living at 14 Hanover Street and then John Findlay bought land in Royal Avenue and built the two houses now known as Arranview. And they moved there somewhere about 1906. I'm not quite sure exactly, but about then. And they had three children. And the interesting thing was that when the flat above the shop became vacant, the flat was called 42 Hanover Street … John Findlay wanted to move round to Hanover Street to live in the flat above the shop, which the family all thought was a strange move. But John Findlay was keen to be near the business, and to be able to stand in the street and see who was going up and down, according to what I hear.

That would help with his Town Council work?

Yes, I suppose so, because he was well known.

So, was your husband, John Findlay's son, was he always destined to go into the business?

Well, no, not really. But he had an elder brother, John, who died when he was about a year old, and John was to have been the outfitter. However, he died when he was a child and thereafter Kenny Findlay was named as the person to be the shopkeeper. It wasn't, I think, what he wanted, but that was how things were to be.

He would have his War service?

Yes, that's correct. He was away during the War and during that time it was Alex Stevenson who ran the shop. Alex Stevenson had been excused military service on health grounds, and while Kenny Findlay was away in the forces Alex Stevenson ran the shop.

How many people did John Findlay employ?

I'm not sure how many he would have at one time, not more than about six or so. The names of the people that were employed in the shop are all on record. There was a John McCloy was one of the first early employees and then there was Sam Campbell and Alex Stevenson, whom I have already mentioned. There was a Billy McCovan, who was killed in a road accident on the A75. A Charlie Stewart, John Agnew, Robbie Rice, Ralph McLaughlin, Graham Anderson and Hugh McCloy. Now, that is all I can remember in the way of menfolk. As far as the women are concerned there was a Mary McCloy, a Mary McKnight. Betty Davidson, a Betty Keeler, a Marie Wallace, Heather Croucher, somebody called Yvonne, an Irene Adams, Betty Murray, Grace Irvine, Dorothy Murphy … . There were a lot of people involved in the shop, but how many at any one time I am not quite clear.

He obviously employed people from the same family, like McCloy.

Yes, I think John McCloy and Hugh McCloy would be related. The McCloy family had a shop of their own in Stranraer at one stage. … the same thing, outfitting … I think it was further along Hanover Street, but I'm not quite clear.

I know from Mrs Brownhill that at one point there were 12 drapers in Stranraer, so it must have been well drapered?

Yes, well to get back to what I was saying earlier, it was to do with the fact that it was difficult for people to get to Ayr or Glasgow to do their shopping, so there was a ready market for stuff in Stranraer.

Now, I know you wouldn't remember the war years, obviously, but you must have heard anecdotes about what it was like during the War with coupons and stuff like that.

Oh, yes, indeed. The stock was run right down because it just wasn't possible to get goods to sell. But the other side of it was that anything you could get hold of, sold. You didn't need fancy advertising to get things to sell.

And they did advertise regularly?

They didn't have to. There were adverts in the *Free Press*. If you look back the old *Free Press*'s, but there wasn't much need for advertising during the War.

What did they do about coupons and things?

… There were coupons found in the shop when I was clearing it … . They must have dealt with coupons.

Did that not cause a lot of extra work?

Well, I suppose it did but I don't really know. I wasn't around at that time, but it would … yes. But talking about rules and regulations and so on, one of the things that I found quite interesting was there was a notice up in the shop dated January 1935 which was to do with the hours that the apprentices were allowed to work. And it names four young people, Mary or Molly Lamb, Sam Campbell, Kinnoch Findlay or Kenny Findlay and Robin Gibb. And they used to start work early in the morning, about half past eight, and had a little break for lunch and they worked on till about half past five at night. They got a half day on a Wednesday, but on Saturday nights they worked till eight forty-five at night. Very, very long hours. And they started work in the shop at fourteen. It's very different to what life is like nowadays for 14 year olds. There can't have been time for much juvenile delinquency!

Have you any idea how much they were paid?

No, I haven't … I've got nothing about wages.

They must have had insurance stamps and things like that?

Oh, yes, they would.

Looking on to the time that you remember, can you tell us about the business then, once you became involved?

Well, by the time I came back to Stranraer, Kenny Findlay was in charge of the shop and Alex Stevenson had moved off and started up on his own. Immediately after the War, the stock was run down considerably and, of course, had to be all built up again. Kenny's parents had died. John Findlay had died just immediately after the War, and so it really was like starting from scratch. And Kenny had been away in the forces, in the Royal Marines, for four or five years and so hadn't any recent experience really in outfitting. But he built up the stock. I suppose he would get a gratuity from the forces which would help him to start up on his own. He could have gone on and done other things, he was interested in electronics. But his father and mother were both poorly by this time and he felt that he ought to come back and get into the business. It was expected of him anyway. And his father handed the business over to him on the 26th March 1946 … just after he was demobbed.

His father would be able to put him in the way of suppliers and stuff like that?

Oh, yes. And, of course, there were customers in the town who knew the shop and kept in touch.

And was there any specific changes that Kenny made?

Yes, the main thing that he did was to cut down the number of lines that his father had stocked. … There were less household goods, less drapery and it was more outfitting, ladies and gents outfitting really. Because, by this time, people were looking for choice in the shops. So you couldn't just stock a little of everything and hope that the goods would walk out of the shop. You had to cut it down and give people choice in what you were stocking. He also began doing more camping goods, and scout and guide uniforms.

Of course, he was very involved in scouting. Was he the only Scout and Guide provider in the town?

I think so … . In fact there is a Thanks badge somewhere or other for having stocked all the stuff for the Scouts … . The Scout Movement issue a Thanks badge to people who have provided a service for the movement.

Is it something that can be put up in the shop?

No, no, it is just a little badge, which will go to his grandson.

What memories do you have of the shop?

When I first came to Stranraer the first thing I noticed was that there was a shop that was stocking Kayser Bondor,[4] which was much to my pleasement, as they say in this area. Something else that I remember very vividly are the red chairs that were in the front shop. People used to come in, perhaps to buy things and look at what was in the shop, but also just for a chat. And it was a great feature of the shop, I think, that the staff didn't force their sales on people. And so, it was a very friendly kind of social centre. And I used to say that there was more social work done in Findlay's shop than I ever did in the Social Work Department.

Every business has its financial troubles. I'm meaning in particular bad debts or perhaps dishonest employees. I take it Findlay's wasn't immune from this?

Well, of course, there are always people who don't pay their bills. And in Stranraer, of course, I think we suffered from what we used to call the 'milk cheque' business [whereby] … sometimes the farmers didn't pay till the milk cheque came in. Which didn't help us because we had to buy the goods to sell in the shop, and they had to be paid for … . Mainly they settled, though when the shop closed there were some outstanding accounts which were never paid.

Did you ever have any trouble with employees? Were there any, like there are nowadays, trade union health and safety regulations?

Yes, there were. I remember having to put in ventilators, and then the VAT returns which had to be done [and] which every shop had to cope with. I, in fact, used to do the VAT returns myself … . The shop was supposed to be at a certain temperature. I don't think it was, but there wasn't much in the way of inspection as far as I can remember.

What about time off for the employees?

Oh, yes, the employees had to get their annual holidays, which, of course, was very difficult for us because they mainly wanted their holidays in the summer and, of course, so did we.

Again, the hours would be better than the hours for the apprentices?

Oh, yes. We've gone on past that a number of years … . By the time I knew the shop, people were working reasonable sort of hours. It would be nine to five, more or less, and half day on Wednesday as far as I remember.

… This is about the time when the new shop front was put in. There had been money inherited from New Zealand and this was used to put in a new shop front and Alex Donnan from Port William who was a Findlay cousin, came up and fitted the new shop window. We had a rather funny incident one day when Kenny Findlay's elder son, Christopher, was lost, not to be found anywhere. And then was discovered in the front window, dressed in his pyjamas shaping lumps of putty, with the passers-by all laughing at him.

What was the shop front like before the new shop front [which is now McAndrew's]?

Yes, it's now McAndrew's. Well, it was just much plainer. There wasn't as much wood to it, it didn't look nearly so solid. It was, in fact, beginning to rot and really had to be replaced.

But it was a plate glass window?

Oh, yes. Yes.

Can you remember anything else that happened during your sojourn with the business when you were in Hanover Street?

Well, I used to go into the shop at Christmas sometimes to help out if they were very busy. But generally speaking I didn't work in the shop. One of the things that always amused me was that if you were serving the ladies in particular they always had to tell you that they had great difficulty getting things to fit because they had round shoulders or a narrow waist or a long neck … there was always something that made it difficult. But we usually managed to get them fitted.

When you say you helped out at Christmas, what kind of things, it wasn't just clothes, did you sell … ?

Oh, well, we sold handkerchiefs and scarves [and socks] but gone were the days when we had lots of haberdashery or linoleum or carpets, rugs, doormats, that was all away.

Tell me about the rundown of the business.

Well, the business ran really on full tilt until Kenny Findlay died and that was the 18th June 1980. I kept it going, but really it was Margaret McCloy who was in charge, who did most of the work. And we kept it going because the stock was already ordered for Christmas 1980. And we ran the business till we had the Christmas and then, in February 1981, we closed the door. [… and we had a sale before we closed.] We advertised that everything was to go at halfprice. We got advice from the Retail Drapers' Association and they said that that was the best thing to do. One of the things I remember about closing down the shop was that we had the pavement lined with all sorts of things that we were chucking out, and a lady came past and she sort of shook her head and sighed and said, 'Oh, it's been a long Findlay's, hasn't it?'

… When you say you had things out on the pavement, was that allowed?

It must have been. But we never had things on the pavement in my day. There's a photograph of Findlay's further back. I suppose not long after they had moved into 44 Hanover Street, and there are things out on the pavement then.

7

Community Life

Although not a focus for any particular interviews, items relating to religious practice and social activities did feature in the interviews and a number of examples relating to this theme are given in this chapter.

The first extracts deal with religious practice and give an indication of how different Sundays were in the days before Sunday shopping was common.

Interview extracts follow relating to repairing the Simpson Memorial Clock in Stranraer and community support before the introduction of Social Security. This is followed by an extract from the interview with Archie Bell, who reflects on his role within the community. Archie was instrumental in enabling the purchase of the first inshore lifeboat in the Rhins in 1974. He subsequently served as both a crew member of the lifeboat and deputy launching officer. Archie also talks about the work he undertook to refurbish the Lord Provost's lamps.

This selection finishes with two short pieces relating to local entertainment. The first is about the Miltonians and the second curling.

Taken together, these extracts give us a glimpse of community life in the Stranraer area in the middle decades of the twentieth century.

George McClymont, Portpatrick

Everybody went to the church in those days. My mother was a great believer in sending all her children to Sunday School.

That would get them out of the house?

Absolutely, it got rid of them on a Sunday. We were all sent to Sunday School. It started at about eleven o'clock, followed by the latter part of the church service. [You] came home and had your dinner and then you went to the Youth Fellowship in the afternoon followed by the Gospel. So that was three times on a Sunday, and sometimes you had nothing else to do and then you would go to the evening service. There were three churches, there was the parish church, there was the English Church and there was the Gospel Hall. The Gospel Hall was still round Barrack Street. It's still there yet to this day, so is the little English Church.

Who was the minister?

The minister was a fellow called George Paterson Graham. Hence my name is George Paterson Graham McClymont. I was his first christening in the village and that's how I got my name.

Bill McCaig, Stranraer

The church played a large part in our lives. Both my grandfathers were elders, and my father and mother were very regular attenders at the church. If it was possible, they never missed a church service in the daytime. Somebody would always be there. When we were children it was just assumed that we would go to church. We were at Sunday School at half past ten and then we went in and had a church service, which lasted till about one. We came home and had lunch and then if there was an evening service, some of us were expected to turn out to it. The evening service was once a month, and I think when we were children the Agnew[5] influence still held and there was a service in the Galdenoch Hall, that's where Rosemary McCall is, in the Galdenoch Hall, once a month – for the convenience of the outlying community. The Plymouth Brethren had a wee hall half way along the Ervie road, it's demolished now. There was what was known as the Wee Hall, and the Plymouth Brethren had their services there. So there was the UF Church, the Plymouth Brethren, and the parish church as well.

Hugh Aitken, Stranraer

I am now moving on to the War years when the Glasgow evacuees came down to Stranraer. Our house had two attic rooms which were declared suitable. We had one mother and a child in the front attic, and a mother and two children in the back attic. They arrived on a Saturday and the next day, Sunday, was a beautiful sunny day. I think the noise of the children running up and down the stairs was too much for my mother so my sister and I were allowed out to play with the evacuees on the Clayhole beach. The first time ever we had been allowed out on a Sunday to play. However, this did not last long as the evacuees, after about two weeks, returned to Glasgow.

Mr Aitken's family business, a jeweller's, dated back to at least 1870. In 1889 his grandfather acquired a number of properties on George Street which were demolished and rebuilt for the business. Hugh trained as a watch repairer and subsequently looked after the town clocks in Stranraer.

> I had an occasion when the clock at the Simpson Memorial at the harbour broke down. And the hands of the clock with the facing up King Street, the hands were not in the correct position for the hour, etc. I hired a ladder and placed it up and sorted the hands to a different position. I can remember it very well because it was an exceptionally windy day. My hat flew off my head first of all, and I thought I had better come down out of this danger. As I got down, the ladder came off the wall and fell over a lorry that was parked on the weighbridge at the side of the memorial building.

Isabelle Shaw, Drummore

> I tell you, the village [Drummore] was different [then]. Everybody knew everybody and if there was anything happened, everybody heard. Now this Lizzie Craig with all her children, she lived in the wee end one, next to Archie and James Gorman. And the boys were three in a bed – I think they were reading their comics or something, at night, with a candle on the pillow, and it just went on fire. She had always put one wallpaper on top of another till it was thick. That night the thing just went round and burned all the curtains and burned all the paper. Well, the people in the village just took these people in and my Auntie Annie had [the] three girls and Lizzie and somebody else took the boys. Then the next day, everybody gave [something] – there was no Social Security [then] – you were on the parish. So Annie and Alex gave materials for curtains, and Jake McGaw gave the paper and all the rest. And the kids got that much, and they got it all fixed up in the day and then they were back in the next night. So everybody helped, and that sort of thing.

Archie Bell

> I was in at the beginning of Lochryan Sailing Club in Stranraer harbour. We had, I think, if I remember rightly, 13 GP14 dingies, mostly home built, and a clubhouse down the pier. And an ex-RAF shed on the Breastwork. After that the club moved to Wig Bay slipway and built the existing clubhouse. I was also in the Young Farmers' Club for a few years and was elected to Stranraer Rotary Club in 1967. Dr Robin Scott, Peter

Brown and myself, along with Andrew Murray, all being sailing enthusiasts, realised that there was a serious gap in the inshore rescue services in
the Rhins area. We had great difficulty in convincing the RNLI and the
local authority that this was the case. ... . The Rotary Club financed the
purchase of the first inshore lifeboat in 1974 to commemorate their 25th
anniversary. This inshore lifeboat [ILB] was unique in its day. Normally
the ILB was limited to operating in a five mile radius from its station. We
put our ILB on a trailer, towed it with a Land Rover and owing to the
unique shape of the Rhins, we could cover about 120 miles of coastline
within about 20 minutes. I was delighted to serve on the crew for seven
years and then, for another ten years, as a deputy launching officer.

...

*Can I ask you about the town Provost's lamps? ... were you approached to refurbish
them, or was this off your own bat?*

Originally, when the Town Council was disbanded and taken over by a
regional council in 1974, the Provost's lights were erected outside the old
parish church. I thought they were in a sorry state, there was only one
existing painted glass for the front and I offered then to refurbish them.
But I went up a ladder and had a close look at them and said, no way can I
work on these up on the top of a lamp post considering the state they were
in. And they were left. When the old parish church closed, two years ago,
the lights were taken to the Burgh yard and the posts were erected in front
of what was then St Andrew's Church, now the Town Kirk. As the lights
were then removed from the posts, I once again offered to rebuild them
and they were brought up to my workshop. And I found that they were in
a considerably worse state than I had originally thought. They had been
beautifully made over a hundred years ago, in copper, but [sorely] abused
since. They were rebuilt. The whole top of one had to be taken apart.
There were 32 folded and soldered pieces of copper in it. This had to be
straightened out and all the joints re-soldered, and that was done. That
was fine until I took the bottom half of the other one apart and found it
was even worse. The metal angles for it, and everything else, had to be
remade. It was actually made from copper from a hot water tank out of my
son's flat in Edinburgh, which I had been saving for some years. That was
rebuilt, then two new painted glasses for the front were made. They were
copied from a photocopy of the original cracked glass, which I had saved
so many years before and put in the museum.

Who painted the actual lantern part?

I painted it. The reversed photocopy was put on top of a lightbox, the glass
put on top of that and the painting done on the inside of the sandblasted
glass. It was done with special glass-painting paints which I hope will last
for years, but time will tell.

Margaret Clark

In 2005 Mrs Clark was interviewed by Nancy McLucas about the Miltonians (previously the Murrayfield Partisans) which was started by her uncle and aunt and which developed over a number of years. Performed in the garden to begin with, the troupe later toured around.

> The ladies were very versatile. For one chorus, we had the same satin blouses and had little red skirts, trimmed with gold and different strappings down the bodice and different epaulettes for the shoulders, and different hats, so it looked like a completely different costume. Our shoes, we even had our shoemaker who used to put the taps on our shoes. And there was one chorus, a 'Dutch chorus' which we did the Cowboy, the Picallil, the Dutch and so forth, and he made us all our clogs for the Dutch dance … Duncan McKinnon was his name.

Bill McCaig

… I think you said you used to curl, Leswalt people, you used to curl up there on the loch itself?
> Yes, on the loch. Just off the road actually. But in the 1947 freeze-up we curled in under the castle. There were rinks made there and that was quite good, but generally speaking we just stopped the cars on the road and just curled across the road. Many and many a curling game we've had there. The curling hut, I think, is still there so that would be another of Sir Andrew's buildings. He built a wee hut for the curlers.

8

Education

Schools could be one-teacher local provision or much more substantial town-based establishments and many of the interviewees talked about their early experiences of education. Regardless of the size, the popular themes remained the same: the journey to school (which was often, both long and taken on foot) and classroom punishment. Teachers who were especially fond of using the ruler or belt are remembered here, most poignantly perhaps by John Carruth, who recalls the lasting consequences of being hit with the ruler each time he reached for the chalk with his left hand.

Isabelle Shaw

My aunt's mother was born up at a place called Darnamoullie, away up in the hills beyond New Luce. And she was one of a big family and when they went to school they all took their peat under their arm to the school fire, so they could get a fire in the school.

Mrs J B Lammie

I can't imagine a better place to grow up in than Craigton Hill. We went to the country school Buittle, which meant walking, I would say a mile and a half over fields and hills, but we didn't think in those days anything about it. That was just the way it was done. Wet weather or dry weather, you went just the same. The teacher was wonderful. I was a shy wee thing but she put me right.

Was it a one-teacher school?

Yes, at that time it was one teacher and I just loved that little school. Any day that was wet when we came in, we stood in front of a huge fire which, of course, was the only means of heating the school. And I used to think, 'Now, just look at all that steam'.

George McClymont

… tell me about your school days in Portpatrick.

Well, Portpatrick was not a very busy school. There was four classes, four teachers. John Smith was the headmaster, Miss Donaldson was the primary, the infants, and then we had Mary McCleary and a Mrs Johnston. Four teachers and four classes. The classes were big classes in those days, maybe 35 to 40 pupils in each class, and if you passed the 11-plus then you went on to the High School in Stranraer. I was never clever enough to pass the 11-plus.

The discipline would be quite different?

Very much so. The people in the village you feared most was the headmaster of the school and the local policeman. Those were people you held in high esteem.

What like was the discipline?

Well, you certainly wouldn't get away with anything at school then that you would get away with today.

What I mean is, were you belted?

Oh, aye. We got strapped quite regularly. Mr Smith took great pleasure in giving you a few whacks of the belt.

What did you do for sports and gym at school?

I always remember there was a gym teacher came from Stranraer once a week … . But that was it, there was no football teams. We made our own games in the playground in those days.

…

And what did you do if it was raining?

Well, they would go into what was the cookery room. There was the back where they had the soup kitchen, and you could do a little bit in there. Highland and country dancing was another thing that was taught at the school. Miss Donaldson, she took the country dancing.

And how did you like that?

Well, not too bad, a couple of left feet sometimes. I always can remember her trying to teach me the Petronella and it wasn't very clever. …

Did you ever have any school parties?

Oh aye, Christmas parties was always a big thing.

And what happened, who provided the food?

I don't know where the food came from. There was always plenty of it. The teachers did a lot of the catering. They always served you. I don't know whether I should tell you this story or not, but there was a fella called Donald Alexander at one particular Christmas party and John Smith, the headmaster, was going round, he had a big teapot and he was going up and down, 'More tea, any more tea?' and he came to Donald, and said 'More tea, Donald?' 'Yes, sir, just a wee drop in the arse of the cup.'

…

Now, you said a soup kitchen, your mother helped out at the soup kitchen?

My mother did that. She made the soup and I think most of the school would have soup every day, and I think it cost a halfpenny or a penny a bowl.

That was before school dinners?

Before school dinners. My mother, she was the lady who made the soup and it was always made in a great big copper urn.

And that was for all the children that came a distance?

Oh, aye, they came a tremendous distance. They came from Killantringan Lighthouse and Colfin Creamery. You're talking about kids walking three and four miles, morning and night. It was always said in the wintertime that kids coming from Killantringan Lighthouse started off in the dark and got home in the dark. They walked over the golf course, through the wood, right down over … to the lighthouse. Then, latterly, I think there was a car provided for them. That's when taxis became fashionable and the taxi went out to Killantringan to meet them, and Colfin. But prior to that they had to walk.

Mrs Muir and Mrs McKie

In 2006, Nancy interviewed Mrs Muir and Mrs McKie, who were both residents in Thorney Croft, about their schooldays. Mrs Muir had gone to school in Glasgow and remembered that she had only to pop round the corner from her home to get to the school. It was quite different for Mrs McKie, as she remembered:

We all lived at Wellhouse, a farm up in Kirkcolm area, and I went to school with my brother and sister. I was four and a half years old. As my mother was working I had to go somewhere. My mother had the house and milking.

So you went to school early?

Yes.

And did you walk to school?

Yes. Nearly three miles.

Every day?

Yes.

Three miles there, and three miles back, at four and a half year old … . Hail, rain and shine?

Yes.

What did you do on wet days? ... what did you do with your wet clothes?
  Well, we had nothing, except just hang them and hope that they dried. ...
So ... they might still be damp when you left to go home?
  Yes.

Their experiences of school punishment were also quite different. Mrs Muir thought the boys might have got the belt, but she didn't remember ever getting the belt herself. Again, Mrs McKie had a different experience at school in Kirkcolm:

How long were you in the first room?
  About two or three years. About year two I would think and then there
  was a middle room, that was Miss Mathieson, she liked to use her belt.
Oh, did she? [laughter] And did she use it on you?
  Yes.
What for?
  If I did wrong.
What kind of wrong? Naughty, or your sums and things?
  Sums.

John Barr

When I was a young fella going to the school at Stranraer Academy we used to go by bus and we got the Caledonian bus at the road end. ... and it was eight pence per week, return. We would get the bus at nine o'clock, and we would go into the town and I cannae just remember where we got off, but I think it went up Queen Street. And I think we maybe got off at the Cross, and we would walk up Lewis Street to the school.
  ... Getting to the Academy, it was a very imposing building and, of course, the masters in they days were very strict. In my day it was Mr Rae that was the headmaster. And Miss Kirkpatrick was there, of course, and Miss Hannay. And they were very, very strict and I think that's what we're missing today. One of the classrooms was actually in kinda steps, and it was very interesting. But, as I say, they were very, very strict. At dinner time we went down to Mrs Bigham's who had a small hotel and ... we got soup there. And her premises were opposite Archie Bell's shop, the butcher's shop, just on the other side of the street. And we went there for a while. But later on from that we went to the British Restaurant, which was opened up just at the start of the War to serve the troops, and it was a self-service and it was very, very popular.

John Carruth

Although John Carruth recalled that the teachers in the High School in Stranraer had been very nice, he had encountered problems when he first went to school:

> I went to school in 1926 when I was five years old and I was left-handed. And, of course it was slate and chalk then and every time I reached for the chalk with my left hand I got the ruler across my fingers. Because the pens were the old pen that you dipped in the inkwell with the nib and, of course, if you were left-handed you were pushing the pen across the paper and the ink splattered all over the place. So, you had to learn to write with your right hand. It took some time to get me to stop using my left hand. And after that I developed a stammer which I was told was because the balance of my brain had been upset. However, the stammer left me when I was about 12 years of age. And I left school when I was 16 and went to work for my father in Peter Davidson, the grocer. And then, of course, the War came and that was it. So that was, more or less, my school days. I wouldn't say … that they were the happiest of my life.

Mary Downie

> When I started at Kirkcolm in 1931 I was very left-handed. I was smacked over the back of the hand each time [the teacher] came on me holding the chalk in my left hand. The slate was on its way out then but I vividly remember the slate with a wooden surround. It was a war of wills between youth and age. I thought then that [the teacher] was ancient but on look-ing back now she wasn't old at all. Anyhow, thinking that smacks were something to put up with each day I carried on using my left hand. When [she] saw that smacks were not going to have an effect she moved on to the ruler. After many cracks on my left knuckles I succumbed and tried, repeat tried, to use my right hand.

Agnes Lamb

Can we go back to your childhood for a minute. When you were living in St John Street, where did you go to school?
> Well, I was only a year old, but ma brothers an sisters went to the old Academy. A went to the Academy as well …
From St John Street?
> No, no, no, I was only a year old when we went away. A went from the

Drums. But in old days they didn't leave on transport … .There was a service bus, but you had to buy a ticket for a week, for the school.

And you came into Stranraer, rather than go to Leswalt?

Well, … I suppose you had an option, but there wasn't transport to Leswalt, you couldnae get a bus to Leswalt. And the Barr family lived at Auchneel an A took them all to the school, because we all stood an waited on the bus at the road end. And you didnae have school meals or anything. And you were probably were soakin when you came into the school, and you had to be wet all day. And I think that is why a lot of people of my age had arthritis and so forth, because you were soaked.

So did you carry a piece at lunchtime?

Well, you could if you liked. A cannae remember, Mrs McLucas. But you had your meal when you came home at night, because I remember ye [were] always starvin and you couldnae belt home quick enough. Because you had to walk from the shore up to the road, and if it was a wet day you were pretty wet by time you got the bus.

Where did the bus drop you off in Stranraer?

I suppose it dropped you off, I cannae remember. The bus office was in what was Trades Street then. Now you might not remember that, Trade Street. Wait to I think. If you went doon, now that's Millhill Street isn't it, where the car park is? Well, Greenvale Street would come out aboot, you know where the fire station is? Well it was a road that came up there, an it went in off Dalrymple Street, an there was a laundry along there, quite a big employment bit, it was a laundry, and quite a few people lived here, and then you went on up Greenvale Street. But lots of people remember it. … . It was there 50 years ago.

Do you remember [any] of your teachers?

Joe Hood. Mr Hood was one teacher. He was the headmaster and a very severe headmaster he was … . He used the strap a lot, very much so. And John Evans taught me at the school, and his wife. A can remember quite a lot of them. Miss Hannah, a Miss Robertson. Aye, I can remember quite a lot of them. But, you see, when you came to the, what you called the qualifying class then, you moved on to the High – or whatever was the High [then]. But in my case, an A could've done, because I'd passed well enough to go, but I was needed at home. You werenae allowed to choose what you wanted to do, or what your education was. Because if you were needed, you had to go home an help. That was the way it was long ago.

John McColm

I attended the Central School until I was 11 and after that I … had one year at Stranraer Academy. Each Monday morning I got the bus from Drummore to Stranraer and during that time I stayed in Stranraer with my aunt, Mrs Harper, at Roslyn in London Road. After one year at the Academy, when Jimmy Stewart taught me in the 11-plus, I had two years at Stranraer Academy. I had a very happy time living with the Harper family. My father collected me after school on a Friday and I spent the weekend at home. While at school, I had some very good friends, schoolmates, Stuart Hogarth, Steen Purdie, Bill McCormack, and they became great friends and were for many years, and still are. The school time was very happy. I had made up my mind I was going to become a vet. I had an uncle a vet in Dundee and I liked his lifestyle but, unfortunately, I had to leave the high school. My father, whose health was never very good, took ill and I had to leave school.

Miss Margaret Templeton and Miss Jean Templeton

In June 2007 Nancy McLucas visited the Templeton sisters to ask them about their childhood memories and their father's business as an optician. The sisters explained their father's reasons for choosing Stranraer as his base and talked about how he would travel about the area, often staying in a room in a private house while he worked. Reminding us of the impact of World War II, the sisters remarked that around the time of Dunkirk, their father would formally say 'goodbye' to each of his landladies as he left them because he thought he might not see them again. The sisters also spoke about the effect the War had on their daily lives, including soldiers billeted in the school buildings and the blackout.

Both sisters often answered the questions together and so the transcription does not attribute the answers to a particular sister unless the information being given is specific to one or other lady.

Ladies, you don't actually belong to Stranraer? When did you come to the town?
September 1929.
And what brought you here?
Well, father wanted to open up an optical business of his own and he studied charts and various things and discovered that there was no qualified optician in this area. So he thought Stranraer would be the place.
Now when you say 'in this area' do you mean the town of Stranraer or Wigtownshire generally?
Wigtownshire.
There was nobody in Newton Stewart?
No.
So where was the nearest one after Stranraer?

I think it would be Ayr and Castle Douglas. As far as I remember there was McEwan's in Castle Douglas when we came to Stranraer.

So people would have to travel to your father, obviously, from quite a distance?

Yes, and he went to them. A little later on, he went to Whithorn, Newton Stewart and Wigtown, to each place, one afternoon per month. And he took equipment with him, and set up there.

He would obviously have a car to do that?

Oh, yes, yes. That's why we got the car. I don't know what he did at the very beginning. He must've travelled by bus a few times. But very soon he got one of these cars with the hood and the plastic windows you put up when the rain came on. A Citroen … . He got the saloon car, I think, in about 1936 or '7.

What happened then during the War?

Oh, everything went on as usual. He could keep the car, and got a petrol allowance for business, once the basic ration was taken off. Up until June 1942, you got a basic ration. You didn't need to be in business or anything, but after that until the end of the War people who were allowed it, and he was one of them, got a basic petrol allowance. But, of course, you couldn't go off in the car to Portpatrick for a wee run or anything like that. It was strictly business. We went to a private house in each place, they let us into the rooms. I am saying us because I [Margaret] eventually worked with him, but that is how it always was. And he told me later that each time, about 1940 or '41 about the time of Dunkirk, for several months he [would] quite officially and seriously [say] 'goodbye' to each of his landladies, because he didn't know if he would be back the next month. But, you know the rest, it all worked out alright.

How long did your father continue in business?

He retired in September 1961. So, that was from September 1929.

By that time were there other opticians in the town?

Oh, yes, oh, yes. I'm not certain about this, but I think there was always a visiting optician through the Co-operative …

Now this would be before the National Health Service?

Oh, yes.

Have you any remembrance of how your father worked the business?

… By this time Mr Irving, he was an optician at the corner of Hanover Square, in the premises that had been previously occupied by my father.

So your father didn't start off in Hanover Street?

Not in 15 Hanover Street. It was at the corner, where the jeweller is now. You know as you go into Hanover Square, with the rounded windows.

I thought that was always Irving, the jewellers.

No. They were along a wee bit, more opposite Barbours, in a smaller shop with a door and a window side by side. Then that whole building was up for sale. And by sheer chance my father spoke to H P McLaughlin, who was in the process of demolishing three small cottages in Hanover Street to build two shops, and my father was given the promise of one of them. So we went straight from the corner of Hanover Square to 15 Hanover Street in 1936 or '37 …

Obviously school children would have their eyes tested at school but what else did your father do, obviously people paid to have their eyes tested?

Oh, yes. Or didn't, or didn't! We always had bad debt. And then … the health scheme started, [and] on the day it was due to start we had never been issued with the official forms to be filled in … eventually they came, and it all worked out alright.

Did you find a great increase in business?

Oh, yes. Oh, yes. A great many people – the first question, 'When did you last have your eyes tested?' and it was really surprising the number of people who said, 'Oh, I just picked up a pair in Woolworth's', or, 'I got a pair from the doctor'. Or, you know, various other places they got them from. In fact, when I asked this one old man, when did you last have your eyes tested [he said], 'Oh, now let me think. It was coming back fae the Boer War'. [*laughter*] One of the questions was, 'What was your identity number?' – which was rather strange. And we got all sorts of variations … . That was a bit of a problem. And, 'What is your age?' to begin with, and it was changed to [ask for] your date of birth. People were more inclined to give their date of birth, than to state their actual age – which was stupid. Did somebody not say, 'Oh, do you want to know how old I am?' when he said, 'What is your date of birth?' And [father] said, 'I don't want to know, but Mr Aneurin Bevan wants to know'. The thing is people were coy about it, not them all, some people. You wrote down their age and instantly forgot about it. I didn't go about the town thinking, Mrs So-and-so is such, and, such an age. It was just a routine question, and that was it.

When you came here you would be ready for school?

MT: I was three.

JT: And I was five. I was five in January but didn't go [to school] till after Easter.

And what school did you go to, and where did you live?

Stranraer Academy … . We were in rooms for a short time above, I was going to say above Aitken's the jewellers but where they were before, above May the Chemists at the top of George Street. We had rooms there, and then we managed to get a house in Marine Gardens at the bottom of Bowling Green Road. So we have been in Bowling Green Road since 1930 … . We moved up here at the beginning of 1949.

So you went to Stranraer Academy which, of course, is now gone, the old one. Can you remember much about your infant class?

Not really very much. I mean, I remember sitting in it, and I remember Miss Lamb the teacher, Agnes Lamb, telling us the different letters of the alphabet. And we got wee cards to sew on. There was always a bundle of raffia in a corner and we did something like a table mat I think. … In Miss Lamb's class there was the big side and the wee side. We didn't all turn five at the right time for the school opening, so that there seemed to [be] more leeway about starting then. Because in my class there would be older people and younger people. And in the class above, somebody a full year older or a full year younger, haphazard.

And who was the Headmaster and what like was he?

Mr Joseph Hood, Joe Hood. I don't think he ever spoke to me the whole time I was there. He was the headmaster, you were frightened of him. He didn't ever give us trouble … . When he came into the classroom we all stood up and said 'Good morning, Sir,' which I think was a very good idea. Then Mr Rae came, I liked Mr Rae better. [And] that building has gone. I remember in Miss Lamb's class it was the only class where the seats were round in a semicircle …

Can you remember how many were in your class?

I think it would be between 40 and 50. I have always been able to spell accommodation because each class had 'Accommodation for this room is so-and-so', usually 60 I think. It was never full, but it was always a decent party at the Academy …

Was Miss Lamb the only infant teacher?

She was the infant teacher. There was Miss McCaig, who became Mrs Tom Harper. The children loved Miss McCaig and the next one up was Miss Bryden. Now, she came off farming people from down Whithorn way … . I met up with her brother once down in Whithorn, we were doing the Whithorn run. He was in lodgings in the house where we had our rooms. I remember … I said something about Miss Bryden. 'Oh, did you know Nellie?' He was so pleased, because I had been taught by Nellie. Of course, I didn't know her Christian name then. She was Miss Bryden.

Were there any men teachers in the primary, can you remember?

Yes, Mr Stewart. James Stewart.

Beaky?

How do you know that?

Because my children started with Mr Stewart at Rephad.

He was well liked. He was a good teacher. There was also, in those days, what we called the Advanced Division. Ones who didn't pass the Control, who didn't want to go to the High. And there were two men teachers there. John Evans who married Bunty Love and Mr … Ogilvy, whose son, George, was a dental mechanic for Gardner Kerr. And George went to Newton Stewart when James Reid, the dentist, moved to Newton Stewart.

Those were the three men teachers.

So you had Miss Lamb, Miss McCaig, Miss Bryden and who else?

Miss Matheson. She didn't belong to the town, I don't think. No, she married and went to live in Fiji. So I have always known where Fiji was.

Were you ever punished? Were you never strapped?

No, we seemed to get through … . Too mim. We were good, and we did our homework. No, we didn't get strapped. No, we were always submissive. Don't you think they should bring it back? [No.] Maybe some took advantage. No, we were never been badly treated, never.

Did you have any visiting teachers? Art, music, gym?

We had a gym teacher, Miss Murray … . We called it drill in those days. And, then Miss Barclay, who eventually became Mrs Gait whose husband had the Cree Mills.

These drill teachers, did they actually wear shorts or … gym tunics?

No, the first Miss Murray wore ordinary clothes. Of course, we weren't getting taught very much. I distinctly remember she had an awful nice angora jersey, I liked that angora jersey …

No sewing teacher?

Oh, yes … . Miss Gillespie. Jessie Gillespie … for Domestic Science. When we were in class six, that was Mr Stewart's class, the girls went into Miss Gillespie for sewing and the boys, did they get joinery or handicraft … something like that?

So Miss Gillespie was actually also working in the advanced division?

Both, because we got sewing. We didn't get cooking. The Advanced Division girls got cooking. So she would teach them to cook. And she was a Gillespie of Gillespie the bakers, and she lived in Mountryan in High Street …

After you left the Academy you went to the High School?

… It was on my birthday I think that I went to the High School, 29th August 1939 I went to the High School, and the War broke out a week later, and the school was closed for several days. But then it was re-opened and that was that.

Who was the Head Teacher at the High School?

John A MacDonald. He was the Rector. Yes, … Miss Digney for French and Miss Thomson for French, Maths [was] Miss Reid and Mr Wallace. English, Mr Hendry and Miss Henderson [for] Science, Dr Hill and Mr Sutherland, Herbert, and don't forget Miss Graham, the lady who became his wife, Miss Ann Graham, she taught English and History.

She didn't teach Latin?

Yes, she did … . I had her once, when the Rector was off, for Latin. I heard she was very good, and it was much clearer what it was all about when the Rector was off … . I don't think any of us got on very well with it. Nobody got on very well with Latin. The Rector was inclined to tell stories about the First War. He preferred that to teaching. I don't think he was awfully good at putting it over, and then maybe we weren't all that interested. [*laughter*] Art, Miss Florence Gillespie ... the same Gillespies as in the primary. Jessie Gillespie was Jack's sister, and Miss Florence Gillespie was the aunt of Ian Gillespie ... so it's the same family. And talking of Gillespies, the same Gillespie family were in business in Stranraer when we came in 1929, as were Simpsons, Jack's the butcher and Aitken the jeweller. And they are still in business, all in the same premises except Aitken's who have moved down the street a bit. But they were all there in 1929, when we came, and still the same family ...

Who took you for gym?

Miss Barclay. Oh no, not all the time. She married and it was Miss Hogarth .... I had her for a very short time.

The War must have made some difference because I can remember it making quite a difference to my secondary. I mean there would be very few men or the young men would be away.

... When I went to the High in 1939 it was the first time that the High School had a Commercial course. There used to be just A and B but there was a C class in 1939, and it was Commercial. Remember, there was another teacher ... Mr Lawson, he was called up to the Navy. Doc Hill was called up eventually, that was after we left. ... St Joseph's School. Now some of the schools were closed, and in the High School there were two classrooms downstairs occupied by another school, and I think it must have been St Joseph's. I remember the gym was occupied by the forces. Not all the time, no ... because we had operettas.

How do you mean occupied by the forces?

Well, they took it over. At one stage the gym at the High School was full of, blankets, I think it was said.

Service men didn't live there?

No, they didn't live there. But it was requisitioned ... and part of the Annexe. And because we didn't get gym we got extra Arithmetic, and it didn't do me one bit of good. [*laughter*]

How long did that go on?

I don't think very long. You see there were some pupils who only had half a day. Listen, the whole of the old Academy building was occupied, because Park School was used. And the pupils from each school had to share the same school, and they went for half a day each. But I think they started earlier in the morning.

How long did this go on for?

I can't remember. It must have been a year or two.

... Stranraer was packed ... from 1940, I would say. I remember, in

May 1940, we were living down at the foot of the road there, and one day, in lovely hot summer weather, we heard trains. There was always another train going down there, you could hear them. And in the end I got the binoculars and went down to the wall down there and had a look. And I remember going back in and saying, 'They are full of soldiers. They're hanging over the rails'. And it was the evacuation from Dunkirk. They were taking them to camps in Ireland, they had to do something with them … . The boats were going back and forth all the time, and the trains. … . And it was very hot sunny weather, lovely weather …

So there would be an awful lot of service men in Stranraer?

Oh, yes, you've no idea. At the Ivy Leaf café for a while, every day at two o'clock, there was a queue of airmen. They shut for a wee while between two and three, I think. And when I was going back to work there would be this blue queue, every day except Sunday of course, of airmen. The ones with some money, no doubt.

Waiting for what?

Food, teas, coffees.

Was there no NAAFI?

Yes, there were NAAFIs. But you could get haddock and chips there, war or no war. They got the haddock from Gibson's, better fish than they could get now. So, oh, Stranraer was occupied, you've no idea. There was a camp at Wig Bay, a camp at Cairnryan, Drummuckloch, the Freugh. Mysterious things went on in the woods up at Lochnaw and over there at the golf course, it was occupied … . And Bay House … was the garrison engineer's office, and Craigenelder was occupied by the Air Force, it was requisitioned. And another house, Ann House, it was [occupied by] the RAF again. And the long since demolished King's Arms had the Navy in it.

Where did the people, for instance, from Ann House and Craigenelder go?

They just went to relatives or wherever they could. Do you remember Jean Ralston? Of course, she and her mother lived in one of the semi-detached houses on Cairnryan Road and their house was requisitioned. And they stayed with the McHarrie's in Westwood. Mrs Ralston and Mrs McHarrie were sisters.

Supposing you had nobody to go to?

I don't know, maybe you could be excused, I don't know. Even a house in Royal … Crescent. It was the movement control. It was the Army who had it. And there were other places.

What about Dunnard, next door?

Dunnard had soldiers billeted. Some big houses had people billeted on them, and other houses had to let rooms to married couples. The Craigenelder Hotel – that had been bought by Captain and Mrs Fergusson who lived round Royal Crescent a wee bit. But they never got into it for it was requisitioned straight away, and they had to wait till after the War.

Was that the Captain Fergusson that went down with the boat?

It was. Kenneth Fergusson, he was in my class at the school. They had to wait the five years or whatever, to get into the house they had bought.

What happened with the education offices?

They were occupied by somebody, because the county library, believe it or not, was in the downstairs part. When you think of the size of the library now, but that's all it occupied was the downstairs part of the education office. And it was moved to a church hall in Dalrymple Street … . It was briefly, I think, in the gym, the library. I think so – in the gym at the High School. I remember I was sent on an errand, I don't remember what it was, but I was told, 'Oh, I don't know where they are. They might be in the gym or they might be in the Annexe'. I went in to the Annexe and looked in a room. Here it was filling with airmen – and others – lying in their beds, so I beat a hasty retreat. The Annexe being the present St Joseph's school … the annexe to the old Academy. It was built as an annexe to the old Academy.

So where were the St Joseph's pupils?

They had their own school, behind the … presbytery. Another school – do you ever hear mentioned, Lewis Street school? It became the labour exchange, now demolished. There was no Ashwood Drive then and we were all frightened of the Lewis Street pupils, they were all bad – 'Run, the Lewis Street pupils are coming'.

Because you would be wearing blazers, of course.

… Oh, no, we had no uniform. But it was introduced before I left. It wasn't compulsory. It was a navy blue blazer with a badge, and it would have a hat. I had a hat, I liked it. I think that was the year I left, maybe. At the High School, again it wasn't compulsory, but there was a tie and a girdle for the House you were in.

Tell me about shop hours please?

Oh yes, all the shops closed between one and two because everyone, schools and all, went home for their dinner in those days. And it was dinner, not lunch. On a Saturday shops remained open til eight o'clock. And it was on a Saturday only, I think, that the Salvation Army played at the head of Hanover Square. The town was so packed with people that everyone walked on the roadway, which was safe enough then. And I understand that sometimes a special train came in from Whithorn. And, of course, down at Portrodie it was just a mass of buses and people … . Jose's father, George Adami, often had to oblige people by keeping parcels for them because they were going on a later bus and they didn't want to carry them about. But he was a bit annoyed once when someone presented him with a roll of linoleum and asked him to keep it. I don't know whether he did or not.

Where were the Salvation Army in those days?

… Their headquarters? There was a hall … at the foot of Park Lane … . It would be demolished when the flats were built.

And they played every Saturday?

As far as I know … . It didn't continue after or during the War.

How did the blackout affect Stranraer?

Well, it was blacked out. And on a very dark night, if you were going out, you took your torch with you. We weren't the least bit afraid to go out. Not a bit, and we were teenagers during the War. It was lovely on a starry night, you could see the stars and even if there was no moon if it was clear and starry, it was alright. And, of course, there was practically no traffic. And what traffic there was had to have one headlight blacked out completely, and the other one masked. There was very little light.

Was there not lights at the camps for instance at the Wig. Did they not have lights?

Well, of course, we were never past them in the dark. They would keep them as dark as they could, I'm quite sure … .When you were down at the foot of the loch, you couldn't see any lights anywhere. And there were camps on each side of the loch … . I remember, after the War, to look round the loch and see the lights, or if you were coming down the way to look at Stranraer and, you know, the string of lights …

What about the planes that came in. There must have been some lights guiding them?

Yes there would be lights … . But the seaplanes … trainee pilots sometimes had to do night flights practising landing and taking off. And sometimes we thought the roof was going to be taken off … when we were still down at Marine Gardens … . It wasn't unusual for the neighbours to say, 'Oh, wasn't it a terrible night, last night. I thought the plane was going to land on the roof'. That sort of thing. I don't know how long that lasted. And then, you see, Wig Bay was a mass of seaplanes because apparently it was the base for the whole of Great Britain for the maintenance of seaplanes … . Short Brothers, they were there.

The shops must have been very busy?

They just had their rations like everyone else, unless they got a bigger allowance sometimes. I remember we did hear from a girl who came to the office, and she'd been in Girvan, at the Roman Catholic School there. And she said when she was there during the War, in Girvan in the shops, you could get cakes and other kind of things that you could hardly lay hands on here. Because Girvan got quotas because of the increased population in the summer, you know, they would be able to claim bigger quotas, according to their trade … . They didn't have military people round about them, but we were stuck with them. There were queues all over the place.

The butchers were only open two or three days a week. They hadn't the meat. It wasn't worth keeping open. That's when the shops closed at five at night, it used to be six .... And they stayed open all day on a Friday ... that was market day .... In our days of going to the school, to the Academy, we had to beware on a Friday because that was cow day. Cows came in off the boat, there was a layerage down there, and sometimes they were being transported – well they weren't being transported they had to walk – from the layerage down there, up to the station to go away .... And when we were going back to the school, here were cows. Sometimes we popped in to somebody's front garden till the cows got past.

... The story about the bull. It was in a shop, Thomson's shop ... two or three people inside the shop, and a man came in, 'Have any of you fellows seen a bull?' [*laughter*] This was on a Friday [and] a bull had escaped from somewhere. Whether the bull was ever found I don't know. I don't think it could have done any damage, but that was the tale.

9

Health

The following selection of extracts relates to health and well-being. John Carruth remembers that the doctor often seemed keen to make a house call, when the charges were higher, while Agnes Lamb, Mrs Lammie and John McColm all relate their experiences from a time when childhood illnesses were more prevalent and treatments less assured of success.

John Carruth

There were several doctors in the town. In Hanover Street there was Dr Harper. His house was where Fidlers the furnishers now are. Then, going down Hanover Street and turning into Castle Street, there was Dr Dale. He only had a doorway on the street, as he lived up above the shops. And I can remember he had an old … car which was driven by a chauffeur, and it had [a] sort of basketwork body and the handbrake was outside on the running board. And it had a barrel-shaped nose on the front, containing the engine of course. It was really a wonderful machine to look at. Then there was Dr Munro, in Lewis Street, whose practice was eventually taken over by Dr Richard, and is now a dwelling house. Further up Lewis Street next to the house, Rowan Tree, was Dr Andrew McCredie. He also had a chemist shop in George Street, part of which is now the Millennium Centre. Then, going round into Academy Street, was Dr Peter McCredie who was also the local surgeon. And he combined his practice with surgery in the Garrick Hospital.

I can remember when I was a boy my mother taking me to the doctor, and you were charged 2/6d for the consultation. He took your temperature and looked in your throat and then said, 'Take him home to bed and I'll come and see him in the morning'. That, of course, was because when the doctor did a house visit, instead of being 2/6d at the surgery it was 3/6d for a house visit. They always liked to come and see you the next morning at home.

Agnes Lamb

Of course, by this time there wouldnae be nine, because my eldest sister died at fourteen. Now, that is quite interesting in a way, because A never knew what she died with. But my elder sister in Canada said that in those days, you didnae talk about what anybody had. Folk were ... families were very, very close about things. But she imagined, ... she says she was a very active girl, she was a wonderful horsewoman and everything. And she took ill, and sis says she imagines that she had TB, but she was never told.

There was a brother between Willie an I, my father [never] saw him, because he was born when ma father was away abroad in the War. And ma sister could also tell me this as well .... He was the loveliest baby you ever saw, and she was holdin him till ma mother bathed him. She was getting his bath ready in St John Street .... But there was four children in St John Street, were all vaccinated the same day, and they all died in one week. Because I never could understand why A was never vaccinated, and this was why. Now, nowadays that would have been a right rumpus, wouldn't it? .... But nothing was done about it .... They never questioned. An these four children died all in that street, in one week.

Mrs J B Lammie

So you had no ill effects from having diptheria when you were younger?
It took me a while to get over that. It affected the heart. Things I could do, like running at school, jumping at sports and that sort of thing, I could no longer do. That was out completely.
Can you remember what kind of treatment you got when you had diptheria?
I don't remember any special medical treatment at all. I remember how kind they all were to me. They gave me sewing to do in the hospital, in Castle Douglas. I would be maybe the last to be in that hospital, I think, with diptheria. I think I am right in saying that. It was very good, it was a different slant on hospitals then to what it is now. Nurses were very much caring for you. Now it is quite different.
Then, after you married?
After I got married we came to a farm in Wigtownshire, that was our first step into Wigtownshire. And I had a son called Bill, and he was born at Craigton Hill because mother wanted to look after us – and you did need someone to look after you then. It was different having a baby. You had a district nurse then, but it was a home confinement.

Mr John McColm

When I became five I started school at Central School at Drunmore and
we walked a mile and a half each day to the school and while there I
walked to Hillcrest at Kirkmaiden village and had lunch with my grandmother McColm and her daughter, Aunt Jenny. That was a very happy
time. On my arriving at the school I wasn't very happy for a time and we
had a very strict teacher. Between Christmas and New Year, after I'd been
at the school for three or four months, I took very ill and the two doctors
who were attending me, Dr Clark from Drummore and Dr Matthews
from Glenluce, [they] couldn't make up their mind what was wrong with
me. And when they did it was too late, my appendix had burst. A surgeon
came from Dumfries and operated on me on the kitchen table at
Cairngarroch. I was very fortunate to survive. For quite some weeks I had
two nurses looking after me. Nurse Maxwell from Dumfries, who later
became matron at Thornhill Fever Hospital, and the other nurse was Mrs
Harvie from Drummore. They nursed me night and day for weeks and I
got out of bed at Easter that year. I was one of the lucky ones that survived
this awful thing.

10

Travel and Transport

Whether by boat, horse, truck, bus, motorbike, train or car, travelling and the provision of transport is a key component in enabling the people and businesses in any given area to function and thrive. The following extracts recall how transportation has changed over time. For example, Hugh Aitken spoke about the coal fire which fuelled the steam-driven Wyllie's lorries, while Agnes Lamb recalled the novelty of getting a lift in a car. A number of the extracts relate to the railway, including Mr and Mrs Darroch, who remembered what life was like for the railwayman and his family.

The diverse range of experiences described in these extracts illustrates again how quickly change can happen and the complexity of factors which can drive that change.

Andrew Hannay

[Talking about shipping oats to Groaten Ltd]
The flaked oats, in the early days, were taken down by train. Sometimes they were shipped in a small type of vessel, like a small tugboat. I can't remember what it was called. Sometimes they were shipped down there because it was much cheaper than sending by rail down to Bristol. They were packed into cardboard containers in Bristol and sold throughout the south-west of England by Groaten Ltd.

Hugh Aitken

Having lived down in the Clayhole all my life, I saw many changes. On the Breastwork, Wyllie's shed used to be there before it was transferred to a big building at the foot of Princes Street and Fisher Street. Wyllie's trucks used to go about and they were old, old ones with a radiator in the front, but it wasn't as you would see on a normal vehicle. It was open and it was a coal fire and the lorries were steam-driven and you could see the burning coals from the front of the lorries.

John Barr

Mr Barr, whose father bought Auchneel in 1920, recalled the transportation of goods at a time when, in his own words, 'Stranraer ... was very dependent on agriculture'.

The horse and cart was the main source of transport to and from the station, where several goods trains arrived and departed daily, carting coal, cattle feeding, manure and all goods required by local traders. Outgoing would be scrap metal, live an dead stock, potatoes, milk, etc. The station was the hub of the community.

George McClymont

You said your mother occasionally came into Stranraer. Tell me about how you got in and out of Stranraer?
The buses were only beginning when I was a boy, the buses were running very irregular, maybe once a day or something, but the train was the mode of transport in them days. And there were maybe two trains in the morning and two in the afternoon and there was always an evening service too, which we used to go to the pictures, for instance, on a Saturday night. And the last train came in on a Saturday at about 11 at nights. But most people used the train.
Have you any memory of how much it cost?
6d was the return fare. I think it was about 4d or 5d to get into the pictures and you'd 2d for a bag of chips.
Was 6d a child's fare?
I should think it probably, but there wouldn't be much difference from that of an adult.
You don't remember what the bus cost?
No, I don't think I ever used the bus when I was a child, until latterly. I don't think there was many buses ran during the War even. It was always the train, so I couldn't tell you what the bus fare was.
Did many folk in Portpatrick work on the railways?
Aye, there was quite a few, I remember there was four surfacemen. They all lived throughout the village, Barrack Street, Colonel Street. Until Eastcliff was built, and then they all got houses up there. There was a cousin of

mine, Willy Campbell and there was Tommy Smith and there was Willy
McCubbin. There was the McCracken fellow who was the porter. There
was Mr [Mc…] who was the station master, and I think that was them.
Maybe about seven or eight people worked at the railway at the station.
And you had the carters too, two carters, Sandy McCracken and Johnny
Anderson. They also had the coal merchant business. Delivered the coals
round the village, and then they carted all the goods from the station
round the shops and various places.

When you say carters, would they take things like trunks further afield?

I never really remember them going out of the village. Maybe to the farms?
That would be as far. But I don't remember them going out of the village
much. There was plenty of stuff coming and going by train, and there was
all the coal coming in, and there was cattle trains, and all the fish went out
by train too. It was busy, particularly in the summertime when the herring
fleet came in. And a lot of herring went by train, and also the visitors.

These visitors must have meant a lot of extra income to the village?

Tremendous. The summer started at the beginning of June right through to
the beginning of September, but it was very busy with visitors and I would
say 90–95 per cent would come by train. It used to be a great thing on a
Saturday, they all came, and we would go up there and humph their cases
and bags down. We used to borrow the station barrow and earn sixpence or
whatever for carrying their cases to the various houses or hotels.

*What about the big Portpatrick Hotel, did it not have its own charabanc or
something?*

It had its own lorry. You never got humphing up there, thank goodness. It
would have been quite a pull. But they had a wee lorry and it always met
the train coming in. Of course, they had it and a charabanc, and they took
their customers up by charaban to the hotel.

… I also believe you made some extra money at the [Portpatrick] golf course?

It was another job for us, was caddying. Caddying from very young boys. I
remember caddying around about 1939, I would only be nine years old.
But bags were very light, they were only pencil bags with a few clubs in
them. We spent a lot of time caddying. They were very generous. You got
two shillings, and if you were a good client you got 2/6, but if you got one
at 2/6 you held on to him for a fortnight so you could make good money.
Money was always put by and in the summer, and what we earned in the
summer was put by, my mother used to take us into town before the
school opened for the winter and clothed us all with the money we earned.

So it was your own money that bought your school clothes?

Absolutely.

Did you ever get any to spend?

Oh yes, we always got pennies and we used to go to Dan Campbell's for a wee bottle of lemonade and what we used to call a [...] biscuit, a sort of chocolate biscuit, and that was after a round of golf you had two or three pence.

...

My mother could always find us jobs. There was nobody in our family was allowed to be idle. Jobs down the harbour when the herring fleet was in. Helping load lorries and humphing empty boxes, there were hundreds of little jobs.

John Carruth

For several years before the War the railway company organised and ran trips to Glasgow on a Saturday, leaving Stranraer at four o'clock in the afternoon. This, of course, only happened in the summer months of May, June, July and August. And the train returned, leaving Glasgow at ten o'clock at night, arriving in Stranraer around midnight, or shortly after. The fare was 4/6 return, four shillings and sixpence that is. I can remember that I was on one trip, and I think it probably was the first one that took place, and would be about 1935. As we trooped off the train and went through the ticket collector at St Enoch's Station one of the old men in front of me said to the ticket collector, 'You'll be very busy in Glasgow tonight'. The ticket collector said, 'Oh?' The old man said, 'Aye, this is a big trip in from Stranraer. There will be maybe 400 on this train. That'll make you very busy'. [*laughter*]

Mr and Mrs William Darroch

Here, Mrs Darroch recalled how difficult it was for her husband to gain promotion in the railway service and the impact his job had on family life:

When Willie came back [from the War] he was just a fireman and he had to pass out again, but then there was a seniority business ... this was service way, and you had almost to wait for someone retiring so that there was a vacancy for a driver. But then there was various things happened. Someone else would come in that was senior from another station, with the result for a long while he was driving or could drive and did do odd jobs, [but] he wasn't what was termed stationed as a driver. Eventually he did get that, but after a long time. It would be well into the sixties. But, then again, they altered the wages and everybody got the same. I think by that time the job went off ... they didn't drive as far as Carlisle ... but that

159

wasn't due to nationalisation at all. It was after that that the wages improved. Eventually, he did get what was termed stationed as a driver ... . Of course they did goods jobs as well as passengers, there was quite a lot of goods work, which is all gone now.

Just to Glasgow, not to places like Stirling or further afield?

No, it would be Glasgow. They did one that they took so far ... and they changed drivers and it went through to Edinburgh. That was one of the big jobs that they did. I forget where they changed drivers. Before Willie finished up he would be in about 13 different shifts [and] he did a week on each. In fact, some of them, he would start maybe early morning and finish up on night shift before the week was out. He had a different shift every day.

That must have been quite complicated for you?

Yes, very complicated. And it was very difficult with the children as well. I didn't drive and there would be activities, 'Well, can dad take me so and so?', 'No, he's sleeping', or 'No, he's just gone out to his shift'. Something like that, and it was very difficult. And then the children had to be shushed, 'Dad's sleeping'. It had an [impact] on the whole life. It wasn't just nine to five.

Did you have a notice pinned up in the kitchen giving his hours or did you just know?

Yes, we needed to have notifications, because we couldn't remember from day to day. But that's not to say it might change if somebody was off ill or whatever. Sometimes there would be an extra shift needed, because there wasn't a driver available. They had to cover for that if they were available. It was voluntary, but they were expected to do it.

Agnes Lamb

... when A wis young, the first person I remember havin a car was Billy McCaig's father, at the Challoch. And it was a great, great thing if Mr McCaig picked you up to give you a lift into school. You were some nob sittin up in a car. You cannae imagine that now, can you?

Not now.

You can't. I mean it reminds me a bit too, if this is interesting, that youngsters ... I suppose young fellas. If you'd [a] fancy car, [you] thought that was great, [an] showed off. Well, when I was young, it was the same with horses. If you'd a better horse than somebody else, you were somebody ... . There was a farmer at Leswalt, and ma father and him were very jealous of each other. An he was very good at pickin me up ... with the horse and machine, into town, wi this high stepping horse. And we worked it out that he knew that I'd go home an tell ma dad what a lovely horse [he had] ... It's funny, isn't it, how youngsters would brag about what they have.

Mrs J B Lammie

… I had to travel by bus, walk to Dalbeattie, three miles, and get a bus there to Dumfries each day, and that became a bit laborious. A cousin of mine was selling his motorbike and my father said, 'Would you like the motorbike, because I'll buy it for you if you would like it?' I said, 'Yes, I would' and I used that to drive to Dumfries.

And what age were you at that time?

I was 17. I was just age to get a licence really.

That would be in the 1920 ? … Did you need to sit a test?

No, no tests then. I just got on the motorbike and drove. The same happened when we got a car, once we started farming and could afford a car. I could drive a car without a test.

Have you ever had a driving test?

… I took an advanced driver's test at one stage, a long time afterwards. But, not at the time when I was young. I enjoyed driving.

War

War, and especially World War II, unsurprisingly features heavily in a number of interviews and has been the subject of a number of the publications produced by the Stranraer and District Local History Trust. Encompassing the experiences of those who were children when Stranraer was transformed into a significant military base and also those whose experience of war took them far from home, the extracts presented here provide interesting insights into some of the many ways that the War impacted on the local community. War pervaded every aspect of life in the area. Many interviewees recalled how dark it was during the blackout: which was a particular necessity given Stranraer's proximity to Belfast. The experience of war could be very different for those living in a rural or urban environment. As Agnes Lamb recalled, if you were not living in the town you were not so aware of the impact of, for example, the large number of Army personnel in the area. Others, like George McClymont, recalled the huge impact the GIs made in Portpatrick: they were generous with the children and boosted the local economy – three of his sisters ended up marrying Americans. Margaret Clark and John McColm both recalled the prisoners of war (POWs) who were billeted to work on farms in the area, while Betty Murray remembered her own Land Army days.

This selection also includes an extended extract from the interview with James Blair, who served in the Navy during World War II and whose war experiences took him far from home. This chapter finishes with a transcription from the interview with Geoffrey Wardley, who was stationed at Wig Bay in 1950 following his call-up in 1948.

Agnes Lamb

Now you would be about 18 when the War started Mrs Lamb?
    Aye. The War started in '39 …
There must have been awful changes in Stranraer?
    Well, it was very dramatic – let's put it that way – if I can cast ma mind

back. A can remember the morning [war] was declared an ma brother was ploughin and A ran across the fields to tell him the War had been declared. But he wasnae called-up because you see in them days, if you were working the ground you were needed, as it were. And it annoyed me very much because A wasnae allowed to be called-up either. Because all ma friends were away in the Wrens or the WAAFs or somethin and A wanted to be a driver in the ATS, but A wasnae allowed to go because A was needed ... . It wasnae only me, hundreds o people like me, they wanted to help.

But there must have been quite a lot of changes in Stranraer?

Well, I don't know how you want [me] to explain that. For instance, ma friends that were away, one in the WAAFs and one in the Wrens, if they were comin home on leave, you had to go ... [This] was ... up at the cross, Robertson had a shoe shop, and you had to go there to get a pass to get down the pier. You couldnae go down without it, to meet anybody. [There were] a lot o restrictions like that.

You got the pass out the shoe shop?

Well, actually he was actually a councillor, Jimmy Robertson, and he was allowed to give them out. Petrol was rationed, again which was very difficult. Sweets were rationed, clothes were rationed. All these things.

There must have been an awful ... influx of service men?

Yes, well, they had huts out where the rugby club is, and quite a few places they had these army huts. And the NAAFI had, across the road there where the library was for a while, that was a NAAFI place as well. An volunteers were cookin for troops [that] passed through. There was a lot [of] troops passin through ... . Of course, the blackout was the big thing. You had to get all your windows blacked out.

There must have been an awful lot of service men in the town?

Yes, there was. But in saying that Mrs McLucas, I wasnae livin in the town an you weren't in, you were only in doing your shoppin ... . If you [were] living in the town, you would have been more aware of it.

Did you not go to dances?

Well, we went to dances but that was at Leswalt. And they had dances there ... . A lot o the fellas from Wig Bay came there. But not in Stranraer, no ... . You must remember, you had to get back and forward. And petrol was rationed, you really only had to use it for necessary things. I shouldnae put this on a tape really, because the fact was, you know where the Castle Green [is]? ... Well, there were shops there, and A & L Douglas that were merchants had a shop there, we called it the 'dog shop' ... that's where people went to pay accounts. And one of my friends worked in it and once the War started and, em, I forget what they call the man, but it was to do wi transport an that, had a wee office at the back. He tested you for driving for a while, it was him that tested me as it happened. He was allowed coupons to give out, you know, to merchants that … they had to have a reason to get them like. And he was awful good, he was a nice man, and he used tae slip you a few odd coupons if you had a car. And I was always very popular, because I had plenty of coupons. But it is maybe not right to say it, but it is funny. He's dead now anyway, so he cannae be pulled back. Petrol was quite a thing.

Archie Bell

… I remember the German bombers going over when Belfast was bombed and the distinctive sound of them. I also remember my father was in the ARP and he didn't know what it was, but we saw a glow from Westcott, over the Cairnryan hills, and my parents thought this was Clydebank catching it again. And only recently when talking to the Women's Rural in Cairnryan, an elderly lady said, 'Oh, you're wrong'. That was the German bombers going to Belfast and they dropped incendiaries on the hills above Cairnryan to set them alight and this was a marker for them coming home [from] Belfast. They saw the fire, headed for that and that was them on their way home. I also remember mother being very worried that I would get out the gate because there was a continual stream of heavy lorries, or heavy lorries for those days, going from Colfin Creamery out to Wig Bay with rock for the construction of Wig Bay.

Betty Murray
[on Land Army days at Lochinch]

Did you live out there?
    Yes, the bothy in those days was … along the canal, and it was my first experience of an oil lamp. No electricity, no hot water, a range for cooking – which none of us could cook …. Mrs McKnight, who was [the wife of] one of the gamekeepers, he was away to war, and she came down and made the dinner. Which, in those days you had your dinner at dinner time, twelve or one o'clock. She cooked that and that was the only cooked meal we had. The rest I suppose was beans on toast and whatever was easily done. …
If you had no hot water, was there a bathroom?
    No. There was an outside toilet, away up the garden.
That must have been pretty primitive?
    It was, definitely.
How did you wash?

I think we must have heated water on the range in the morning and then just washed ourselves at the sink, because that was all there was. The water for drinking … you go along the canal, outside that gate there was a well and that is where we got the water for drinking. So we had to walk from the bothy right along there, fill the pail with water, bring it back to the bothy and that was your drinking water. For the water that came out of the tap was [only] for boiling.

[When you had time off did you], like the forces, [did you] get chits for your travel or anything?

No, the Land Army was different in a way. It was more just a job, although it was still, you were called up and that sort of thing, but you didn't get the benefits that the forces got at all.

Can you remember what you were paid?

I think it was £2 5/- a week, and I think there was so much taken off for the coke that we got for the fire. I think it was 5/- or something, I think we got £2. I think that was what it was if I can remember rightly. That sort of rings a bell. …

[In the bothy] we had a wireless and it worked by a battery, and you had two batteries. So we brought a battery into Patterson's in Hanover Street on a Saturday and we left the battery in. And it cost 6d. And we left one battery and collected the other one and did that every week, and that cost us 6d a week for the battery. That wireless belonged to Ciss Drummond [another land girl] … she had brought it with her.

George McClymont

The War made a difference to Portpatrick?

A big difference. Just after War broke out there was a contingent of soldiers and they were all based in the old church hall, and possibly the School Brae. There was a big contingent, about 100, which they were used to guard the radio station, the coastguard station with sentries round the harbour, as they normally would in wartime. Then, when America came into the War there was a lot of GIs came and they took over the whole of the Roslyn Hotel and the top portion of Portpatrick Hotel. There were probably 100. They were operating a radio station up at Lochnaw. I think the big mast is probably still there and that's where they were, but they were all stationed in the village. They made a big difference to the village. They were very generous, they were good to the kids. At Christmas time there were packets of sweets for every child in school … . It was the Americans that provided them. Economy in the village would rise greatly when they were there, for they spent a lot of money.

Of course, you have a family connection.

I have three sisters who finished up marrying Americans. Two married GIs and one married and she emigrated to America, but Lily and Bob McAulay, they courted all the time Bob was in Portpatrick, and then he got stationed down in England somewhere. He came back one time and he got accommodation at Roslyn, and I've still got his receipt for a month I think, 10/- a week for his accommodation, full board. But he had to bring his own ration book and towel. That was the stipulation, it said that on the little receipt.

So, while the War was on there would be no fishing out of Portpatrick?

We fished away, they did. Fortunately, there was never any contact with the enemy shipping, but they still fished. The herring fleet didn't come in during the War but there was what they called a steamer and it would pick up all the herring from the small boats at the Isle of Man, and it brought all the fish in.

That was quite dangerous.

It must have been …

Were they escorted?

No, there were no escorts. They just came in and unloaded, and went back the next day for another load. They came in about every day.

And nobody thought anything of that?

No, not one bit. I can remember during the War too, all the convoys that was going, Russian convoys, they all assembled off Portpatrick. And there was hundreds and hundreds of tankers and cargo ships, all sorts of ships … Destroyers and Corvettes.

Where could you see this?

Just off Portpatrick … . we were living at Eastcliff and you looked down over the sea and they were only a mile off … all assembled there. It was quite a sight.

Nowadays, you see, they would be looking for spies and terrorists. Was there any extra police?

There was a contingent of military police. They were always in the village.

That was really for the soldiers, not the civilians?

That's correct. But life just went on as per normal.

The food situation?

We never seemed to have much problem because we could always get fish and living in the village there was always plenty of farm produce … and you could always buy a bit of butter at a farm, and there was always plenty of grub available.

What about the blackout?

They were very strict with the blackout because we used to watch the German aircraft going over the village to bomb Belfast. And on moonlight

nights you could see droves and droves of these German aircraft. And we
stood and watched the bombing and the searchlights on the beach.

Could you actually see the fires?

Absolutely, you could see the fires.

And you stood outside and watched. You weren't hiding in a shelter?

No, we stood and watched. You could see the aeroplanes going over and
coming back.

Were there any shelters in Portpatrick?

Not to my knowledge, no. There was air-raid shelters.

So, if they had dropped one in Portpatrick that was tough?

One was dropped near the Freugh. Somebody was unloading and
probably one stuck, jammed or something, and let it go over the Freugh.
That was the only bomb I ever remember landing in this area.

    … the blackouts. The air-raid warden used to go round and [shout],
'Put the light out'.

Could you still go into the pictures?

You could still go to the pictures, but the trains were all blacked out. I
don't know why because I'm quite sure from the air they could see the fires
from the engines. However, everything was blacked out.

What like was Stranraer in the blackout?

Oh, terrible. It was very, very dark in wintertime. There was no street
lights, no lights from windows and by instinct you got back and forwards
from the pictures to the station.

The station at that time would be in Station Street?

It was the top station, aye.

John McColm

During the War years we were very short of staff and we often had, during
the harvest time, Italian prisoners helping for the harvest. They weren't
very happy. But two of them lived on the farm and to satisfy them my
mother made, what they would term pasta, for those Italian prisoners.
And they were very thankful for it. Towards the end of the War we had
many army lads to help at the harvest. They got leave from the Army.

Margaret Clark

… where did the German prisoners stay?

Well, they were stationed at just where I live out here across Fairway, there
was a big POW camp, and also one up in the high road next to Sheuchan

School – which later became a housing place …
And what did the German prisoners do?

Well, they worked on the farms. I remember working on the farms after school hours, or at weekends and holidays. We were encouraged to go out and do a bit lifting potatoes, thinning turnips. And I remember we used to have our lunch with them. We weren't fraternising with them, but we were kids. But they used to sign in their language. They used to sing their songs to us and probably [thought] a lot of their homeland and folks and families they had left behind, because they were really young men I would imagine.

James Blair

In 2004 Mr Blair recorded an interview relating his own active War service with the Navy. Some extracts from this interview are given here.

On November 14th 1940 I travelled from Stranraer to Skegness. I had never seen such flat country as Lincolnshire. Scarcely a tree to be seen as far as the distant horizon, and I realised this was it. The landscape was so depressing it brought to me the thought of how I might never see home again. I felt like weeping. At Skegness the barracks were named HMS Royal Arthur, a former Butlin's Holiday camp which had been taken over for the Navy. It was there we were rigged out in sailor's kit consisting of two suits, one working uniform and one dress uniform. Then we were issued with a sheet of brown paper, this was to parcel up our civvy clothes to be sent home.

… Our last memory of Skegness – the Sunday before leaving for Chatham there was a church service in which we sang 'Eternal Father' and began to realise what we were all in for. Just have a look at the words. All sung with deep feeling by several hundred young recruits, all in the same boat. It was very moving and never to be forgotten – just like the three times running around the camp at six-thirty every morning having shaved in lukewarm water in the air-raid shelter.

…

[In November 1941, James was in Campbeltown on an anti-submarine course and this enabled him to travel home for Christmas leave. The journey, however, proved very difficult.]

That course completed, we set out for home by bus to Tarbert on a snowy Saturday morning and from there by boat to Wemyss Bay. The snow was now very heavy but I got the train to Glasgow, only to find I had missed the last one to Stranraer and the bus service was only getting as far south as

Girvan. So I called up a cousin, Jim Christine, and he and Jean put me up overnight. There were no trains on Sunday, so I tried the bus service which by then had only managed as far as Ballantrae. I took a chance on it but there was no joy as the road was still impassable at Glenapp, so back I went to Girvan [and] caught a train to Kilmarnock and from there got as far as Carlisle. From Carlisle I took the early morning paper train to Dumfries and eventually arrived in Stranraer by bus Sunday midday. What I didn't realise at the time was that there was a flying service from Machrihanish, which is only a stone's throw from Campbeltown, to West Freugh, five miles from Stranraer … . I could have flown over in about 15 minutes!

[James went on to serve with the *Derwent* and was based out in the Red Sea escorting convoys at the time of this next extract.]

Derwent only lasted three months from January to March 1943. On that date we were at anchor in Tripoli harbour, the second night there was to be our last. It was a muggy night, you could hardly see a hand before your face. Suddenly the noise of attacking aircraft and explosions in the harbour sent us to action stations. I was on the pom-pom platform,[6] but we could see nothing when the ship was hit below the waterline by a circling torpedo. This was a devilish device which, when dropped went round in increasing circles until it hit some object, and it could cause tremendous damage. I was airborne in fact, but alas the lad within a few feet of me was never seen again … . There but for the grace of God.

We did have casualties, some of them fatal [and] with the loss of engine power we could do nothing, but fortunately the ship settled upright on the bottom. Another of these torpedoes hit a merchant ship, the *Ocean Voyager*, which was carrying 3000 tons of aviation spirit and 2500 tons of high explosives. The whole harbour was ablaze so we could see plenty now – a solid wall of flame, and in the slight breeze it was floating down in our direction. The captain sent most of the ship's company ashore but the officers remained. First job was to empty our ready-use lockers and ditch all the ammunition from the deck. The captain's plan was to use bearing-out spars to push the flaming jerry cans around the ship as they approached us. It was a very hot job but it worked so well that at the last stage the *Derwent* was completely surrounded but eventually it was all cleared ashore.

Geoffrey Wardley

Mr Wardley was called up in 1948 and was stationed to Wig Bay in January 1950.

He shared some of his experiences with Nancy McLucas in June 2015, including his first impressions of Stranraer and details about the crafts he helped repair and maintain.

Did you know what you were being sent here for?
> Yes, more or less. I was the only one of the course in Calshot in 1949 and didn't get moved on until after Christmas that year in 1950. I arrived here and thought I'd come to the end of the world. It was a stormy day. And, of course the train wouldn't go any further because of the weather. It was the *Princess Margaret* was lying there. I had to wait till after eight o'clock before they came and picked me up. That is when the boat train came in early in the morning.

Were you the only one or were you part of a group?
> No, I was the only one at the time. Another chap came later on.

So you were actually sent here on your own. Had you ever heard of Wigtownshire before?
> No, or Stranraer …
>
> …

How many boats were on the loch when you arrived?
> We had to guard about 100. And where Kirkcolm school is built now, that was all flat. Scaur Point we call it. There was about 100-odd flying boats there because they were bringing them up then for a death-bed.
>
> …

Have you any idea what happened to the flying boats?
> They all got scrapped. A few of them went to South Africa, or somewhere. I think some went on to New Zealand because they have a very long range on fueling and it's a pity they didn't still have them when the Falkland's War was on. They would be handy to land on the water and take off. They wouldn't be like a sitting target like the boats are.
>
> …

… what were you doing at Cairnryan?
> On the boats again, repairing damaged boats or anything like that. Because they used to take all the ammunition out [on] them and dump it in Beaufort's Dyke … . Old landing barges had to roll the stuff off …
>
> … [These] were steel boats, landing barges … . I repaired the runways they used [when] rolling the bombs off.

12

Princess Victoria disaster

The *Princess Victoria* disaster is an integral part of the collective history of Stranraer and is also the subject of a Stranraer and District Local History Trust publication, 'The Loss of the *Princess Victoria*'. The interview extracts given here, although short, bring us very close to how it must have felt to be in Stranraer on 31 January 1953.

Mhairi Mitchell

Mhairi's grandfather, father and husband were all involved with the lifeboats. Her father had retired by the time of the *Princess Victoria* disaster, and her husband was away in Fraserburgh, but here Mhairi shared her own memories of that day:

… you must remember the Princess Victoria *[disaster]?*
 Yes, I remember that … . My sister and I listened to it on the old wireless set and we got the shipping band, and we listened to all about the *Victoria* on this shipping band, and it was the *Pass of Drumochter*, the *Orchy* were two of the main ships that came to the rescue. They were away up north, I think, and they came to the rescue.
So, it must have been pretty horrible listening?
 Oh, it was a terrible, terrible day. And it was a north wind, and usually here it is a south-westerly that is our bad wind for the sea. But it was north that day and when our lifeboat went out from the inner harbour to the outer harbour, even then you could hardly see it before it got out to the mouth of the opening there. You could hardly see it. It was ferocious.
And how long was the boat out?
 Well, it was a bit unfortunate. They didn't get the signal till about ten o'clock in the morning and they picked up two survivors and they took them to either Larne or Belfast and the boat did not come back till the next day.

So how did people in Portpatrick hear? Was it the rockets going off or what alerted them?

Yes. There was only the rockets in those days.

When did they find out [that] it was the boat from Stranraer?

That I don't know.

And you were listening to the shipping?

Yes. But you see the boat had gone down at – they got the message about seven in the morning, but our lifeboat didn't go out till ten o'clock. There was something. I don't know what it was. The Girvan [one] was out, the Donaghadee one was out, and our one was out. But our one went out later, about ten o'clock …

…

… there was always a standby crew but there was always a secretary to call out the boat, but there was the coxswain and a mechanic, and, I think, it was another six.

And how did they get in touch with them?

Well, just by phone, and then the rockets went off. And one was for the coastguards, and two rockets for the lifeboat. And if the [coastguard] crew and the lifeboat crew had to go out, there was three rockets went off. Nowadays they have all these pagers.

Heather Short and Margaret Short

Both women worked with the telephone exchange in Stranraer.

… were you both in the exchange at the time of the Princess Victoria*? You weren't Heather, but you were Margaret?*

MS: Yes, I was.

Now, what are your memories of that?

MS: I was on duty that morning the boat went down, and I remember the ship's radio, Portpatrick 311, and 209, the coastguard, kept in touch … . All emergency numbers were listed on one back board so that they got priority treatment. I remember them telling us that the ship was in trouble but we couldn't believe it. It was a dull, very dreich morning, wasn't it, stormy, just unbelievable. We still couldn't believe it was happening because she was in trouble. She left Stranraer about nine-thirty, which was her normal sailing time, and she was outside the loch before they realised how serious the trouble was, and by that time we had heard about it, she was drifting and they were sending out lifeboats.

…

And how many of you were on duty that morning?

MS: Was there about four on a Saturday morning? There would normally be about four of us on a Saturday morning. A skeleton staff. We would go off duty, that would be our half-day, and it was only after that we realised the ship had gone about two o'clock, two-thirty. As I say it was such a shock to us. It hit us more when we were at home and people came to the door, people who had relatives on the ship. And they came to the door that night, I remember, asking if I had heard any news of their relatives and what was happening and so forth. So others that had been on duty with me, day staff, set off that night [and] went down to the telephone exchange, which was just chaos, to relieve those who were on duty. There was just no break at all, and we worked right through the morning.

And where were these calls coming from?

MS: All over, because it was a manual board you understand, they were coming from England, Scotland, they were coming from all over. And the incoming position was just ablaze and we could hear people crying in the background.

HS: … You were dealing with, how many calls Margaret, on a switch-board … you were dealing with 12 calls all diversified to different types of calls and all over the country. … not a lot of people can cope with it. You know the old-fashioned exchanges, when you had the big high board like they had in Coatbridge, where you jumped to put the cords in. These cords that you would deal with, I wasn't there then, they would be every-where. It was a very concentrated thing, if you didn't have a break after so many hours, you would be ill.

13

The Storm in the Winter
of 1947–48

The weather, unsurprisingly, featured in a number of interviews. Here are just two extracts, both relating to the same storm but from different viewpoints. These extracts remind us of the value of first-person accounts in enabling us to build a more complex history of a shared experience.

John Carruth

On Wednesday, 12th March, 1947, a crowd of young fellas like myself went to Glasgow to a football match which was the Scottish League versus the English League. After the game we left St Enoch's Station at ten past five, and by the time we got to Irvine station there was a little snow on the platform. By the time we got to Troon, the platform was covered. By the time we got to Prestwick, the platform was even deeper covered. Time we got to Maybole it was well covered and Barrhill, it was really bad. Then we stopped at Glenwhilly station and after we came out of Glenwhilly station the train got stuck at the first cutting south of the station. We were in the train from Wednesday evening until Friday morning. Some of us were in compartments where the weight of the snow broke the glass and, fortunately, some of us were in compartments where the glass was not broken. So we all crowded into each other's compartments, and we were reasonably comfortable. There were a number of boxes of Lyons' cakes which were consigned to West Freugh for the airmen. That was the only food that was on the train, and we tried to persuade the guard to let us have some food on the Thursday, because we were all very hungry. But he refused to open the guards' van to let us have access to the cakes. However, some of the men got a hold of the guard and went into his pockets and took the key out and opened the guards' van and we got in to the cakes, opened up the boxes, and the cakes were distributed to all the passengers which, I think, was about 140 on the train. So, all the eight boxes of cakes were devoured. [*laughter*] We then spent the Thursday night on the train, very cold, but some of us were quite young, like myself, and we managed to overcome the cold. But it was very bad for some of the older ladies. On the Friday morning we got out of … the train and jumped down into the snow. There would be about 30 or 40 of us and we started to walk from Glenwhilly through the snow, as near to the railway line as we possibly could, and arrived at New Luce station between five and six in the evening. There was a train of coal wagons with a big squad of men with shovels, and they were shoveling the snow into the coal wagons … . When the train was loaded with the snow it set off and we got back into Stranraer about seven o'clock at night. The train was then shunted back out of Stranraer town station and the wagons were taken down to the pier station where the snow was unloaded into the sea. The remainder of the passengers, the elderly women and the young women [who] remained with the elderly women … they didn't get back into Stranraer until Saturday evening. All in all it was quite an experience.

Willie Darroch (railwayman)

Mr Darroch recalled the same incident.

> There is quite a story about that … the 1947 snow. And I was on the snow plough and the others were sitting in the bothy, in the shed. And I said to the chief, 'What about someone else having a go at this now?' … We went out, two engines and a snow plough, and it's quite a story about that, because there was flat couplings in some of the engines. One of the engines was the worst and when you hit a bank of snow when you went to this place Swansneck, about three or four different curves and high cutting and they were filling with snow. [They] finally got prisoners of war, who were stationed in Stranraer, to come and dig parts out of the snow so we could have another bash at it. And, with the slack couplings and the engines, the first engine hit the snow. There was a long coupling between the two, the second engine hit the first engine, and it wasn't very comfortable, and we dug in three or four times before we got through. There was another snow plough coming from Ayr direction, from the Girvan direction, and it hit something heavy. I think it was frozen snow and such like. … The guard used to stay across the road there … he decided he would take some of the ones who were fit, quite fit, he pointed out what it would be like. He brought them from Glenwhilly station where they were [stranded], he brought them down through the snow, and some waited …

14

Ghostly Happenings

Hugh Reid

When they met for their interview in January 2006, and before he told Nancy about his poaching adventures, Hugh Reid entertained her with anecdotes about some of the ghostly incidents and mysterious occurrences that had happened in Stranraer.

Mr Reid, you said there was a murder in the Backrampart, was this when you were a boy?

> A boy, yes. Well, this man wis the rent collector and here he went a-missin an they didnae know who done the murder, but years later on these people in the Backrampart – they were Irish people – and they more or less got the blame o killin him, but they couldn't prove it. And when this Irishman died, the horse and the hearse … came doon the Backrampart and they put the coffin in the hearse an the horses wouldn't pull it. The horses went down on their knees. So Andy McClelland, he took the horses back out and he marched them to the top o the Backrampart and then marched them back down again, locked them back into the hearse, but still they refused it. After that, I don't know how – ah, mean A wis young then – they got him away, or took him away. But later on, my father … and mother stayed up in one of the rooms with my Uncle Alex. And here, one night – he worked on the oyster boats, my father – he woke up in the bed. And he'd only my brother at the time, Robert, and here he felt th[is] weight in his legs an he got up […] an here, it wis the man that hid got murdered. It was his ghost, or spirit or something. So, he never said anything. He said, 'I couldn't say anythin to your mother because we hid no place to go, because we'd hae cleared out'. So, he says, '[I used to be up at] night-time and I watched him walkin from the mantelpiece to the door'.

The ghost of the murdered rent collector?

> Yes, he used to walk back and forrit. And, he said, my mother was telling a

lady one time about one of the girls [...] of the same family, and she hid
been in the room across fae where they lived and she was chased out of the
room ... by the ghost of the man.

Was this before you were born?

No, no. I wis only about seven years old at the time. And, my father's
brother used tae come up for him at five o'clock in the morning, for tae go
down tae the boat. So this morning he come up and he got crushed in the
stairhead. He telt me father, he said, 'I'm not coming back up here again,'
he says, 'Whoever got me gave me an awful squeezing on the stair head' ...
So this man John Higgins, he'd been comin up the Backrampart an the
same thing happened to him. He got crushed too. And they have a good
idea who done the murder but they couldnae blame it on the person. But
they knew, my mother and my father, they knew who done the killing.

Is that building away now?

I don't know if that building is away or not, down there at the
Backrampart. There used to be a big stone at it. I used to hear them talkin
about the big stone.

Did anybody every call the police or the doctor or anybody like that?

Well, in them days ... they wir desperate days. I heard my father talkin
about them. They made a law o their own. There was a man called Stuart
... and they all carried guns. Old poachers. And they made their own law.
.... But, the police wid come mibby ... they weren't the same as this
present day. They hadnae the same thing to [investigate] murders and they
were more or less jist policemen, they werenae detectives.

*And when you were a wee boy, did you every feel this ghost about where you were
living?*

It niver bothered me, anyway. There was only one [it bothered], my father.
It didn't bother with our family.

... It didn't bother your mother?

My mother used to tell me aboot when my father had a good drink in him
an he used to mainly lie out on the street, at the door. And as just as far as
my memory cries me back, a woman called Melanie Higgins ... she said
she could hear this thing dancing round about ma father where he was
lying [there]. This thumping about wi a boot. And she said, many a time
she thought he'd be kicked to death. She had been lookin at him in the
morning, an he was alright .... Whatever this thing was that danced
round about him and you could hear the thumpin about. And we thought
... lyin drunk, there he'd be kicked tae death, but he wis alright. But the
spirit never bothered our family but it bothered the other family, the
Irishmen. It bothered them.

*Have you any idea why he was murdered. Was it because he was the rent collector
[and he had money]?*

Yes, he was the rent collector … and he had the money. That's what it was
…

… And, was the rent collector a local man?

I believe he was. I heard his name an all … I don't know if it wis
McClelland they called him, or something.

There must have been an investigation?

Aye, there wid be, yes, but they never found out who done the murder
anyway. But the people that lived there, they had a good idea who done it.
Because the ghost was there anyway, the spirit was there. And still my
Uncle Alex lived in that room, it never bothered him. An he lived there for
years. An he saw it umpteen times, and it niver bothered him. After my
father got another house and it still lived in the house, and it wouldn't
leave the house – and it never bothered him.

Now you know some other ghost stories?

Oh yes, aye. Well, I tell you the truth this was what happened to my father.
He was courting ma mother at the time and it was up where the Galloway
Creamery is now. It was just barren land then – that was before my time.
And he worked on the oyster boats and he always carried a big knife then,
for openin the oysters. And this night they were lying on the bank across
fae the old nursery … .There was a nursery up there, where the big grocer's
shop is now. Jist wild country, and they were lying on the bank and he seen
this fellow comin across from the nursery an he said, 'I looked at him. I
thought he had been watching me, what I was doing'. So, he says, 'I got up
and walked forrit and [this man] walked across the road and I kept
followin behind him. An just when I got to the hedge, I was gonna put the
knife in him'. Oh, yes, in them days they didn't care. They aa carried
knives and guns. An then, he said, as he got to the hedge, [sound of the
wind whooshing] a whoosh of wind. 'I knew then what I'd tackled' he
says. 'I happened to [have] this half bottle o whisky … had in my pocket
and drank it' he says. And, he says, '[I] knew I'd tackled something beyond
my means,' he says.

And had he any idea who this person was?

He never said who it was, but he said it was unearthly anyway.

But not somebody he knew … like the rent man?

No, nothin like that. At the same place years ago, I was 13 or 14 then,
[Anonymous] and me wir poachin wi dogs an we killed a few rabbits an
that. And we used to hide them an then go back at night-time an get
them, ken, tae avoid the police. So this night, here's a man about 40 or 50
years of age, and, we went away out to get these rabbits an come in … . An
when we come in we walked down past the Creamery, just the same bit, an
here we heard this chain rattling. [Anonymous] said, it must be one of the
farmer's dogs who'd broke away [an] it wis trailin the chain behin it. So,

anyway, when we got down a wee bit further this chain got closer and closer tae us till we got to near where it stopped. I jist remember it was a dog, about that height, an its eens were blazin. An this man and me, he said, 'Run for your life, if you run tonight'. And we ran right down to Pritty Mill Close and he told his wife about it, what we'd seen, this dog. It wis the size o a cuddy ... I had an idea it was the devil, that's what it was. It was unearthly. It was a bad place the Galloway Creamery. They said that, up there at that nursery there. I've heard men saying that before.

So where the Creamery is now was a place that was haunted? ... Had something happen[ed] there that made it a bad place?

I couldn't say if anythin happened there before, or no. I wis workin with [a] man called Willie Pirrie, an he was kinda [foreman] for the toon, and he heard me telling this story to some chap when we were workin up there. And he said, 'Who told you that?' ... I says, 'Ma father'. And then he believed me, because he'd seen the same thing ... at the same place.

Any more?

Yes. Well, one night there wis, [Anonymous 1], [Anonymous 2] and myself an we were poaching. An we'd been in the Approach there, early, at six o'clock at night and we came back out again.

The Approach?

Yes, Culhorn. And we got a good few rabbits. And we came out there at the Wee Aird, Loves of the Wee Aird. There were no houses or nothin else then, just the barren ground. So [Anonymous 1] went in tae get a flask, an somethin tae eat. So this chap and me, we went to the back of hedge ... it was a cold night. So I said, 'Give me a knock when [Anonymous 1] comes out'. So I was lying at the back o the dyke. He went, 'Hey. Hey'. 'What?' 'Look at this,' he says. Comin up McMasters Road, this lady wis dressed in pure white, jist walked right up the road, about from here to the window. Passed us there, right round the Loves of the Wee Aird and away down by Cairney's Corner. And I said ... 'Don't tell to [Anonymous 1] when he comes out. He'll say we're scared, we're feart'. So we never mentioned it to him. So, we got on to the bikes, [Anonymous 1] came out and we went down to the shore and up round Archie Douglas's farm, up the hill, an we went in to Balker ... to poach. An here, this chap, when we're pittin the nets out, he says, 'Mind thon woman we seen?' 'Aye'. 'When we went through Archie Douglas's farm there,' he says, 'She passed between your bike and mine, right through the farm'. He says, 'I seen her again'.

Who was this?

I don't know, don't know who she was.

So you've seen quite a few apparitions?

Oh, yes.

... are you the seventh son of the seventh son or something like that?

No. I don't know what I am … Ma brother … he was a man like that. He could hae seen things. He could have told you any place where there wis evilness.

There were never good ghosts then?

No, no … . Well I'll tell you a story about my brother, an his wife an all knew this was the truth. This is no lie or nothing. Him and me had a good drink, it was Hogmanay time. And we came up tae his house, and the two brothers, McDowalls they called them – the one was dead and [my brother had been] great mates with him – and one stayed his self. So he left his wife and me together, and he said 'I have to go along and wish Peter a Happy New Year now' … . They lived along John Simpson Drive. Here, he went along and [when] he come back, he was due sober. His wife said, 'Be God, you weren't long sobering up, boy'. 'Jean,' he says, 'I'm gaun tae my bed, an don't waken me the night, please.' She said, 'That's funny. There must be somethin wrong wi him. I don't know, Hogmanay an gaun tae his bed'. So a long while after it, I asked Jean, did he ever tell ye what happened that night. She said, 'He did, and you ask him an he'll tell you the same thing' … . He said he went along to see the brother an when he went in, he sat down beside the brother and they had a drink. And, he said, they had two or three drinks and he said, 'You know, about ten minutes after it the other brother was sittin beside me, that was dead' … . It sobered him up. He could … see death. He could tell you anything, he was gifted that way. He was very strong. He went once into my brother's house tae drink … and he went in the door. He says 'I'm not comin into this house, boys.' He said to my brothers, 'This is an evil house boys'. Evil – I thought they were goin tae fight. 'Don't tell me that my house is evil.' Well, his wife was an awful woman for cursin an swearin. His wife said some terrible things. I didnae like her. The language that she used, ye ken, was bad … . This woman up the stair, her daughter worked in the George Hotel, and she said they heard the row last night down there 'with your brothers, your brother telling them it was an evil house'. But, she said, 'That's funny, for my daughter was going out at five o'clock in the morning, goin to her work, and she said when she went out a little lady walked up the steps with her – to the road – and [so] she turned and came back and battered on the door to get back, in again'.

And who was this?

I don't know, couldnae say who it was. My brother … he could have told you something, he seen things. Sometime he scared me myself. I said, 'Don't start that again, boy'. Well, this is true. He was in the Navy, and he was in the … convoys going to Archangel and he was in the first trip, and he was in the second trip. He wrote a letter to his wife from the ship and told her he was goin to be torpedoed at a certain time. [The] night he wid be torpedoed. And he wrote the letter and sealed it and said to all the men, 'I'm gettin all my clothes ready for whenever we're hit'. She kept the letter, and on that day and date, that night, he was torpedoed … . He survived [and] they fished him out of the water. But he knew the day it was going to happen, and she kept that letter for a long time, and showed it to people. How did he know the night he was going to be torpedoed? An he knew, he told the men in the boat, he said, 'We'll get hit at a certain time'. And they just laughed at him, and they did get hit.

You never were tempted, in that case, to put money on the horses … if your brother could see what was happening?

No, he wasnae a gambler. He never bothered with horses or gambling or playing cards … . He might have took a drink and that …

It was really unpleasant things that he saw.

He was a great man for a joke an that, but … he seemed he could feel where there was danger some places. He had that kin o inclination, that there was danger about some place.

Have you any more stories?

Ma faither … in his day there wis some evil things done. My mother used to tell me about these things that people [did]. There was a man called Stewart and that, and they just took the law into their own hands, an they all carried guns. They mair or less made their own law. An he was sayin one night, he wanted to do a bit poachin about the Dochra moor. And he had to walk up the railway line, and he had the dog with him for chasin the rabbits into the net, [the dog] didn't catch them it just chased them in. And he went up onto the line at the Galloway Creamery to walk up the line to come out at the viaduct … . He had to walk up the viaduct then, and out to get tae the woods to poach. An, he said when he was a good bit up the line he heard this man walkin, comin down the other way. And he thought maybe it was a surfaceman. He said the dog was on that side … and the dog was very vicious. If anybody [did anythin] he would have went for them. The man was walking in the middlest sleepers, so you could hear them being tramped down. He said, 'The man passed me by and I never even seen him'.

Now this would be on the old Portpatrick line?

Yes, that's right. He says, the dog never noticed or touched him. If he'd been a gamekeeper the dog would have went for him right away. The dog just ignored him … . He could hear the footsteps. He thought it was maybe the surface men working on the railway line. He said, 'I never saw anybody'. [That wis] at the same bit, at the Creamery again.

Now there is some story about Cairnryan Road?

That was a story that was a story that was told to ma father … . My father was a fisherman and … my mother's mother had told her about this man

Dr Orgle, who was a doctor. And he always went oot at night-time, and
the horses were shod wi rubber and the coach was shod wi rubber, so you
couldn't hear them. And they said if there had been anybody on the road
… they would have picked you up and you were took to Dr Orgle, and he
experimented on you. An he said that they were coming back from the
fishing, and they had to leave their boats at Ballantrae and had to walk
back into Stranraer. You see they were sailing boats in them days. And he
said he met this stallion driver with the horse, and he kent my father and
his brother. He said 'Will you be passing by the house, Joe, the night'.
'Aye.' 'I wonder if you would go in and see if the daughter is alright.' He
says, 'She wasn't just keeping [the best of health in] her head and all that'.
And his wife was dead. So [they] said that [they] would call in and see her.
So they went and knocked on the door and she was there, the girl. They
went in and she made them a cup tea and they weren't long in till the
coach drew up at the door. [They] heard him. And, he said, 'If we hadn't
been in they would have got their hands in, but [they] flew back up the
road with the horses'. Dr Orgle.

Dr Who?

Dr Orgle. Dr Orgle they called him. She was telling me once what her
mother had told her. Paddy Cooke and [them] they used to play cards. It
wasn't for money, it was for hens, at Whitelees. She said we had to go and
look for Paddy, and we got him and fetched him back. And we came into
the town and seen the coach, and she says to Paddy, 'Paddy, son, if you've
ever run in your life – run tonight'. An they ran down into Princes Street,
and if they hadn't have gone into Princes Street they'd have got them too.
Seems the same as Burke and Hare you see. I always remember the name,
Dr Orgle …

And did he live in Stranraer?

… Yes, and the coach worked in Stranraer too. It was shod with rubber
and the horses feet were shod with rubber too, [so] that you couldn't hear
them.

Did nobody ever do anything about this?

I couldn't say, mistress, to tell you the truth. But, ma mother told me
things that her mother told her, and you couldn't really believe the things
that really happened. Because they made their own law, she says.

*… Now we are in Mr and Mrs Jack Findlay's house and Mrs Findlay has remem-
bered another ghost story that her father told her. Annabelle?*

Right, this happened round about the time of the First World War. In
Hanover Street there was a shoemaker and his son went, I think he went
around the beginning of the First World War, and he was subsequently
killed. Now, my father told me that people would not walk past that shop

at night because they could see the image of this young man on the screen of the shop inside. The shoemaker had taken on an assistant and, because there was a basement in the building, the young man went down into it and came back up and protested that [the shoemaker] already had someone employed. When he described the person in the basement, who at that time he saw him was wearing uniform, the old man said that was his son who had been killed, I think, probably about a year before. But, it was a well-known story in Stranraer because the majority of people of my father's age were too frightened to go past.

Thank you. And you have another story?

When I worked in the telephone exchange, latterly I trained girls. And I was up in this room at the top of the building training girls, and when they finished their day's work they would go and I would be left to clear up all the paraphernalia. Now, I knew about the ghost [McGibney's ghost] but it had never bothered me. I never thought anything about it until this day in winter which, by that time it was dark. I heard heavy feet on the stairs, thought nothing of it, and saw the door handle turn, and I thought, 'Right, okay, who's coming to bother me now.' And I went over to the door and opened it and there was no one there at all, no one on the stairs. [I] went down to the exchange, and when I said to them, no one had left the switchroom. So I must have experienced a ghost. It was a creepy experience.

Now back to Mr Reid.

Mrs McMillan and me, we were great friends with her husband and we visited them a lot. She had a son on the boat, David McMillan.

This is the Princess Victoria?

She was always complaining about her hands being cold, Mrs McMillan, and I said 'I'm going to buy you a pair of gloves'. I was going to buy these gloves at all costs, they weren't dear in those days, but I would get her a pair of gloves for her hands. So I went away to some place and I got the gloves, black gloves, and I said 'There's the gloves I got you'. So she put the gloves on and I thought on after. That's when the *Victoria* went down, a fortnight after it. And she lost her son on it. And that was a coincidence, me buying the black gloves. I thought on it after that … now there you are, me buying a pair of black gloves for her and there's her son David drowned on the boat. Now, what made me buy her a pair of black gloves.

And any other colour would have done.

I thought on it after it, I never mentioned it to her, there you are. I went and bought that woman a pair of black gloves and there's her son lost on the boat, David. It was a kind of coincidence … me buying a pair of black gloves, never bought her anything else but a pair of black gloves, the lady.

She lost her son after it on the boat, David.

... Another story?

This was the murder caused ... through in Black's pub at the Cross yonder, Petrucci's got it now. And they were all in joking. They were all poachers, with their guns an their dogs. And one happened to say to Jimmy Douglas, 'They tell me your father is leaving the house to Jock'. 'Oh no, he cannae leave the house to him, I'm the oldest son'. ... 'Well', he says, 'he's leaving the house to him. He's the man getting the house'. 'Oh, well. I'll see about that.' So he went up [to see] and the old man, [who] was in the house. He says, 'Father, what about this house? ... They tell me you're leaving the house to Jock'. 'No, son, I'm no leaving the house to nobody. I never mention these things'. He says, 'If anybody gets it, you'll be the yin.' 'Oh no, father,' he says. An he took the gun like that, out, an blew the old man's head off. And then he just stepped back, like that, and below his own chin – and blew his head off his self. And Jock, he cleared out to Drummore, never came back. That was the murder in Glebe Street.

When was that?

Oh, that was before my time. My father knew all about it. And the old house, when we were boys we were used to this man coming in and it was only just the ruins. It wasn't worth any money, it was just ruins of a house in them days. He used to come in and red it up, and clean it up, and tidied it up – the old ruins – and then he walked away back to Drummore.

That's some walk.

Aye. He thought nothin of it.

15

Stranraer in Photograph
by Donnie Nelson

Donnie Nelson spent his professional life working with the *Stranraer and Wigtownshire Free Press* and was a founding member of the Stranraer and District Local History Trust. During his time at the *Free Press*, his keen interest in history, and photographs, led him to run a column 'A Peep At The Past' which printed photographs relating to the area, along with the known contextual information. Readers would often reply to Donnie, providing more information on where or when images were taken, or the people or events depicted.

This selection, and Donnie's commentaries, reflect his interest in community life as well as wartime Stranraer. His contribution illustrates the valuable way in which images can help historians and ethnologists to construct a more nuanced understanding of a particular time and place. As well as the physical evidence presented in the chosen image, we also have Donnie's own experience and knowledge to help us to understand and interpret the content. The final item, about the *Marquis of Hartington*, is a particularly good example of this approach. All images are reproduced with kind permission of the Nelson Collection.

11 February 1982 (A)

This photograph was possibly the oldest photograph of a stage production in Stranraer ever published in the *Free Press*. Nothing is known, unfortunately, of the play or where and when it was produced, though it is known that the players were a group of young people belonging to St Joseph's Church, Stranraer, and it was staged as part of an entertainment arranged by the congregation of the church.

It is quite evidently a deathbed setting and was possibly the final scene of a religious play. Six of the young people shown in the image could be named. Standing on the left with the candle is Miss Cissy McGeoch, of Portpatrick and Stranraer. Beside her, dressed as a priest and carrying a crucifix, is her cousin Miss Helen (Nelly) Hughes of Stranraer, and kneeling on the far left in the front row is Helen's sister, Miss Isabella

Young Players, St Joseph's Church, Stranraer.

Hughes. On the right of the back row is Miss Bessie Walls of Stranraer and the little boy kneeling in front with his back to the camera is Hugh (Sonny) McDavitt of Stranraer.

The central figure on the couch is Miss Agnes O'Neill of Stranraer, a cousin of Miss McGeoch and the Hughes girls. Miss McGeoch was the eldest daughter of Peter McGeoch of Fairview (now the Thistle public house) in Dalrymple Street, Stranraer, and Fernhill, Portpatrick. Peter, who died in 1902, made a considerable fortune in the United States as a young man and returned to Stranraer to establish a reputation as a very successful farmer and cattle dealer. The daughter pictured here became Mrs Mercer. Helen Hughes emigrated to Canada and later moved to the United States where she died in New York in 1948. She never married. Her sister Isabella became Mrs Peter Hannay and with her husband owned the Grapes Hotel in Stranraer in the 1930s. She was the fourth member of her family to be connected with the Grapes, her grandfather, Laurence Hughes, having built the original inn of that name in the town.

Miss Walls was later Mrs Cullen and Hugh McDavitt was the son of Dan McDavitt who had a pawnbroking establishment in Queen Street and a considerable reputation as a larger-than-life figure in the community. Miss O'Neill, later Mrs Murray, was the daughter of Pat O'Neill, a member of another local family of influence with their ownership of several ships which plied from the Old Pier in connection with their coal business. An assessment of the meagre knowledge of the players shown here has led to a tentative dating of 1894–96 for this photograph.

Stranraer and District Amateur Operatic Society, production of *At The White Horse Inn*, 1971.

At the White Horse Inn (B)

'There's joy the whole summer through' was the promise of the next line of the popular stage production's opening chorus. There certainly was, and enjoyment as well, when the Stranraer and District Amateur Operatic Society presented their fourth show to the public in 1971 in Stranraer Academy Hall.

It was at a meeting held on 17th May 1967 that a decision was taken to set up the society, the brainchild of Harry Beeby, a man who had come to live in the area shortly before with his wife and family. Harry's wife, Jane, was a music teacher at the Academy and Harry persuaded Mr Gordon Teale, the headmaster of the school, to take on the duties of chairman of the society they hoped to bring into being. The meeting, attended by 42 people, a few of whom had already committed themselves to undertake places on the committee or production group, agreed without hesitation that such a society would fulfil a need in Stranraer and could encourage others to join.

The rest, as they say, is history. In February of the following year *Brigadoon* became the society's first production and it is on record that after the first show of a four-night run all the tickets for the remainder of the week were sold out the next morning. And it was a success that was largely founded on the expertise of the 'Wilson and Wilson' hands on the wheel: Ailie Millar Wilson was the producer and Eric G Wilson the musical director. Both put in a tremendous amount of hard work and inspired others to give the same commitment. Four-night runs very quickly became a full week for each show and every night was a sell-out.

The reputation of the society was enhanced not only by the singing and acting of those on stage. The locally recruited orchestra and the magnificent stage settings and scenery commanded a great deal of respect and there were occasions when backcloths were passed on to other societies who were only too eager to use the talents further. This photograph, taken during the dress rehearsal, shows the cast, all in costume and make-up, against one of the backcloths painted by a member of the stage crew.

Almost 60 members were on stage for this production and the enthusiasm which the society had built on would last for almost 40 years before things suddenly got tighter and players and backstage crew became difficult to gather. When key personnel became really scarce there was a wise decision to withdraw from the scene for a few years rather than attempt productions which lacked support and it was then that the society did become history.

Anyone for tennis? (C)

First mention of a tennis club in the Stranraer area is in the *Free Press* of 6 May 1886, when there is an intriguing reference to the Stranraer Lawn Tennis Club 'recommencing'. Three months later the paper, for two successive weeks, mentioned the club's 'second annual tournament'.

Stranraer. Lawn Tennis Club, c. 1906

Where exactly this club operated in the town is not stated but for many years it was understood by members that the first club had lawn courts at Sun Street, on ground which had belonged originally to the bowling club which later became the West End Bowling Club.

It is known that the Sun Street courts were changed to blaes surfaces in 1906. There are plenty of references to annual tournaments and matches with other clubs during the remainder of the 1880s and right through the last decade of the nineteenth century. A special day in the club's story took place in 1893 when a match was played against the Bellevue Club of Ayr.

This photograph is not dated but is thought to have been taken around the opening of the new blaes courts in 1906 and that date would certainly fit with the identification of the young Eric Anderson, fifth from the left in the back row. In later years he was more familiar to Stranraer people as Dr Anderson and he has been picked out in a few other tennis photographs taken around this time.

The location of the photograph is definitely the Sun Street courts and the small pavilion behind the group and off to the right has been compared and matched with other prints of the earliest pavilion there. It seems to have been an all-wooden erection and the peculiar lattice-type paneling behind the small viewing balcony also helps to identify it.

Following World War I the club seemed to become much more active with tournaments, open days and sales of work to gather in funds. In 1920 it is recorded that a Stranraer tennis team visited Larne for a friendly match and two years later we find the Irish players coming to Sun Street for a return match. It is known that a fair number of visits, back and forward, kept the clubs in touch between the two wars.

The club carried on a quiet existence after the war years and there was a spell under the guidance of Mr Percy Jordan, club secretary for many years, when attempts were made to establish an open championships as an annual event. It did not last however and when Percy and his family went off to Australia the club lost a very hard-working member. Some years later the club came to an arrangement to use the municipal courts at Stair Park and the ground at Sun Street was subsequently used for a housing development.

The members of the Sun Street club were very fortunate for many years in the way their club had come into existence and also because of the attitude towards it by the people who owned the ground which was occupied by the pavilion with its balcony, changing rooms and general lounge and the three playing courts. As mentioned above, the area had originally been used for bowling until the club were able to purchase a more suitable site to the west of the town.

The owners of the three large houses on the opposite side of Sun

Street had purchased the ground initially and leased it for bowling as it meant their wonderful view of Loch Ryan was saved from any development which might impinge on this. The owners were quite happy to continue the lease for tennis as their view was again preserved. In return, the yearly rental to the tennis players was quite cheap.

One of the three owners was Mr Roland Adair, a local solicitor, and it was one of the duties of the captain of the tennis club to cross Sun Street once a year and hand over the rental to Mr Adair. The old gentleman would accept the cheque offered to him, give the captain of the club tea and cakes and chat with him about how the club was progressing and enquire about new members. He also promised to return the visit shortly as he felt he should keep in touch with the members. True to his word, Mr Adair would drop into the club one evening in the following week and be introduced to new members and exchange greetings with those he knew. And, as he left later, he would hand back the cheque he had been given the week before and indicate it was a donation to the club. It was little wonder that Stranraer Tennis Club was a happy place for members and players.

Royal visits to Stranraer, 1955 (D)

The year 1955 was a memorable one for the people of Stranraer and District. In April that year the Queen Mother had a short holiday at Lochinch Castle as a guest of Lord and Lady Stair and though there were no public functions to interrupt what was a private break she did visit the town council offices at Dunbae House where she met Provost Alf Walker and his fellow councillors on an informal basis.

A few months later, in August, there were much more reasons for the people of Stranraer and Wigtownshire to celebrate royal occasions when the Queen and Prince Philip visited the town and were officially received at a civic reception by Provost Walker and the councillors and their wives at the Town Hall. The royal guests signed the burgh visitors' book and spent some time with the councillors and their wives before going off on a tour around various sites in the county.

The royal party, which included Prince Charles, Princess Anne and Prince Michael of Kent, had sailed into Cairnryan earlier that morning aboard the Royal Yacht *Britannia* and the children stayed at Lochinch while the Queen and Prince Philip were engaged in public functions which included a visit to the local Agricultural Society's annual livestock show in Stranraer.

While all these various functions were taking place yet another royal visitor was arriving. This was Princess Margaret who flew into the RAF

Royal visit to Stranraer, 1955.

base at West Freugh, prior to joining the rest of the royal party at Lochinch for a meal before they all sailed off again later in the day from Cairnryan, on their way up the west coast before enjoying the usual royal holiday at Balmoral.

This photograph shows the Queen and Prince Philip touring the park on their arrival at what the locals always refer to as 'the cattle show'. This took place after their morning tour around the various parts of the county, which had included a stop at Whithorn to visit the excavations at the site of St Ninian's first chapel there. Later, at the cattle show, the royal party met quite a few of the winners in the various sections of the show and the Queen actually presented some of the trophies and cups for the more important classes. Along with Prince Philip she also spent a fair amount of time chatting with some of the retired farm workers present as guests, and the Queen handed over long service medals to those who had qualified for these awards.

It was a wonderful day for the people of Stranraer and pretty smart planning by those who organised the cattle show. With the co-operation of the farmers from the Machars district of Wigtownshire the two organisations shifted the dates of their shows and the Stranraer show took place on what had been the traditional date for the Wigtown function. This meant that the Stranraer show slotted neatly into the same date as the royal visit and Her Majesty graciously accepted the invitation to spend some time there. The photograph shows the reaction of the people of Stranraer: a packed arena and the most successful show ever.

And later, on a calm and peaceful evening, the crowds gathered again, this time at Cairnryan and on the road running along the east side of the loch, to cheer the royal guests away as the tender picked up the last of them from the port and carried them to the royal yacht which was lying off the harbour. As it slipped out of the loch and headed north many cheers were heard as the people marked the end of a perfect day.

Those magnificent men ... in their flying machines (E)

In August 1913, the farm of Cults, Castle Kennedy, was chosen for a use which was far removed from anything connected with agriculture. One of its fields had been earmarked as a landing ground for the flying machines which had been introduced to the world within the last dozen years or so; machines which were receiving great attention but which had still never been seen by most of the people of Scotland. Wigtownshire was to see its first ever aeroplane when No 2 Squadron of the Royal Flying Corps would use it as a landing and take-off point for their aircraft which would be crossing the North Channel to take part in military manoeuvres at The Curragh in Ireland.

In this photograph we see that first aircraft to land in Wigtownshire, a Maurice Farman Longhorn, the name given to it because of the skids

First aircraft to land in Wigtownshire, Cults farm, 1913.

and struts which protruded forward from the unlikely looking flying machine. And in the open air pilot's seat is Captain G W P Dawes, the first man to fly into Wigtownshire. Captain Dawes had been an officer in the Royal Engineers and transferred to the Royal Flying Corps when it came into being.

In the background on the left we can see one of the other aircraft which was part of the group of six which flew from Montrose to take part in the annual exercises. The Longhorn, a French-built aircraft, was the only one of its kind in the group and it was accompanied by five BE2 biplanes, BE being a shortened class-name meaning British Experimental. One of the reasons for using the Cults was, of course, to shorten the leg of the flight over the North Channel, but another reason was that the aircraft would be fitted there with 'floats' in case they came down in the sea. The four long cylindrical floats can be seen here, fastened under the wing of the Longhorn.

As it turned out, the floats were not called into use, all the aircraft safely crossing into Ireland, though it was noted that only five returned via the Cults the following month, one of the BE2s having crashed during the exercises.

Following that first use of the field at the Cults, the area was then listed by the Royal Flying Corps as a designated flying ground for the Corps' purposes. However, it was never used again by them and it never knew the sound of aero engines again until World War II brought the Royal Air Force into the area.

It was in June 1941, that Training Command took over the original field, and quite a large additional area, and established a gunnery school there. In December 1942, it was passed over to 17 Group Coastal Command whose jurisdiction lasted until September 1943, and thereafter Flight Training Command was in charge until May 1945. Ten years later the aero engines rumbled again at Castle Kennedy, this time for peaceful purposes as Silver City Airways used it for a short time for their flights to Ireland.

How they brought the good news – And its aftermath in Stranraer (F)

Thomson's shop sold a variety of goods as can be seen from the window displays here along with the wall advertising. Its situation also helped business, as the shop was on a busy corner of Hanover Street where most of the traffic from the south Rhins came into town off Dalrymple Street. This was a time when newspaper hoardings boldly pushed their individual takes on the latest crises of the rapidly expanding World War II.

Thomson's shop, Hanover Street, Stranraer.

The late Tom Miller took this photograph, his imagination inspired by the exultant declarations on the newspapers' 'scream sheets'. Every morning, after getting off the Glenluce bus, Tom would take different ways to his place of work in the county council offices, taking photos along the way. On the day he took the Hanover Street route this display made him reach for his camera as he saw the opportunity for an unusual picture.

Giving a copy of the photograph many years later, for use in the *Free Press* 'Peep at the Past' series, Tom explained that he had been absolutely amazed at the run of Allied successes, so much so that he felt he had to record them himself. It was only a few days later that these successes were shown to be hollow victories and the Germans had killed off any hopes of Norway and its allies winning the battle for the north-west of Europe. But even before that setback Tom found himself in the firing line. Having successfully taken his photo, he was feeling particularly pleased as he marched into the office where he worked, only to find two policemen were waiting for him and insisting that he accompany them to the local police station. When he got there he was shocked to find that no less a person than the chief of the county force wished to interrogate him. Someone, it seemed, had spotted him using a camera and reported to the police that there was a spy in town. Tom, through his work, knew the boss of the county police, so thought this could be sorted out quickly. Alas! It seemed that a possible spy would be treated as such and Tom underwent a grilling from a stern-faced police officer who had to think long and hard about every answer he got. What was he doing with a camera? A hobby? Where had he got film when there was none for sale in the shops? Why had he bought large supplies of film when the War started? What made him think it might get scarce? What was he going to do with the photograph? On and on it went, question after question, with Tom getting the feeling that it would only take one wrong answer for a firing squad to be summoned from wherever they were waiting with their rifles at the ready.

But eventually the ordeal ended. Tom maintained that it was with obvious reluctance the police accepted his story. He was reprimanded for having a camera, for having film, and for using both. It was pointed out to him that he was very fortunate to live in a country where his explanation was accepted. Tom apologised, promised not to be a naughty boy again and was set free. But, he vowed he would never speak to the head of the police force again. He had the feeling that every time he saw the man his interrogation was being thought about again and the decision being queried.

As well as having a story to go with this photograph, it also portrays a style of shop, long gone from the local scene in every sense of the word. In the years after World War II the build-up of traffic became too much for roads which had been laid down originally for horse-drawn carts. In the post-war period speed restrictions, parking and lane widths all had to be reconsidered and changes made. Exits and entrances from busier roads to rural areas caused a great deal of concern and corner buildings at such locations became targets for demolition in order to enable the construction of new traffic flow systems. The narrow neck from Hanover Street into Dalrymple Street was widened by the demolition of two corner buildings and better pavements added to the wider roadway.

A royal salute – in more ways than one (G)

Cairnryan was a quiet little fishing village on the shores of Loch Ryan until wartime necessities in the 1940s brought changes to the place and its population: changes which banished the placid life previously enjoyed by the small number of locals and created a massive port which would point to a new future for 'the Cairn'.

The original intention behind the decision to build a port here was the dangerous possibility that ports on the Clyde or the Mersey might be bombed by the enemy or put out of action in some other way, so it was decided that two emergency military ports should be provided on the west coast of the United Kingdom.

The labour needed for the construction of the two large piers and the lairage and the roadways and railway sidings which were linked up to them and the existing railway connection to Stranraer was provided mostly by the men from the Royal Pioneer Corps, the Royal Engineers and the Royal Army Service Corps.

HMS *Phoebe*, Loch Ryan.

The story behind this picture relates to a couple of days in the early life of Cairnryan Military Port: a time when the place was not yet fully functioning but the authorities, aware of what was being built up, decided to make first use of the facilities and help a couple of royal visitors with part of their transport problems.

The whole thing started when a Royal Navy cruiser, HMS *Phoebe*, lying at anchor in Scapa Flow, suddenly received orders to sail immediately to Loch Ryan and pick up two Very Important Passengers who were to be taken to Belfast. As the *Phoebe* steamed southwards on what was at first assumed to be a secret mission, somehow word got out and was spreading that in fact it was the King and Queen who were being picked up.

Not surprisingly, the news about the identity of the travellers was also being broadcast around Cairnryan and district, so much so that I was suddenly ordered to grab a jacket and join my mother and a friend of hers for a walk to Innermessan where the military railway line to Cairnryan crossed the main road to the same destination. When we arrived there we found around 100 people waiting, and wondering, if it was true that King George and Queen Elizabeth were coming. So much for security.

They certainly were on their way and after waiting for about 20 minutes. excitement reached fever pitch when an engine with a couple of carriages was spotted and quite a cheer went up as it swept past the crowd at the level crossing. Moving fairly fast, but not too fast, I can say that a lady with a large hat on had waved to us from one of the carriages as the train went past.

Well, fun and games over, or so we thought. It was around 65 years later that a national newspaper carried this photograph and the story from a marine who had been aboard the *Phoebe* when it sailed with the royal couple from Stranraer. Stranraer? Yes, that's what the man said, and it was only after I got in touch with him that the whole complicated mix-up was finally unravelled.

It turned out that the crew of the *Phoebe* somehow thought that they were travelling to Stranraer for the pick-up and when they docked very briefly and sailed off again so quickly this wrong destination had stuck with them. When they made the return journey from Belfast, it was at Cairnryan again that they stopped at briefly to let the King and Queen away and things got even more complicated for most of the crew. It seems that His Majesty, grateful for the Navy's help, suggested to the skipper of the *Phoebe* that he might grant his crew an hour ashore to let them have a pint. The cruiser's captain agreed and when the royal couple had departed the thirsty sailors scrambled ashore, asking a dockyard matey there where the pub was. His reply killed their hopes stone dead. There hadn't been a pub there for a couple of hundred years.

End of shore leave! But not the end of story: if you look closely at the photograph of the *Phoebe* and her wonderful array of flags you will see that it seemed that the skipper, when he discovered the identity of the passengers he was getting, decided to respond to such a magnificent occasion with a spectacular display for his ship. He was flying the Navy's White Ensign, of course, but added the Union Jack, an Admiralty bunting and a Royal Standard. The story ended with the captain getting a severe reprimand from the Admiralty for going over the top with his idea of a royal salute.

When the Cavalry came to Cairnryan (H)

This photograph of uniformed and mounted troops, known to have been taken in the vicinity of Cairnryan, Wigtownshire, in the earlier days of World War II, was used to illustrate an article in the *Free Press* in the series, 'Wait till your father comes home on leave'. Little was known about the photograph beyond the location, and the caption which accompanied it queried the use of horses at a time when the soldiers being drafted into the village were understood to be there for the purpose of creating a port and also the camps for the men who would build and run the complex.

The article triggered an immediate response from Mrs Isobel Fiddes, whose father was shepherd at High Croach on the southern shoulder of Cairn Hill just south of the village at the time. She recalled the day when a dozen soldiers, each with a white horse, had arrived at the farm where her father, Mr McInnes, had been asked to find the men space to pitch the tents which would house them and some kind of accommodation for the

Cavalry, possible Scots Greys, High Croach, 1941.

horses. Mrs Fiddes also recognised one of the soldiers in the photograph as he had returned regularly in later years and kept up a mutual friendship with her family. It was a friendship which would last for 65 years: George Rawlinson, the young soldier from Middlesbrough, who first set foot on High Croach on 19th May 1941, returned almost every year after the War until he died in 2006. It was because of this that Mrs Fiddes knew him immediately she saw the photograph in the *Free Press* and she recalled that George and the other soldiers, who, she thought, were in the Scots Greys, were always willing to let her and her little sister Catherine have a ride on the horses.

She also cleared up the mystery of the Army sending cavalry to Cairnryan. The men were going to be there for just over seven weeks to plan and establish a water supply system from Loch Ree up on the moors to the camps which were being established around Cairnryan and with no road in the area of the loch it was easier to use the horses for transport of men and materials. The iron piping which would deliver the water was hauled on what looked like homemade sledges and the horses provided the power to haul these delivery vehicles over the hills of Craigammin Ridge.

She remembered too that her father went further than merely finding space for the men to pitch their tents; deciding that they deserved better than living under canvas he cleared a barn loft for them to use as sleeping quarters. The farm also provided stabling for the horses and Mrs Fiddes recalled that she and her sister Catherine would help the soldiers when they worked with and exercised the horses, taking them up to the burn above the farm or down to the shore. One horse she remembered was called Dolly and she thought that more than one had the name of Buster.

Their part in the creation of the Cairnryan camps and what would become the country's No 2 Military Port complete, the soldiers and their mounts left High Croach and the McInnes family on the 11 July 1941, to report back to Redford Barracks in Edinburgh. This date, and the others, were easily checked by Mrs Fiddes as she still had her mother's diary: a treasured and happy reminder of what had been exciting times for a little girl more than 70 years ago.

The epic voyage of the *Marquess* (I)

She was no beauty. In fact, looking at the tattered old photograph among my souvenirs it would be fair to describe her bluntly as an ugly little ship. I was not at all sure of her technical details but probably she could be described as a coaster.

She sat low in the water, showing little freeboard, and was painted a nondescript grey with the only relief a plain black boot-topping on her single funnel, which itself always suggested it was too long and too narrow to match the rest of her deck clutter.

One thing she had going for her: her magnificent name. For such a plain unpretentious little vessel the title of *Marquess of Hartington* rolled richly off the tongue. I was aware that for their water transport fleet the Royal Army Service Corps (RASC) had different groups of names, given according to the size and use of the vessel and they reserved the really aristocratic titles for these coasters which were real workhorses and were given the bulk of the dirty and dangerous jobs. And there was nothing more dangerous for these little ships than the deep sea ammunition and explosives dumping which they carried out after World War II from Cairnryan Military Port. I can recall a sister ship of the *Marquess* which was called the *Sir Evelyn Wood*, just as small as the *Marquess* and every bit as ugly.

I'm not sure what place in history these gentlemen had but their namesakes at least sounded better than the even smaller harbour runabouts of the RASC fleet which were called after Derby winners. Imagine being in charge of a boat called *The Fuss-Buzz*, another of the Cairnryan fleet.

But, back to the *Marquess*. As the Lord made them He certainly matched them and the skipper of our redoubtable craft was a man named A E Corvin, with the Albert familiarly shortened to Bert for shore staff and his hardy crew. He was also, however, known as Crash because of his eccentric method of berthing the ship. Invariably he had one of his crew on the little bridge of the *Marquess*, ostensibly being coached in navigation and seamanship, and the deckie was allowed to bring her into the pierside and would ask the skipper as the ship glided in 'Shall I ring down "finished with engines"?' Crash would take the wheel, give it a bit of left-hand down, and, as the *Marquess* rattled against the pier, would say with satisfaction 'They know we're finished with engines'.

Then came the day of what can only be described as the *Marquess'* epic voyage; one which would go down as a rich chapter in the glorious history of the RASC. The few crew members lounging about on deck, waiting for their skipper to arrive, groaned in concert when they spotted him marching smartly down the pier. Crash was wearing his No 1 uniform and they all knew what that portended. He would step aboard as if he was taking command of the flagship of the Home Fleet, cast a critical eye over the *Marquess* and decide that the scruffy little workhorse needed a funnel repaint job. That would mean at least a couple of the crew would be kept busy before they even sailed out of Loch Ryan on their way to the dumping area where they would get rid of another dangerous cargo of unwanted ordnance or explosives.

The painting went well, the voyage went off with nothing untoward happening and the little ship turned back for its home port with everyone pleasantly anticipating an early docking, an early tea, and a trip into Stranraer for a few well-earned beers to round off another day.

Marquees of Hartington, Carinryan Military Port.

The crew should have known better; things rarely going smoothly for Crash. So, as the *Marquess* sailed into Loch Ryan and past the site of the old oyster tanks a mile or so to the north of Cairnryan, Crash pulled on the lanyard of the ship's whistle, his agreed signal with his wife Harriet, to let her know he would be home for tea within the hour. She and Crash lived in a caravan on the site of the old sheds.

Unfortunately, the lanyard broke and Crash, appreciating immediately that a continuous, piercing whistle blast was not a friendly noise, ordered one of the crew to climb the funnel, catch the broken end of the lanyard and restore silence.

One by one the crew members politely declined. They were not normally a mutinous lot but they pointed out that the paint on the funnel was still wet – as well as warm almost to the point of boiling – and they democratically decided this was a job best left to their skipper. He, of course, still in his best uniform, agreed that the whistle would have to be left until it ran out of steam.

One small detail no one had remembered was that after their delicate cargo had gone over the side into deep water they had all forgotten to haul down the red flag which signified their dangerous mission and warned other shipping to stand well away.

So there they were: sailing into Cairnryan with red flag flying and hooter going continuously and all aboard the *Marquess* were really puzzled as they rounded the point of the South Deep Pier to see the immense amount of activity taking place. Ships were being evacuated, with personnel hurrying down the pier and driving vehicles away, while at the same time fire engines were arriving on the pier and dozens of soldiers were running here and there, unrolling hoses, carrying stretchers and first-aid equipment and generally not panicking with great style.

It was only after Crash docked with his usual skill that all was revealed. And it was said afterwards, admittedly with great glee among the fleet personnel, that the faces of the crew of the old *Marquess* matched the red flag they had flown so proudly on that epic voyage.

There were many other stories told of the reactions of everyone around the port the day that the *Marquess* sailed serenely into the harbour, causing perhaps the biggest upset since the earliest days of World War II, but, one thing is certain, the calmest people around would be those aboard the little vessel. They were used to upsets and alarms when their skipper set sail but they had also learned that he faced all these with a calmness and equanimity that defied fate and they had developed his habit of shrugging these episodes aside and ignoring the blistering expressions of rage and wrath from those higher up the chain of command.

What's in a name?

The things that Crash felt strongly about were few in number and were soon worked out by the members of his crew, but they were never quite sure of the priority or order of importance in which to place his wife Harriet, his ship the *Marquess*, or, his only recreation, the game of cricket. There was also the old bicycle he used to get him from his caravan to the ship or the cricket match but it was a fixed-cog machine, something he never quite mastered, and he fell off it so often that his features seemed to be permanently marked with bumps and bruises.

His love for his ship was never hidden and it was a cause for concern with his crew that he would lavish as much pride on the appearance of the *Marquess* as many an admiral would have for his flagship. And it was not only the appearance of the *Marquess* that was important to him; its title was of great consequence too and he rarely shortened it to the familiar form used here.

An instance of this occurred once when the ship, for whatever reason, had sailed across the Solway Firth and tied up at Whitehaven on the Cumbrian coast for a few days. When their business in England had been sorted out it was towards the end of a normal working day and the crew felt it would be quite appropriate to have a few jars ashore and then sail home the following morning. Crash, however, had been long enough away from Harriet and decided that they should slip moorings immediately and sail through the night to arrive as early as possible the next day at Cairnryan. It was not a happy ship which sailed away from Whitehaven that night and when the *Marquess*, striking north-west across the firth, ran into heavy fog, there was quite a lot of satisfaction expressed on the lower deck. The skipper prudently heaved-to, set a deckwatch, and the rest of the happy gang got their heads down in the foggy darkness.

They wakened in the morning to a glorious sight: the warm sun lighting up a glittering blue sea which showed ne'er a ripple, a paler blue sky above, and, surprise, surprise! a shoreline about half a mile away which was fringed by a luxurious growth of trees. The usual lower deck conference discussed this interesting-looking landfall, loud enough for the skipper to be aware of their suggestions and very shortly afterwards one of the deckies was rowing Crash ashore. Hauling their dinghy up on the beach they discovered that just through the fringe of trees there was a well-kept roadway running roughly parallel with the beach. A shrug of the shoulders sent them left rather than right along the road and after about half a mile they rounded a gentle bend and stood staring like a couple of Elizabethan explorers at a brilliant red Post Office phone box. Opening the door they found that everything inside was as it should be and Crash looked enquiringly at his companion as he read out the location tab fixed above the phone. 'Gatehouse of Fleet' he said, only to get a wide-hands gesture and a shrug of the shoulders as the deckie signalled he hadn't a clue as to name or location.

Only one thing for it. Crash lifted the phone and within seconds a pleasant female voice asked 'Number please?' 'Can you please put me in touch with the headquarters of Cairnryan port near Stranraer?' said Crash. 'Certainly sir. Who's speaking please?' Crash, still staring at the strange name tab above the phone, suddenly adopted a very grand tone and declaimed 'This is the Marquess of Hartington and at present I am with my friend here, Gatehouse of Fleet'.

The deckie, who had been hanging over his shoulder to hear what transpired, had given up by this time and had discreetly withdrawn to have a smoke so the rest of the conversation with the bewildered telephone exchange lady was not recorded.

Lost again

That was not the only occasion when Crash got lost but it has to be recorded that the idea that he might worry about it never seemed to strike home with him and he had a unique ability to wriggle out of the trickiest situations with great aplomb.

Returning one time from the upper reaches of the Clyde the *Marquess* again found herself sailing into foggy conditions and at the time of the day when the light was starting to fade. Crash was determined to get back to the Cairn that night and insisted that it could be done.

When darkness fell completely and with the crew nearing the mutinous stage and pointing out that they were sailing across near gale-force winds and along a dangerous coast, Crash compromised. He cut the ship's speed and sent the Peggy – the youngest deckhand and the equivalent of a cabin boy – for'ard into the bows of the *Marquess* with a bucket of coal and instructions to throw a lump of it well ahead of the ship every two or three minutes and listen carefully for the splash. If there was no splash the ship would be brought to a standstill immediately!

This went on for some time, the ship crawling through the darkness, until Crash had to admit there was a considerable risk and the engines of the *Marquess* were stopped. The anchor was dropped and to everyone's surprise it held so the ship's company were stood down and most of them went quite happily to their bunks.

When morning broke there was still a fair thickness of fog and it was decided it would be safer to remain as they were until the weather cleared.

A deckwatch was set and the Peggy went to the bows again with orders to let the bridge know immediately if he heard another ship approaching.

Within minutes the puzzled youngster reported that he couldn't hear any other ships but he had heard motor cars and also voices. Another deckie confirmed that this was the case and just then the mist thinned and the last tendrils of its blanket were swept away and Crash and his crew found themselves looking at the early morning traffic passing through Ballantrae, with a few people from the village also wondering why the little boat was anchored so close to the mouth of the Stinchar.

APPENDIX

Stranraer and District Local History Trust and List of Interviewees

Stranraer and District Local History Trust was formed in 1998 with the intention of publishing books of local interest and authored by invited local historians. At their first meeting they established an oral history subgroup and Harriet Collins, a member of the subgroup, went on to complete the first interview, recorded in January 1999, with Mrs Helen Davies. Trust members John MacQueen and Jack Hunter completed further interviews and then, in November 2000 Nancy McLucas was volunteered for this task. She took up the mantle and subsequently recorded all but one of the recordings made after that time. Many of the recordings were made on an open reel tape machine and the recordings were transferred onto compact disc by E W Wilson, with the museum and library each receiving one copy of the script and disc. The copy in the library is available to the general public. A further copy was also given to the contributor. Most often, the group would identify who they wanted to interview and then approach them. As Nancy explained in 2016, interviews often took a long time to organise because the interviewees would often feel they had little to contribute. However, as the interviews demonstrate, this was simply natural reticence on the part of the interviewee. Nancy recalled that, although she was nervous of using the recording equipment, she also had great fun. She spoke with great affection about many of the people she had interviewed, including the Misses Templeton, who laid out the very best china for her visit and Margaret Clark, who told such scurrilous tales about her time at the telephone exchange that the recording machine often had to be hastily turned off. Although now retired from fieldwork Nancy, now 86, reflected that she still had her eye on a few potential interviewees.

The core membership of the Trust, all volunteers, has remained constant through nearly 20 years of activity. In this time they have published 31 books which are sold around the world. When Christine Wilson, Trust Secretary, was interviewed in December 2014 she recalled the leap of faith taken by the group when they undertook to publish their first book. Each committee member pledged to donate £100 to cover the cost of the publication and when the manuscript was sent off to the publisher each prepared to make their contribution. Happily, the print run of 1000 books sold out within three weeks and subsequently reprinted to meet demand and so the costs were covered. The books are all prepared for publication by committee members and the only payment made is in kind to the author, who receives ten copies of their publication. Once printed, the books are stored in committee members' homes and distributed from there: no small undertaking when you consider that there are 31 titles and 100 books equates to six or seven boxes. Proceeds from the sales have enabled the Trust to financially support archaeological digs in the Stranraer area as well as providing a bursary scheme to support sixth year students from Stranraer High School and the Douglas Ewart High School intending to go on to study history at university.

For more information about the available Trust publications, please see their website <www.stranraerhistory.org.uk/publications>.

List of Interviewees and key information relating to the themes covered in the individual interviews

Material from each oral history recording made by the Trust has been included in this volume. Some interview transcripts are given in full, while others are represented by the use of extracts within thematic chapters.

The recordings were made by Nancy McLucas unless otherwise indicated.

Interviews which appear in full in this collection:

Mrs Helen Davies
Interviewed in 1999.
Fieldworker: Harriet Collins.
Content: childhood and family life in rural Rhins, schooldays, dairy work.

Mrs Vivien Delf
Interviewed in 2013.
Content: early life, farm work, living conditions.

Mr Hugh Reid
Interviewed in 2006.
Content: local supernatural tales and anecdotes, detailed description of poaching practice.

Mr Bobby Gemmell
Interviewed in 2003.
Content: childhood experiences at Lochnaw, WWII, apprenticeship and career in the building trade.

Mr Ian Jack
Interviewed in 2007.
Content: history of family business, butcher in Stranraer for almost a
century.

Mrs Agnes McClymont
Interviewed in 2008.
Content: working life with the Gas Board in Stranraer.

Mr Alan Smith
Interviewed in 2007.
Content: history of family firm of solicitors in Stranraer, law.

Mrs Betty Findlay
Interviewed in 2008.
Content: history of family business, Findlay's drapers, WWII, shop
community.

Miss Margaret and Miss Jean Templeton
Interviewed in 2007.
Content: Schooldays, father an optician, WWII memories of blackouts
and the sea-planes.

Interviews which are represented by extracts in the thematic chapters:

Mrs Isabelle Shaw
Interviewed in 1999.
Fieldworker: John McQueen.
Content: childhood memories of Drummore, shops, local worthies,
learning to drive, the introduction of electricity.

Mr Andrew Hannay
Interviewed in 1999.
Fieldworker: Jack Hunter.
Content: information about the family firm, millers since 1695, WWI,
Wigtownshire Creamery, Andrew's career in banking.

Mr Bill McCaig
Interviewed in 1999.
Fieldworker: Jack Hunter.
Content: changes in farm life, women's work on the farm, transport,
squatters, curling, church, entertainment, Stair Estates.

Mrs Barbara Hannay
Interviewed in 2000.
Content: early life on the farm, entertainment, work, school, cattle shows, wartime, evacuees, impact of the Americans arriving.

Mr Andrew Love
Interviewed in 2004.
Content: childhood memories of tramps and travellers.

Mrs Anne Brownhill
Interviewed in 2004.
Content: information about the family business, The Glasgow House, including interiors, staffing and Christmas time in the shop, information on other Stranraer shops.

Mrs Margaret McColm
Interviewed in 2004.
Content: schooldays, working in the dairy, Clydesdale horses, horse shows.

Mr James Blair
Interviewed in 2004.
(written recollection).
Content: WWII experiences.

Mrs Agnes Lamb
Interviewed in 2005.
Content: early life on the farm, tattie pickers from Ireland, impact of WWII, wartime wedding, housing.

Mrs Margaret Mitchell
Interviewed in 2005.
Content: family connections with the lifeboat, WWII, the putting green in Portpatrick, *Princess Victoria* disaster.

Miss Margaret Clark
Interviewed in 2005.
Content: local concerts, the Miltonians, POWs during WWII, working at The Glasgow House, working life at the telephone exchange in Stranraer, McGibney's ghost.

Miss Margaret Clark, Miss Heather Short, Miss Margaret Short
Interviewed in 2005.

Content: working at the telephone exchange in Stranraer, *Princess Victoria* disaster.

Mr George McClymont
Interviewed in 2005.
Content: childhood memories of Portpatrick, fishing, catching rabbits, schooldays, early jobs, WWII, blackouts.

Mr John McColm
Interviewed in 2006.
Content: Life in farming, WWII, rural depopulation.

Mrs Muir, Mrs McKie
Interviewed in 2006.
Content: childhood memories.

Mr John Barr
Interviewed in 2006.
Content: Farming, tattie workers, education, transport, Stranraer town life.

Mr and Mrs William Darroch
Interviewed in 2007.
Content: WWII, working on the railways, 1947 snowstorm.

Mrs Nancy McLucas
Recorded her interview in 2007.
Content: life in Bishopburn, travelling vans, community life.

Mrs Catherine Monteith
Interviewed in 2007.
Content: schooldays, WWII, local shops.

Mrs J B Lammie
Interviewed in 2008.
Content: early schooldays, farming, WWII, POWs, post-war developments: electricity, tractors.

Mr Archie Bell
Interviewed in 2008.
Content: family business: butcher, baker, WWII, Rotary, lifeboats, refurbishing the Lord Provost's lamps.

Miss Betty Murray
Interviewed in 2009.
Content: experiences of being in the Land Army, WWII.

Mr Bob Grierson and Mr John McColm
Interviewed in 2009.
Content: farming, especially relating to potato farming and the Irish tattie pickers.

Mr Jim Wallace
Interviewed in 2013.
Content: early life, cattle and sheep, especially showing livestock, judging shows across the country.

Mr John Carruth
Interviewed in 2013.
Content: Stranraer pre-WWII, shops, fishing, housing, health, schooling.

Mr Hugh Aitken
Interviewed in 2014.
Content: early life in Stranraer, WWII evacuees, church, Clayhole, family business, jeweller's shop, fixing the Simpson Memorial clock.

Mrs Olive Murray and Miss Debbie Murray
Interviewed in 2014.
Content: family business, Moodies in Stranraer, change over time.

Mrs Christine Wilson
Interviewed in 2014.
Content: History of the Stranraer and District Local History Trust, publications, oral history work, bursary scheme, grants to local projects of historical interest e.g. funding for a survey of the copper mines at Tonderghie.

Mr Geoffrey Wardley
Interviewed in 2015.
Content: RAF work at Wig Bay after WWII.

Mrs Mary Downie
Interviewed in 2016.
Content: schooldays.

ENDNOTES

1 The images given here are all part of that archive and the stories attached to them have appeared in the *Stranraer and Wigtownshire Free Press* in past years.

2 Also known as Pine Tar, Archangel Tar was often used with livestock as an antiseptic.

3 Animal feed.

4 Kayser Bondor was a very popular hosiery manufacturer at this time.

5 The Agnew family held Lochnaw Estate from 1426.

6 Anti-aircraft cannon used in WWII.

INDEX